The Allyn & Bacon
Teaching Assistant's Handbook

The Allyn & Bacon Teaching Assistant's Handbook

A GUIDE FOR GRADUATE INSTRUCTORS OF WRITING AND LITERATURE

Stephen W. Wilhoit
University of Dayton

New York San Francisco Boston
London Toronto Sydney Tokyo Singapore Madrid
Mexico City Munich Paris Cape Town Hong Kong Montreal

Vice President, Publisher: Eben W. Ludlow
Marketing Manager: Christopher Bennem
Supplements Editor: Donna Campion
Senior Production Manager: Eric Jorgensen
Project Coordination, Text Design, and Electronic Page Makeup: Electronic
    Publishing Services Inc., NYC
Cover Designer/Manager: Wendy Ann Fredericks
Cover Photo: ©Joe Ginsberg/PhotoDisc/PictureQuest
Manufacturing Buyer: Al Dorsey
Printer and Binder: Courier Corporation
Cover Printer: Phoenix Color Corporation

For permission to use copyrighted material, grateful acknowledgment is made to the copyright holders referenced throughout this book, which are hereby made part of this copyright page.

Library of Congress Cataloging-in-Publication Data

Wilhoit, Stephen.
    The Allyn & Bacon teaching assistant's handbook : a guide for graduate instructors of writing and literature / Stephen W. Wilhoit.
        p cm.
    Includes bibliographical references and index.
    ISBN 0-205-33677-9 (pbk.)
        1. English philology--Study and teaching–Handbooks, manuals, etc.
    2. Teachers' assistants--Handbooks, manuals, etc. I. Title: Allyn and Bacon teaching assistant's handbook. II. Title.

    PE65 .W55 2002
    428'.0071'1--dc21   2002067758

Please visit our website at http://www.ablongman.com

ISBN 0-205-33677-9

3 4 5 6 7 8 9   BKM BKM   0987654

DEDICATION

For two of the most important teachers in my life, Momma Betty and Daddy Fred. You will always be with me.

CONTENTS

CHAPTER 2   **Getting Ready to Teach Before Classes Begin   24**

CHAPTER 6   **Grading Student Writing   100**

CHAPTER 7   **Presenting Material in Class   112**

CHAPTER 10   **Holding Conferences with Students**   171

CHAPTER 11   **Teaching Literature**   179

CHAPTER 12   **Growing and Learning
as a Teacher   195**

CHAPTER 13   Preparing for the Academic Job Market   214

PREFACE

The Allyn & Bacon Teaching Assistant's Handbook grew out of my eleven years as the director of Teaching Assistant (TA) Training in the Department of English at the University of Dayton, my years as a TA peer-mentor at Indiana University, my own experience as a TA at three universities, and my examination of a wide survey of the literature on TA education. Though the book is primarily intended to meet the needs of first-year TAs, more experienced graduate instructors may also find the text helpful, especially Chapter 11, which discusses how to teach literature; Chapter 12, which addresses professional development; and Chapter 13, which discusses how to find employment as a professor.

Working closely with TAs for so many years has taught me that graduate student instructors thrive when they have the right kinds of knowledge, freedom, guidance, and support. First, to do their job well, TAs need a lot of information. For example, they need to know how English departments and writing programs are typically structured and staffed, what it is they are supposed to teach, what their students are supposed to learn, and how they can accomplish both goals. Also, because they both teach and take classes, TAs need to learn how to succeed in graduate school, balance the many demands placed on their time and attention, and prepare for their future careers. Second, TAs need freedom. They need multiple opportunities to put knowledge into practice, to design their own syllabi and assignments, to experiment with pedagogy, to succeed—and sometimes fail—as teachers. Like all new teachers, though, TAs must receive adequate guidance if they are to manage this freedom successfully. They need help learning how to sort through their options, plan their classes, organize their time, and learn from their experience. Finally, TAs need support and encouragement. Life can become terribly difficult for TAs—they need to know that their chairs, teaching supervisors, and professors understand and appreciate their contributions to the department.

Faculty who work with TAs can use *The Allyn & Bacon Teaching Assistant's Handbook* in several ways. Some may ask newly hired TAs to read the handbook (or at least certain chapters) prior to any required preservice workshops or courses and keep it on their desks as a reference work. Others may use the book as a primary or supplementary text for in-service workshops or classes. Still others may pair this text with an anthology of readings on composition theory. Though I stress throughout *The Allyn & Bacon Teaching Assistant's Handbook* that classroom practice should be guided by theory, the thrust of this text is clearly pedagogical. Faculty who feel this text slights discussions of theory might consider pairing it with any of the fine anthologies of theoretical work found in the list of "Additional Readings" at the end of Chapter 2.

However this handbook is used, it should complement the instruction that faculty offer TAs, not substitute for it. Many schools have developed handbooks of their own that offer TAs specific information about their school, department, students, and program. This book can supplement those handbooks, providing TAs additional advice on how to succeed in graduate school, how to become an effective classroom instructor, how to engage in a program of professional development, and how to find employment in the academy.

Because the advice I offer in the book is based largely on my experience and the experiences of the TAs I have worked with over the years, few readers will agree with every recommendation I make. When this is the case, I hope the text spurs discussion and debate. Also, because TAs work in such diverse institutions and programs, faculty and TAs using the book will often need to adapt the advice and instruction I offer to suit local circumstances. My greatest hope is that *The Allyn & Bacon Teaching Assistant's Handbook* fosters just this sort of conversation and collaboration, that it helps TAs and their supervisors work together to ensure that all graduate instructors receive the instruction and support they need to succeed as teachers, students, researchers, administrators, and colleagues.

ACKNOWLEDGMENTS

Many thanks to the graduate teaching assistants who responded to various chapters of this book: Greg Gibson, Judith Shroufe, Katie Snarey, and especially Kate Monnin. I would also like to thank William J. Carpenter, Lafayette College; Catherine Latterell, Penn State University, Altoona; and Irene Ward, Kansas State University, who reviewed the manuscript. As always, I could not have completed this project without the help of my wife, Karen, and the patience of my children, Rachel, Sarah, and Rebekah.

CHAPTER 1

Defining a Job, Defining a Role

INTRODUCTION

Now that you have been awarded a graduate teaching assistantship, you are probably curious about your new job and the department in which you will work. This chapter will try to answer some of your questions by providing an overview of the way English departments and writing programs typically staff their introductory writing and literature courses, the various roles teaching assistants (TAs) play in these departments and programs, the typical responsibilities that come with a teaching assistantship, and the support structures English departments and writing programs typically offer TAs. The chapter closes with a discussion of some employment issues you will face as a TA and a set of suggestions on how to balance the various demands placed on a TA's time and attention.

HOW ENGLISH DEPARTMENTS AND WRITING PROGRAMS STAFF THEIR INTRODUCTORY CLASSES

As a TA, you occupy a unique position in your department. Both graduate student and teacher, your life is often filled with contradictions. In some departments, tenured faculty members will accept you as a colleague; in others, faculty will discount your work. Occasionally department chairs and university administrators will praise your efforts, but most of the time you will receive neither the support nor the recognition you deserve. When it comes to paying taxes on your stipend, you are an employee; when it comes to receiving benefits, however, you are a graduate student. Some undergraduate students look on you with suspicion and treat you disrespectfully; others readily accept you as their instructor.

Many of these contradictions arise from the way English departments and writing programs staff their introductory composition and literature classes. Four types of instructors commonly teach introductory writing and literature courses in American universities: full-time tenure-line professors; full-time, nontenure track faculty; part-time faculty; and graduate teaching assistants. At large research universities, only a few full-time tenure-line faculty teach introductory composition or literature classes. When they do teach introductory literature classes, they often lecture in large auditoriums filled with students; TAs assigned to the course work with the students in smaller discussion sections. At comprehensive universities (those offering master's degrees, not doctorates) and four-year colleges, full-time tenured or tenure-track faculty are more likely to teach introductory writing and literature classes.

Increasingly schools are hiring full-time, nontenure track faculty to teach these classes as well. These instructors have advanced degrees in English and often teach three or four courses a term. They typically receive a salary slightly below a beginning professor's and get full benefits, including health insurance and a retirement plan. However, unlike tenured or tenure-track faculty, they are usually not expected to establish a research agenda and cannot get tenure or be promoted. They sign one- or multi-year contracts that can be renewed indefinitely.

Most departments also hire part-time instructors to teach introductory literature and writing classes. Part-time instructors usually teach two or three classes a term, receive relatively low pay, and rarely get benefits. Though most of these instructors have advanced degrees in English, they cannot receive tenure and typically work on yearly contracts. If enrollment falls, they are not rehired. Many part-time instructors, though, work for years at the same institution. Universities will often hire a part-time instructor to teach a specific course, such as business writing, technical writing, or journalism. Because of his or her experience, this person may be more qualified than any faculty member at that school to teach that particular class.

Schools with graduate programs usually rely on TAs to teach many of the introductory writing courses they offer and some of the introductory literature classes as well. TAs may also work as tutors in writing centers or as writing instructors in disciplines other than English if their university has a writing-across-the- curriculum program. TAs are usually paid a small stipend or salary for their work and are typically granted either full or partial tuition remission. Few receive other employment benefits. Though their work is often underappreciated and undercompensated, TAs are vital to the departments that employ them. They provide a wide range of services and play a variety of important roles.

TA ROLES: AN OVERVIEW

As a TA, you will play at least four distinct roles in an English department or writing program: instructor, graduate student, scholar, and colleague, the same roles tenure-line faculty fill. Ideally, these roles complement one another; filling the demands of one role helps you meet the demands of the others. In reality, though, for TAs these roles sometimes conflict, forcing you to set priorities and make choices. Learning how to handle the demands of TA life can be challenging. Yet each role you play also offers its own rewards and joys.

TA as Instructor

In your first year as a TA, this role will likely occupy most of your time and attention. You probably applied for a teaching assistantship because you want to teach. Because you want to do a good job in the classroom, you will likely spend a lot of time preparing every class you teach, grading your students' work, and worrying yourself to distraction if a class does not run as smoothly as you hoped. As a TA, you may be solely responsible for every aspect of teaching: developing your own syllabus, choosing your own textbooks, designing and grading all of the essays you assign, leading class discussions, solving problems in the classroom—the list goes on and on. Your department places a great deal of trust in your ability to perform these tasks well, which is a complement to your talents but also a source of worry. Many new TAs feel pressured to perform like experienced teachers in the classroom and are much too hard on themselves when classroom problems inevitably arise. Yet most TAs rise to the challenge; some even become exemplary teachers.

TA as Graduate Student

Some new TAs forget that they are also graduate students. While your role as a classroom teacher may occupy most of your attention, your role as a graduate student is actually more important: one of the quickest ways to lose a teaching assistantship is to perform poorly as a graduate student. If *your* grades slip or if your professors feel you are spending too little time on your own studies because of the time you spend getting ready to teach your classes, you may well lose your assistantship. Always remember your full title: *graduate* teaching assistant. You are a graduate student who teaches classes.

To succeed as a graduate student, you need to understand what professors expect of you. Professors usually expect their graduate students' work to be sophisticated, thorough, and independent. Many expectations are so basic they go without saying: graduate students will never miss class, they will always be prepared, they will read all required and supplemental texts, and they will turn in professional-quality work. In addition, though, graduate students are expected to make up for any deficiencies in their education: if a professor mentions an author or critic in class, you should find that person's work and read it; if you are taking a literary period course, you should brush up on the history of the time; if an author's work draws heavily on a particular literary, philosophical, or artistic movement, you should begin to study the source texts that author consulted. In short, as a graduate student, you will be expected to master more than just the material the professor covers in class. In examinations and papers, your graduate professors will want you to demonstrate the ability to analyze and evaluate what you have read; to synthesize material in original, interesting ways; and to form and defend your own interpretations of the material you study in class. As a graduate student, you will be expected to engage in real scholarship.

TA as Scholar

In most M.A. and M.F.A. programs and in all Ph.D. programs, graduate teaching assistants are expected to engage in a range of scholarly activities, including research and publication. Many doctoral students today build an impressive resume of publications and conference presentations that helps them land tenure-track jobs when they graduate. But engaging in academic scholarship serves a range of ends, not just improving your employment prospects.

First, venturing into research and publication as a TA helps you decide if a career in academics is what you want. If you get a job at a comprehensive or research university, you will be expected to publish if you hope to get tenure. Participating in these activities as a graduate student can help you determine whether you want to work at a school that emphasizes teaching or one that expects more research and publication. Second, scholarship can complement your graduate course work. As you take your classes, you may find authors, critics, texts, or literary movements that intrigue you. Through your research, you will develop a greater understanding of the material you study in class, placing you in a much better position to enter professional conversations on the topic.

Third, engaging in scholarly activity can improve your classroom teaching. The late Ernest Boyer argues in *Scholarship Reconsidered* that "scholarship" should not be too narrowly defined. In this important book, Boyer discusses four types of scholarship:

Scholarship of Discovery: In this category falls work that typically gets labeled as "research," work that creates or discovers new knowledge. Scholars use their expertise to add to an understanding of the world.

Scholarship of Integration: In this category falls work that involves contextualizing, interpreting, and synthesizing research findings. Scholars use their expertise to interpret what others have discovered.

Scholarship of Application: In this category falls work that typically gets labeled as "service," work that involves interacting with others in the academy and in the community. Scholars use their expertise to serve others.

Scholarship of Teaching: In this category falls work that aids student learning. Scholars use their expertise to develop ways of instructing students more thoroughly and effectively.

As a TA, you can begin to explore all four types of scholarship, determining which you find most rewarding. In fact, once you begin to teach your classes, you will almost surely become a researcher of some sort. For example, whenever you systematically analyze a classroom problem or develop new theories of instruction, you are engaging in the scholarship of discovery. Reading what others have to say about the problem and adapting their ideas to suit the needs of your students involves the scholarship of integration. If you volunteer to work as a tutor in your school's writing center or a community literacy program, you are engaging in the scholarship of application. Revising your course syllabus to better suit your students' needs involves you in the scholarship of teaching.

You may even begin to make this scholarship public through publication. For example, a professor might suggest that you revise a seminar paper for publication or that you present a paper at a conference. Many TAs begin their publishing careers with conference presentations. At local, state, regional, or national conferences, they discuss successful teaching activities or research projects. They then rework the material and submit it to professional journals for publication. Do not be surprised when faculty urge you to become an active, publishing scholar; it is one of the new roles you have taken on.

TA as Colleague

Just being a member of a department or program brings with it a wide range of roles to play. First, you will be interacting daily with your fellow TAs. In most departments, the TAs form a close, supportive community—working together and helping each other whenever possible makes the job easier. Some professors may develop a similar supportive relationship with you. These professors will consider you a junior colleague, treating you in ways they will not treat undergraduate students and other graduate students. They will see you as a fellow teacher, a colleague with whom they can "talk shop." Some TAs have a difficult time adjusting to this new role. Because they occupy a middle ground in the department—teacher and graduate student—they must learn to negotiate this shifting relationship with professors: in the hallway walking to their graduate course, they may be talking with their professor as fellow teacher, but when the class begins, they must assume the role of student again. Seeing yourself as a professional colleague in the department can be especially difficult if you are a TA who was an undergraduate student at the same institution. The relationship you have with your professors changes when you begin graduate study as a TA; roles you have spent years occupying as an undergraduate student in that program can be hard to change and adapt.

As a TA, you may also be asked to assume more official roles in the department or program, such as serving on committees or assisting various program directors. TAs often serve on committees that oversee the composition program or that hire new faculty. In most cases, you will have full voting rights as a member of the committee and will be expected to perform the same work as faculty members. You may also be asked to assume certain administrative roles in your department or program, such as assistant to the director of composition or assistant assessment coordinator. Again, even though you are "only" a TA, faculty members appointing you to these positions or fellow TAs electing you to serve in them will expect you to be an active, informed colleague.

All of these roles are explored in much greater detail throughout this book. The purpose of this brief overview is to alert you to the complex interplay of roles that comes with being a TA. You will embrace some of these roles; others you may try to avoid. Much depends on your goals for the future. As a TA, you can prepare yourself for the career that interests you. The key is to take advantage of the opportunity.

TYPICAL RESPONSIBILITIES OF TAs

TA job descriptions vary greatly from school to school, but some responsibilities remain fairly constant across institutions. Most of these responsibilities arise from your position as a teacher; others, though, involve program administration.

Pedagogical Responsibilities

These responsibilities result from being a classroom teacher. They will vary from school to school and even from TA to TA within a department or program: more experienced TAs typically have more freedom when designing and teaching a course than do less experienced TAs. Below are some of the more common pedagogical responsibilities for TAs.

Designing a Course Syllabus

Some departments give their TAs a syllabus to follow that spells out, day to day, what the TA is supposed to cover in class. Other departments allow

TAs—especially those with some experience—to develop their own course syllabus within established guidelines. These guidelines often spell out the philosophy of composition favored by the department, the number and types of papers students are supposed to write in the course, and the types of readings students are supposed to study. Still other programs allow TAs to develop their own course syllabi without guidance, especially if they are teaching an upper-level class. For more information on designing course syllabi, see Chapter 2.

Choosing a Textbook

Some departments select the books TAs use in their classes, others let TAs choose a text from a departmentally approved list, and a few let TAs choose textbooks on their own, giving them the same freedom enjoyed by professors. If you get the chance to teach an introductory literature class when you are a TA, you will likely choose your own textbooks. For a discussion of how to choose good textbooks and readings, see Chapter 2.

Creating Assignments

Most TAs design their own assignments. Developing expertise in this area of teaching is important because a poorly designed or written assignment will likely lead to poorly written papers. Chapter 4 discusses in detail how to design effective assignments. Remember too that you will always find faculty or experienced TAs willing to share assignments that worked well for them in the past or to critique drafts of your assignments.

Grading Assignments

Once students write those papers, you will have to grade their work. For new TAs, this can be one of the most time-consuming aspects of teaching, especially when they evaluate that first set of student papers. Grading can also be a source of great anxiety. Inexperienced TAs lack a set of standards against which to evaluate student work. With experience, it becomes easier to say, "This is an 'A' paper, or this is a 'C' paper," but learning to make those judgments takes practice. If you are a TA working with a professor who lectures to a large group of students, you may be responsible for grading assignments using a rubric the professor designed. You might even be asked to help the director of composition evaluate placement or exit examinations, usually in a holistic grading session. Evaluating and responding to writing are central to your life as a TA and are discussed in Chapter 5 and Chapter 6.

Developing Effective Teaching Strategies

Once you know which courses you will teach, you need to consider carefully how you will use the time you have with your students. If you teach an introductory composition class that meets three days a week for sixteen weeks, you have roughly forty-five class sessions with your students. How will you use those forty-five meetings to help your students become more effective college readers and writers? What are the best teaching strategies to employ, given the course and students you are teaching? Making wise pedagogical choices throughout the course differentiates effective from ineffective teachers. A range of teaching strategies is discussed in Chapter 7.

Meeting with Students Outside of Class

Much of the instruction you offer students will occur outside of the classroom. Most departments require you to keep a certain number of office hours each week so students know when you will be available for conferences. Maintaining these hours is important. In fact, many teachers make out-of-class teaching a central part of their course. They like to work with students individually in less formal settings, such as at the library or school cafeteria. You will discover that working one-on-one with a student for even five minutes can sometimes be more productive than working with that student and his peers for an hour in class. Working with students outside of class allows you to individualize instruction and give students your undivided attention. Tips on effective conferencing are offered in Chapter 9.

Addressing Students' Questions

As the classroom teacher, you are the first person students will come to if they have questions about the course material or their writing. Yet at some point all new TAs wonder, "What if my students ask me a question, and I don't have the answer?" Quite naturally, new TAs are concerned about losing credibility if they get stumped by a question. Yet, even experienced teachers cannot answer every student question and often give answers they later regret, that are wrong or incomplete. If you do not know the answer to a student's question, part of your job as a TA is to find it. Being a teacher involves constant learning—you are responsible for looking up answers to questions and educating yourself about the topics you teach.

Administrative Responsibilities

Although most of your responsibilities as a TA are connected with your teaching, others may involve administration. As a member of a department or program, you may have additional responsibilities.

Addressing Placement Questions

Most departments and programs have well-established procedures for placing students in the proper introductory writing course. These procedures determine which students are placed in advanced, regular, or developmental writing classes and are based on standardized test scores, writing samples, high school writing portfolios, or some combination of measurements. As a TA, you may play an important role in these placement procedures and decisions. For example, you may help administer placement tests or give your students a diagnostic essay the first week of class to determine if they were placed correctly. Making sure each student gets into the appropriate class is a major responsibility of every teacher and writing program administrator.

Addressing Drop and Add Questions

In many departments, the director of composition oversees the drop-add procedure for first-year writing classes to ensure that no section has too many students. If this is the case, as the classroom teacher you need to direct students to the appropriate administrator if they want to drop or add your class. If you are teaching an introductory literature course, however, adding or dropping students from your class will be your responsibility. In an effort to accommodate students, you have to be careful not to overload your course.

Giving Midterm Grades, Final Grades, and Academic Progress Reports

Almost all colleges and universities still award grades for courses. Calculating and reporting midterm and final grades takes time, and the work almost always falls at a bad point in the semester for TAs. You can count on having to calculate grades just when your own seminar projects and papers are due. School administrators may also ask you to fill out academic progress reports on at-risk students or student athletes. These reports alert administrators that particular students may be struggling in your class and need additional assistance.

Identifying and Working with Special Needs Students

By federal law, teachers have to make every reasonable effort to accommodate students with special needs—students with physical or mental handicaps or students with learning disabilities. Most colleges and universities have a central office and administrator to serve these students. As a teacher, you will likely be notified of any special needs students in your class and told what accommodations to make. However, not all students with learning disabilities like to call attention to themselves, and many do not want special treatment. If you believe that one of your students falls into this category, you need to decide how to approach the matter in a way that is both ethical and legal. Federal law dictates what you may and may not say to this student, so always bring your concerns to your teaching supervisor before approaching the student. Together, you can help ensure that every student in your class gets the type of instruction and support he or she needs.

Assessing Program Outcomes

An increasing number of accrediting agencies are demanding that colleges and universities articulate specific outcomes for their writing programs and assess those outcomes using multiple measures. As a teacher in a composition program, you may be called on to help implement the department's assessment plan. For example, you may be asked to summarize student and faculty survey results, tally questionnaires, or evaluate portfolios of student work. These assessment activities usually occur between terms when you might have other plans. As a member of the teaching staff, you are responsible for helping when asked.

Designing Web Pages

Many schools are asking all of their teachers—TAs included—to build and maintain individual or course Web pages. If you do not know how to build a Web page, most schools offer classes to teach you the basics and tutors to help you solve problems. Just be aware that as a TA, you likely will not be exempt from this requirement. If you are new to the process, constructing a Web page can be time consuming, but it can also be a lot of fun once you learn how. (See Chapter 8 for some advice on building a course Web site.)

TA EDUCATION PROGRAMS

Clearly, as a TA you are required to do much more than just teach your classes and grade your papers. Most universities recognize how overwhelming these responsibilities can be, especially for new TAs, and have developed a range of services to educate, prepare, and support TAs. In her survey of graduate teaching assistant (GTA) education programs across the country, Catherine G. Latterell found remarkable uniformity. Her findings are worth quoting at length:

> What is immediately noticeable about the descriptions of the GTA education programs I received is their rough similarity given a wide range of programmatic possibilities. Of the 36 programs represented in this survey, 23 locate their teacher preparation program in a single course, which may or may not be repeated throughout each term of a GTA's initial year of teaching. Another seven programs have developed a combination of courses which fulfill their teacher preparation requirements, and two more have developed extensive mentoring programs in combination with a course requirement …. Mentoring programs which involve experienced GTAs, part-time instructors, and/or full-time faculty in the professional development of first-year GTAs exist in varying degrees in all programs. Additionally, nearly all of the programs (32) reported that they require a fall orientation for new GTAs …. Of the 32 programs requiring an orientation, half stated that it lasted five days or more—with two programs reporting the GTAs enroll in required writing pedagogy courses during the summer. (10)

Your school may not offer all of these services and educational opportunities, but be sure to take advantage of what is available.

Pre- and In-Service Workshops

As Latterell's study indicates, most English departments and writing programs offer preservice workshops for new TAs; many, in fact, require attendance. The length and structure of these workshops vary greatly from school to school. Some workshops take place a few days before the fall term begins; others last several weeks. Some are department- or program based, whereas others involve TAs from across the curriculum. Regardless of their structure, these workshops tend to have the same goal: to introduce you to the university, the department, and the writing program; to review university and department policies on issues such as attendance, late work, plagiarism, student classroom conduct, and sexual harassment; and to teach you how to design assignments, respond to and grade student writing, present material in class, and hold student conferences.

Once the semester or quarter begins, many schools offer in-service workshops for their TAs and teaching staff. These workshops, held periodically throughout the term, usually focus on one or two aspects of teaching, such as responding to student writing or working with international students. Some programs make attending these workshops optional; some make them mandatory. Some schools pay TAs if they attend these workshops; most do not.

Practica

Most teaching practica involve TAs meeting with their supervisor once a week for an hour or so to discuss their teaching, to address problems, and to plan future class sessions. In larger programs that employ many TAs, the leader of the practicum may be an experienced TA working with a small group of newer TAs. Sometimes TAs get course credit for taking the practicum; sometimes they do not. Practica sessions tend to be informal and practical, addressing day-to-day classroom needs, questions, and concerns. During these sessions, TAs are encouraged to share successful assignments and classroom activities and are allowed to vent when their teaching is not so successful.

Courses

Many programs require TAs to take certain courses as a part of their assistantship both before and while they teach. For example, some departments or programs require TAs to pass a course in writing theory and/or pedagogy the summer before they teach for the first time. At other schools, TAs do not teach a course until the second year of their assistantship, after they have taken several required courses and perhaps observed several teachers in the classroom. Still other programs require TAs to take courses in writing theory and pedagogy as part of their degree program. Universities that offer a doctorate in rhetoric and composition may have a wide range of required courses, including classes in the history of rhetoric, rhetorical theory, composition theory, composition pedagogy, writing program administration, research methodologies in rhetoric and composition, cognitive psychology, and learning theory.

Peer Mentors

Your program may appoint you a peer mentor, an experienced TA you can turn to for help and advice. Peer mentors can answer questions about the courses you are teaching and your degree program. Their advice and guidance can be invaluable since they, like you, are TAs in the program. Peer mentors are especially helpful in answering practical questions about the program and school: which professors have the best reputations, where to purchase your books, how to find an apartment, where to find help for a troubled student, or how to write assessments for midterm reports.

Faculty Mentors

In addition to peer mentors, many writing programs—especially smaller ones—also assign TAs a faculty mentor or teaching advisor. This faculty member works with only one or two TAs and is responsible for answering specific questions they have about teaching. A faculty mentor will likely watch you teach class and offer advice, review a set of papers you have evaluated to check on your grading standards and procedures, and examine the assignments and tests you prepare. Some faculty mentors will seek you out and request this material; others prefer to wait for you to come to them with questions or problems. In some programs, your faculty mentor will write an evaluative letter at the end of the academic year stipulating whether the department should extend your contract another year.

Academic Advisors

Faculty mentors answer questions you have about teaching; academic advisors answer questions you have about your graduate studies. Your faculty mentor may change from year to year, but at most institutions, your academic advisor remains unchanged so he or she can better track the progress you make toward your degree. You should consult your academic advisor when choosing courses, dropping or adding a class, or preparing for the job market. He or she will be an important part of every aspect of your studies. At some schools, especially small ones, one faculty member may serve as both your teaching mentor and academic advisor.

Directors of TA Education

Many departments select one faculty member to supervise the preparation of all the TAs. Whether the director of composition or the director of TA education, this person likely runs the program's pre- and in-service workshops, teaches some of the required courses, and is the first person you will turn to if you have questions about your teaching. Faculty members are typically named to this position because (1) they have a strong background in rhetoric and composition, (2) they work well with new instructors, and (3) they are excellent teachers themselves. Forming a strong working relationship with this faculty member can make your classroom teaching much more productive, much more enjoyable, and far less stressful.

Department Libraries

Good teachers do research. Instead of just reading the required textbook and teaching from it, they consult a range of books, articles, and Web sites for new information and new teaching techniques. Much of this material is available on-line or in your department, especially if your department maintains a library of composition textbooks. Spending a few hours consulting these texts before you teach can help you enter the classroom much better prepared and much more confident.

Collections of Course Material

Most directors of composition maintain a collection of successful course material that TAs can consult as they plan and teach their own classes. These collections often include course syllabi, assignments, examinations, exercises, worksheets, and overheads. Examining these documents can make constructing new course material much easier, offering models you can adapt for your own needs. Studying how other teachers teach can help you gain a deeper, fuller understanding of the profession and discover new instructional techniques. Sometimes this material is stored in folders or binders, but increasingly departments are putting it on disk or on-line.

Web Resources

That some of this successful course material is now on-line opens up a new, expansive resource for TAs: the World Wide Web. Many college and university writing programs around the country place their course and program material on-line, allowing anyone to examine their syllabi, class policy statements, assignments, and exercises. These sites may also contain links to other support material, books or articles, professional organizations such as the Modern Language Association, or on-line tutorials or on-line writing labs. Chapter 8 offers a more extensive overview of Web resources.

Campus Writing Centers

A school's writing center or writing lab offer students the individualized attention they often need to write more successfully. Just as important for TAs, though, is the expertise amassed by writing center directors and tutors. If you have a question about how to reach a particular student or address a particular kind of writing problem in your class, a writing center tutor or its director can offer practical, informed, time-tested advice.

EMPLOYMENT CONCERNS

Most TAs do not think of themselves as employees, and for good reason. Universities themselves seem undecided on this issue: when it comes to tax law, they tend to view TAs as employees, a fact made clear to TAs when they look at the deductions on their first pay check. When it comes to offering benefits, however, most universities view TAs as graduate students, no more entitled to benefits than any other nonteaching graduate student in the department. At universities across the country, TAs have unionized in an effort to improve their working conditions.

Thinking of yourself as an employee goes beyond a concern over salary and benefits, however. Your teaching will be easier and better if you have adequate office space and supplies and access to telephones, photocopying machines, networked computers, travel funds, and secretarial support. Many departments do their best to improve the working conditions of TAs, but others do not, leaving it up to the TAs themselves to push for needed changes.

Stipends and Teaching Load

Your stipend and teaching load should be specified in your contract—you should know exactly how much you are getting paid to teach a certain number of classes. Some departments automatically increase your pay each year; others base raises on a competitive merit pay system. Most merit pay systems are based on an annual review of your teaching, research, service, and progress toward degree. If you work in such a department, be sure you understand the system: who makes the merit pay decisions, and what criteria and standards are employed?

Many TAs find it impossible to live on their stipend alone. They either take out a loan to supplement their income or take on a second job. If you want to get a second job, be sure to check with your department chair or teaching supervisor. Some departments and universities do not want TAs—especially those teaching for the first time—to moonlight. Other TAs prefer to find a second university job—working in a library or cafeteria, for example. Again, check with your department chair or teaching supervisor to see if such employment is going to be a problem, and then check with your school's human resources office to fill out the proper tax forms.

Tuition Remission

Most TA positions carry with them full tuition remission—you do not have to pay tuition for the required classes you take. Schools that do not offer tuition remission often allow TAs to pay for their graduate courses at a reduced rate. If you receive tuition remission as a part of your assistantship and still receive a bill for your classes, see your department secretary or chair. More likely than not, the graduate school that awarded you the assistantship did not send your name to the bursar's office, which sent you the bill. A telephone call from the department chair or secretary usually solves the problem.

Make sure you understand the limits of your tuition remission. Schools typically restrict the number of credit hours you take each academic year without charge—you will have to pay out of pocket for any credit hours you take over that limit. Also, find out if summer courses will be covered under your tuition remission plan and whether your plan covers graduate classes taken outside your major. In most cases they do, but it is best to find out before you sign up for these classes and receive a bill. Finally, be sure you understand how many years your tuition remission will last. Once you complete your required classes, you may need to write a thesis or dissertation. As you complete these projects, you will sign up for enough thesis hours to remain a full-time student. Be sure you understand whether your tuition remission covers these hours as well.

Insurance

Some schools do not offer TAs insurance coverage—TAs must shop the market for a policy they can afford. Other schools allow TAs to purchase health insurance through the university at a discounted rate. Many of these policies have limited benefits, but they might be all you can afford. Your school's personnel or human resources office will be able to give you the information you need to purchase this insurance (some schools will even allow TAs to purchase their plans with pretax dollars, saving you money). You might also want to check on dental insurance. Most university health insurance plans available to TAs do not include dental coverage; it must be purchased separately. Finally, before you purchase insurance on your own, check with your parents. If you are young enough, you might still be able to get coverage under your parents' insurance plans even though you are working as a TA.

Office Space

TAs rarely get a private office. Instead, most have to share office space. Sometimes two or three TAs have to share an office; other times a dozen or more may be placed in a "bull pen," a large office with several desks or tables. At a minimum, you should have your own desk, some sort of filing cabinet so you can store student papers, and a book case. The furniture you get may be second-hand and mismatched, but as the semester goes along, you will be glad you have it.

Telephones

Most departments realize that TAs need telephones in their offices (though in a bull pen, a dozen or more TAs may be sharing the same telephone). If you do not have a telephone in your office, check with your department chair or teaching supervisor to find out what number students should call to contact you or to leave a message.

Mailboxes

Every department should provide each TA with a mailbox, either in the department office or in the TAs' offices. If your department does not provide you with a mailbox, ask where your students should drop off their papers. Having the students slide a paper under your office door is not acceptable— too many papers get lost or thrown away by the cleaning staff when students do this. If your department does not provide you with a mailbox, work with your fellow TAs to set up your own. Your students need a safe place to drop off their work.

Computers

Computers have become an essential teaching tool, especially for writing instructors and TAs. You will use computers to complete assignments and projects for your graduate classes and to prepare material for the classes you are teaching. Many TAs, in fact, build their courses around the computer— they place course material on a Web site, communicate with their students through e-mail, and respond to student work on-line. Although departments are increasingly providing TAs with computers in their offices, many still do not. There are some alternatives.

First, obtain a computer account at your school. This account will allow you to use the university's computers and labs and to set up a university e-mail account. Second, if your department cannot afford to purchase a computer for each TA or for each TA office, see if your chair or supervisor can place a few computers and printers in a central departmental computer "lab" that TAs can share. Third, if you bring your own computer to the office, ask that your office be networked. For a small cost, the department can wire your office for Internet access. You can make a strong case that such access is necessary for your job as a teacher and your success as a graduate student. Fourth, if you want to purchase your own computer, see if your university offers low-cost loans for this purpose. Many do. If all else fails, find out which departments—such as journalism, computer science, or biology—have computer labs you can use and whether your campus library provides access to computers for research and writing.

One caution: if you use a "public" computer, be sure someone has installed a good antivirus program on the machines. Also install a good antivirus program on your own computer if you bring home disks you used at school. An infected disk can wipe out weeks' worth of work.

Research Grants

As a TA, you may be able to apply for several types of research grants. These grants—typically awarded during summer terms—are intended to support your efforts to complete research projects arising from your graduate study (many schools also offer separate grants to support graduate students who are writing their dissertations). These grants are usually awarded competitively; applications typically include a description and defense of the research project, a detailed budget, a time line, and letters of support from faculty.

Over the past few years, the definition of "scholarship" has been changing and a new type of research grant is growing in popularity, one aimed at improving instruction. These "teaching" or "instructional" grants support the faculty's efforts to develop instructional applications of current research, improve existing classes, design new courses, or apply technology in the classroom. Increasingly, TAs are able to compete for these grants as well.

Travel Funds

If one of your papers is accepted for presentation at a professional conference or if you are invited to give a poetry or fiction reading, your department or university may have funds available to subsidize the trip. However, policies on distributing travel funds vary widely. Some schools offer no funding for TAs; other schools offer full or partial funding. Those offering full or partial funding may distribute the money only after you formally apply for the funds and administrators have the opportunity to review your request in light of other requests. Not all requests will be funded. Some schools set aside a separate fund for TA travel expenses—to get this money, TAs compete among themselves. Other schools fund TA travel out of departmental accounts—TAs compete against other TAs and faculty for these funds. To get travel funds, check with your department chair as soon as you receive notice that your work has been accepted for presentation. Do not put off your request, and by all means do not attend the conference at your own expense and then apply for compensation after the fact, unless your department chair tells you to do so.

Getting an early start on funding is important because as a TA, you may have a range of resources available to you. For example, college deans and provosts often maintain supplementary accounts to support TA research and travel. TAs often have to combine funding from several sources to pay for a conference presentation. Doing this takes time but may be the only way you can fund the trip.

Library Privileges

Most college and university libraries treat graduate students and TAs differently than they treat other students when it comes to the services they offer. As a TA, your loan periods might be extended, late fines may be waived, some photocopying may be free, interlibrary loan access may be expanded, and access to special collections may be available. Check with your teaching supervisor or a reference librarian to find out what library privileges are available.

Parking

Just about every campus in the country has a parking problem: too many vehicles, not enough parking spaces. As a TA, though, you will likely move toward the front of the line when parking permits are distributed, you may be allowed to park in faculty or staff lots, and you may receive your pass at a discounted price. Be sure to check with your chair or with your campus's parking services to determine where you are supposed to park and how much a permit should cost.

Keys

As a TA, make sure you have a key to your office and to the building that houses your office. You may need to work late at night or early on weekends when the building might be locked. Also, ask your department chair and teaching supervisor about getting keys for any computer facility you use on a regular basis and for the room that houses the duplicating machine (especially if you teach early in the morning, before secretaries will be available to open the room for you). TAs tend to keep odd hours—you get your work done when you can. Make sure you have access to all the facilities you need.

BALANCING DEMANDS: LIFE AS A TA

Life as a TA can be hectic and demanding—you have many roles to play, many responsibilities to fulfill, and many people depending on you to do a good job. You will also find that your years as a TA offer some of the richest rewards of your professional career. Rarely again will you experience the same excitement of learning and growing; rarely again will you be surrounded by peers focused so intently on improving as teachers; rarely again will you form such strong friendships. Below are a few tips that can help you get the most out of your TA experience.

Get Organized

Without good organizational skills, you will likely fall behind in the classes you are taking and teaching. When this happens, you may feel overwhelmed, unable to ever catch up. Of course, you can and will catch up, but it is better to avoid the problem altogether, and the only way to do this is to stay organized. First, if you do not already have one, purchase a daily course planner to record the dates, times, and locations of all your classes, meetings, and appointments, and the due dates for all your work. Many computers come with calendars as well. If yours does, use it too and begin every morning reviewing what you need to do that day and the next. If necessary, write down the due dates for important projects and post them on your desk or on your office door, someplace you will see them every day.

Second, learn to use lists wisely. On Sunday nights, for example, list the projects that are due the next week. Do the same thing on Fridays—list the tasks you need to complete over the weekend. Marking off tasks as you complete them will give you a sense of progress and accomplishment. If you do not get every task completed, do not worry. List tasks in order of importance—finish the most important projects first, save the rest for later. Finally, try hard not to put off work, especially in your graduate courses. Because so many graduate courses require long projects due the last week of class, it is easy to forget about the assignment the first month or so of the term. That is a mistake. Break big projects into smaller tasks and set due dates for each one. Hitting these deadlines will help you avoid a panicked rush at the end of the course. Staying organized and even a little ahead of due dates is your best bet for avoiding problems.

Set Priorities

As mentioned above, part of getting organized is setting priorities. However, these priorities will change throughout the semester. For example, sometimes your top priority will be getting a set of papers graded and returned to your students. Other times it will be finishing a research project of your own or getting out of town for the weekend. Learning how to weigh and balance these priorities takes time. Remember, though, that family demands trump all other concerns. Sometimes resolving problems in your personal life is more important than anything happening at school. When personal or family conflicts occur, take care of yourself and your family without guilt. School is short and life is long. Your course work and class work will get done eventually. If personal or family problems seriously interfere with your work, do not hesitate to talk to your professors or teaching supervisor about getting help; they have likely faced similar problems.

Set Goals

You will need to set all sorts of goals as a TA: academic and personal; long-term, medium-term, and short-term; specific and abstract. Goals keep you focused and allow you to look back at the end of the day, the end of the week, or the end of a term and assess your progress. Goals help you set needed priorities, choose among competing agendas, and stay organized.

Long-term abstract goals include preparing for future employment, finding more time for your family, or improving as a classroom instructor. You will complete these goals sometime in the future or perhaps work on them the rest of your life. These goals help you refocus when you doubt the direction your life is taking, feel overwhelmed by work, or have to make major life-changing decisions.

Long-term specific goals include completing your degree work, preparing for the Graduate Record Exam, or applying for employment. As a new TA, you need to see the finish line, what you are working toward, to stay organized and motivated. Some time in the future you will complete your degree work, take your qualifying exams, and write your dissertation. Right now, though, you need to prepare yourself to reach those goals. Without working hard now, you never will attain them.

Medium-term goals include those you set for the semester: what you want to accomplish in the classes you are taking and teaching. Some of these goals will be very abstract: you want your students to improve as writers or you want to become a better critic of poetry. Others will be more specific: you want your students to learn MLA citation standards or you want to complete your paper on "Lamia." Other goals might be more personal—by the end of the term, you will complete the short story you started or devote at least two weekends a month to your family.

Short-term goals include those you set for a particular week or day. You may decide that by the end of the week, for example, you will respond to your students' journals and finish reading *Middlemarch*. By the end of the day, you will e-mail the writing center to set up appointments for your students or you will choose a spot for your summer vacation. Setting small, short-term goals is an important part of time management. Without them, it is easy to waste time, and as a TA, you will have little time to waste. Figure 1.1 outlines several of these long-term, medium-term, and short-term goals.

Committing these goals to writing is vital. Taking just a few minutes to jot down your goals will help you clarify your plans, set priorities, and organize your time. When you accomplish a goal, scratch it off the list.

There will be times, every term, when you look at your list and realize you can never get everything done. Do not despair. Instead, get done what

FIGURE 1.1   Sample Goals

	Time Frame	Abstract Goals	Specific goals
Long Term Goals	Accomplish during degree program	Gain expertise in a field Prepare for the job market Become a stronger teacher Focus on academics	Read all of Trollope's novels Publish five papers Improve as a lecturer Complete all required courses
Medium Term Goals	Accomplish during semester/ term	Improve my students' writing Improve skills as a critic Get more of my work done Get home more often	Focus on structure and voice Learn material in poetry class Finish short story Thanksgiving with the folks
Short Term Goals	Accomplish during week/ day	Finish grading student papers Finish research on term paper Jazz up my teaching a little Get more exercise	Grade 5 papers a day Search ERIC and MLA Try group work and reports Go swimming Friday

you can and begin a new list, moving the uncompleted tasks to the top. Learning to set and achieve goals as a TA is one of the most important skills you can acquire.

Use "Down Time" Wisely

As a TA, you will quickly discover the rhythm of college teaching. Periods of hectic activity—grading that first set of student papers, for example—give way to "down time" when the pace is slower. Learn to use this down time wisely. Many new TAs are fooled by the pace of the first few weeks of the term—usually a down time. Their graduate classes are just gearing up, no big projects are due, no student papers need to be graded—this is a time when being a TA seems to be a snap. This is the time, however, when you should be getting ahead on your work—reading the books required in your graduate courses, designing future assignments you will give your students, working on a grant proposal or a conference paper. Midterms and finals are traditionally hectic periods, as are the days right before Thanksgiving or spring break. You may have several sets of papers to grade and several papers of your own to write. If you used your earlier down time wisely, you will get through these busy periods fine. If you did not use it well, these can be difficult, stressful times. Always keep an eye on the academic calendar. Plot out when papers and other projects are due, ones you have to write and ones you have to grade. In the days and weeks between these times, accomplish what you can to get ahead and prepare.

Combine Tasks

Look for ways required tasks might overlap. Can the research you do for a graduate course paper help you prepare for one of the classes you are teaching? Can a class exercise become a research project and possible publication? Are there committee assignments open that will help you prepare yourself for the job market? Look for connections among the various roles you play. When you combine tasks, you save yourself a lot of time. Additionally, you tend to put more care and attention into these projects when you know they serve multiple purposes.

Get Exercise

This imperative may seem out of place, but it is important. Too many TAs develop a "bunker" mentality. They become so consumed by their studies and their teaching that they ignore other vital aspects of their lives, including their health. Getting regular exercise will improve your well being, increase your energy, and relieve stress. Visit the gym or pool whenever possible—shoot baskets, swim a few laps, walk around the block—whatever form of exercise you prefer. One trick to make sure this happens: as you fill out your calendar for the semester, mark in the days you will get exercise.

Treat these times like class meetings or appointments—do not bump them unless you absolutely have to. If you schedule yourself to jog at noon on Monday, Wednesday, and Friday, for example, and a student wants to meet with you then, tell the student you are busy and schedule a different meeting time. Maybe you and a few other TAs can work out together a few times a week. Having a partner can sometimes help you keep to a regular schedule. Finding time for exercise can be hard, but TAs who manage it feel less stressed than those who do not.

Set Aside Time for Your Family

Balancing your life as a TA includes finding time for your family too. Do not neglect the obligations you have toward your spouse, life partner, significant other, or children. Your teaching assistantship may cause them stress as well. I recall going home on many Thanksgiving breaks as a TA with a set of papers to grade. I had to get them done—the members of my family understood this—but they also expected me to put the papers aside from time to time, which I had to understand. When my oldest daughter was two or three years old, she would let me know it was time to stop studying and pay attention to her by crawling in my lap and taking off my glasses. As a TA, it is easy to lose perspective. You become so engrossed in your teaching and studying, you may forget to pay enough attention to your loved ones. As you schedule your life, save time for them too.

Set Aside Time for Yourself

What nonacademic things do you like to do? Read trashy novels? Watch videos? Play the piano? Whatever it is, do not lose it while you are in graduate school. At the end of a long day or long week, return to those things—you need them to maintain a sense of who you are. Are you wasting time? Well perhaps, but you may need to. Having some quiet time alone is important. It lets you refocus, escape your concerns, and recharge. Also, before you became a TA, did you like going to church on Sunday? Did you spend time coaching your kid's soccer team? Did you volunteer at the community center? In many ways, being a TA will define your life—it takes up so much of your time, you may feel like you have no other life to live. Try not to let this happen. Realistically, you probably will not be able to do everything you did before you became a TA. However, you do not have to abandon the life you led before you took on the assistantship. Plus if you are a first-year TA, know that this is likely the busiest you will be. Over the years, as you gain more experience, you will find yourself spending less time on your teaching and grading than you are now. Certain aspects of your life may need to go on hold while you complete your assistantship—especially that first year—and others may have to be scaled back. But to the best of your ability, try to maintain a life outside the university.

CONCLUSION

Your life as a TA can be difficult and challenging, but it can also be rewarding. Use this time to your best advantage by exploring all of the roles you play, teaching a range of courses, experimenting with classroom pedagogy, taking classes from a variety of professors, attending local art exhibits and concerts, and forming friendships with your peers and professors. While a TA, you will have many opportunities to develop your skills as a teacher, scholar, and colleague. Setting goals, staying focused and organized, and using your time wisely will help you make the most of your teaching assistantship

WORKS CITED

Boyer, Ernest L. *Scholarship Reconsidered: Priorities of the Professorate*. Princeton, NJ: Carnegie Foundation for the Advancement of Teaching, 1990.

Latterell, Catherine G. "Training the Workforce: An Overview of GTA Education Curricula." *WPA* 19.3 (1996): 7–23.

ADDITIONAL READINGS

Abbott, Robert D., Donald H. Wulff, and C. Kati Szego. "Review of Research on TA Training." *Teaching Assistant Training in the 1990s*. Eds. Jody D. Nyquist, Robert D. Abbott, and Donald H. Wulff. San Francisco: Jossey-Bass, 1989. 111–24.

Brannon, Lil, and Gordon Pradl. "The Socialization of Writing Teachers." *Journal of Basic Writing* 3 (1984): 28–37.

Lauer, Janice M. "Graduate Students as Active Members of the Profession: Some Questions for Mentoring." *Publishing in Rhetoric and Composition*. Eds. Gary A. Olson and Todd W. Taylor. Albany: State University of New York Press, 1997. 229–35.

Leverenz, Carrie Shively, and Amy Goodburn. "Professionalizing TA Training: Commitment to Teaching or Rhetorical Response to Market Crisis?" *WPA* 22.1–2 (1998): 9–32.

Long, Mark C., Jennifer H. Holberg, and Marcy M. Taylor. "Beyond Apprenticeship: Graduate Students, Professional Development Programs and the Future(s) of English Studies." *WPA* 20 (1996): 66–78.

Nyquist, Jody D., and Jo Sprague. "Thinking Developmentally about TA." *The Professional Development of Graduate Teaching Assistants*. Eds. Michele Marincovich, Jack Prostko, and Frederic Stout. Bolton, MA: Ankor, 1998. 61–88.

Staton, Ann Q., and Ann L. Darling. "Socialization of Teaching Assistants." *Teaching Assistant Training in the 1990s*. Eds. Jody D. Nyquist, Robert D. Abbott, and Donald H. Wulff. San Francisco: Jossey-Bass, 1989. 15–22.

CHAPTER 2

Getting Ready to Teach Before Classes Begin

INTRODUCTION

Teaching for the first time can be intimidating. For most of your life, you have been a student; now you are going to move to the other side of the teacher's desk. Feeling nervous or apprehensive about the situation is normal. In fact, many experienced teachers still get nervous that first day as they meet a new group of students and begin a new class. Many new TAs face an additional source of anxiety: taking graduate classes for the first time. As you begin your program of graduate study, you may not know what to expect, which courses to take, how to fulfill your degree requirements, or what your professors will be like. This chapter is written with the new TA in mind, someone beginning graduate degree work and teaching a course for the first time. No matter how long you have been a TA, though, completing a few tasks before the semester begins will ease your nervousness and help you get off to a successful start.

LEARNING ABOUT YOUR GRADUATE PROGRAM, DEPARTMENT, AND UNIVERSITY

Once you have been accepted into a university's graduate program and awarded a teaching assistantship, familiarize yourself with your department's degree program, making sure you understand which courses you have to take, which examinations you have to pass, and when you should complete these requirements. First, obtain a copy of the school's graduate bulletin (which lays out your degree requirements) and a course catalogue for the upcoming semester (which lists the classes that will be offered) to help you decide which classes you want to take your first semester.

Next, contact the department chair and get the name of your academic advisor, the faculty member who will guide you through your degree requirements. Contact that person right away by letter, e-mail, or telephone and set up an appointment to discuss the classes you will be taking. When you meet, ask your advisor to review the degree requirements with you to be sure you understand them, to approve your course selections for the upcoming term, and to map out a sequence of courses you should take over the next year or so. You need to develop a long-range view of your graduate education, a sense of what courses you will take in what order.

While you are on campus for this appointment, take care of some other important business. For example, check on housing. Many universities have an office of graduate housing that maintains lists of available apartments and rooms, both on campus and off. Some departments keep these lists as well. Perhaps your best source of information on housing, though, is other TAs. Ask the department to send you the names, addresses, telephone numbers, and e-mail addresses of several TAs who would be willing to help you find housing.

Also check on the university's pay schedule. Your contract will specify your salary and teaching load. However, the department chair can tell you when you will receive your first pay check, how often they are issued, and how they are delivered. This information will help you determine your budget for the upcoming year. Now is also the time to check on benefits at the university's human resources office, which should have detailed information on all the insurance policies the university offers TAs. Find out whether medical insurance is available, how much it costs, and when the enrollment period opens.

Check with the chair to find out when you can move into your office. Office assignments are usually made prior to any preservice workshop. Also investigate the university's computer facilities and find out which labs are open to graduate students and how to obtain a university computing account. The department chair can give you information on parking and should be able to tell you about gaining access to the school's athletic facilities. Finally, ask when to report to campus before classes begin. If your school does not offer preservice training, plan to be on campus a few days before classes begin so you will be settled in before meeting your students for the first time.

As you see, there is a lot to do before you take that first graduate class. If you forget or are unable to complete any of these steps, you can take care of most of them once the term begins—you will just have to face longer lines and longer waits. Completing several of these tasks before the term begins makes the first few weeks of classes much easier on you. The tasks you should complete before your graduate courses begin are summarized in Checklist 2.1 at the end of this chapter.

GETTING READY TO TEACH
YOUR CLASSES

Once you are awarded your assistantship, you can also begin preparing material for the classes you will teach. Even if your school requires new TAs to follow a standard course syllabus and use a textbook selected by the department, understanding how to develop a syllabus and how to choose a textbook can still be helpful. As the term gets under way, with the approval of your teaching supervisor, you may want to deviate from the standard department syllabus or choose a supplementary textbook. This chapter offers advice on learning more about the class you will teach, selecting a textbook, preparing a course syllabus and policy sheet, and assuming your new role as a classroom instructor. (Because most new TAs will initially teach composition courses, this chapter focuses on getting ready to teach writing classes. For advice on planning a literature class, see Chapter 11.)

Learning More about the Courses You Will Teach

If your writing program requires new TAs to teach from a standard syllabus and use a common textbook, getting ready to teach is easier than when you have to design your own class and select your own texts. However, you still have some important work to do in the weeks leading up to class. You need to study the required textbooks and course syllabus, examine any available sample assignment sheets, and discuss the class with people who have taught it before.

First, ask the director of composition or the director of TA education to send you a copy of each textbook you will be required to use and read them cover to cover. Once class begins, you do not want to be in the position of staying a chapter ahead of your students. Second, note what each book covers and contains. What aspects of writing does each book address? How is each organized? Do any of the books have suggested writing assignments? Do any of them have student exercises? Are there any parts of the books you find especially difficult or especially interesting? As well as you can judge, are there sections first-year college students might find difficult to follow? Do the books contain sample readings? If so, which readings seem more compelling than others? Which readings might your students find especially interesting or difficult? In short, read the textbooks like a teacher, keeping in mind three important questions:

1. What aspects of writing do the textbooks cover and what do they neglect?
2. How might I use these books as a writing teacher?
3. What parts of each book might especially interest my students?

Third, as soon as possible, get a copy of the course syllabus you are required to follow. These syllabi usually come in one of two forms. One type offers a day-by-day description of what you are to do in class—what papers you will assign, what class activities you will employ, what readings you will cover. Although these syllabi save you from having to develop a course yourself, they also leave you little room for innovation and experimentation once you get more comfortable in the classroom. The other type is a more general syllabus that does not dictate what you will do every day in class. Instead, they outline the number and types of papers you must assign (how you order these assignments is up to you), what textbooks you will use (which parts of the textbooks you assign is up to you), and any other aspects of writing you are required to cover (such as the writing process, critical thinking skills, argumentation, or library research). In either case, carefully examine the department syllabus so you understand what you are being asked to teach and how much freedom you have to develop assignments and other course material on your own.

Also ask the department's director of composition to send you sample assignment sheets instructors have found successful in the past. These assignment sheets will give you a good idea of what the writing program expects you to cover in class, how instructors tend to use the textbooks to teach writing, and which readings in those books the program's instructors have found useful.

Finally, talk to some experienced writing teachers in the program, faculty or TAs who have taught the class in the past. First, ask them to describe the course for you and to identify its most important goals. Second, ask what works well in the course and what does not. In terms of course content and pedagogy, what do the students grasp easily and what is more problematic, which assignments work well and which do not, which teaching techniques prove most successful? Third, ask about the textbooks. What material in each text works best in class? How will they use the textbooks differently the next time they teach the class? What parts of the textbooks do they recommend you not use in class? Fourth, ask about the students. What are they like? What is their educational background and writing experience? What aspects of the course do they tend to enjoy; which ones do they find problematic? Former teachers will be your best source of information about the course you are about to teach. The steps you should take as you get ready to teach your classes are summarized in Checklist 2.2 at the end of this chapter.

Philosophies of Composition: An Introduction

Many new TAs are amazed at the variety of ways writing is taught in college. As they read more about the field, they find widely different and sometimes contradictory advice about the best way to structure a writing course, which assignments to use, how to evaluate student work, and how to interact with students in class. These different approaches to teaching writing arise from different philosophies of composition that guide writing programs across the country. As a beginning TA, you need to understand the philosophy of composition guiding your writing program. As you gain more experience and take classes in rhetoric and composition, you will learn about other philosophies of composition and make some commitments of your own, aligning yourself with one approach or another.

A philosophy of composition entails a set of assumptions concerning the aim of writing instruction and the nature of language and learning. These assumptions guide pedagogy—a teacher's philosophy of composition largely determines the types of writing assignments he or she employs along with his or her grading policies, classroom pedagogies, and selection of textbooks. Informed writing teachers attempt to unify every aspect of their teaching around some central philosophy of composition.

Over the years, several writers have attempted to categorize and classify current philosophies of composition, developing taxonomies that help instructors identify and discuss trends and differences among theories. Discussed here are two taxonomies, one developed by Richard Fulkerson in "Four Philosophies of Composition," because it is readily accessible to new TAs, and one developed by James Berlin in "Contemporary Composition: The Major Pedagogical Theories," because it reflects some important, recent trends in the field. As you gain more classroom experience and prepare to develop your own writing courses, you will want to study the other taxonomies found in the list of "Additional Readings" at the end of this chapter.

In his article, Fulkerson classifies current philosophies of composition around the four elements of written communication: the writer, the reader, the subject, and language. Any piece of prose involves a writer writing to a reader about something using particular language, formats, and conventions. Fulkerson argues that current philosophies of composition tend to emphasize one of these four elements over the others (see Figure 2.1). For example, an **expressivist** philosophy of composition tends to emphasize the voice and interests of the writer. Composition courses embracing this philosophy focus their attention on assignments that call for self-reflection and self-expression while the teachers in these classes help students explore their personal visions of the world and develop a language that captures their unique voices. A **rhetorical** philosophy of composition emphasizes the reader. These composition courses teach students how to achieve their desired effect in writing; teachers tend to emphasize the rhetorical techniques that help writers meet

FIGURE 2.1   Fulkerson's Taxonomy of Philosophies of Compositions

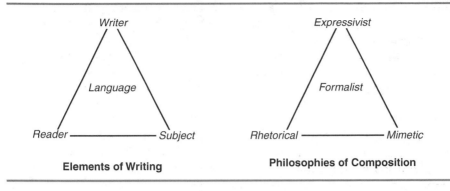

Elements of Writing   Philosophies of Composition

the needs of or sway readers. A writing course emphasizing a **mimetic** philosophy of composition helps students learn how to learn about the world beyond their own experience. Teachers tend to emphasize research strategies and the clear communication of information. Finally, a **formalist** philosophy of composition emphasizes the language, format, and conventions of writing. Composition courses based on this philosophy tend to focus on the mechanical aspects of writing, style, and format; teachers emphasize correct expression, grammar, spelling, and the conventions of written communication.

In his article, Berlin also identifies four major philosophies of composition. However, he disagrees with Fulkerson that each emphasizes one element of the rhetorical situation over the others. Instead, Berlin maintains that each is based on a distinct interpretation of all the elements in the rhetorical situation and a set of beliefs about the nature of reality and knowledge. Writing teachers adopting a *Neo-Aristotelian* or *Classicist* philosophy tend to believe that the world is knowable through sense impressions and understandable through deductive, syllogistic reasoning. When writing, all one need do is find the right words to capture that reality. Teachers adopting a *Positivist* or *Current-Traditional* philosophy also believe that the world is knowable through sense impressions but believe it is understandable through inductive reasoning. When writing, one experiments with different styles to see which most effectively conveys one's understanding of reality to a particular audience. Teachers adopting *Neo-Platonist* or *Expressivist* philosophy believe that the world is knowable only through introspection. When writing, one strives to give voice to his or her unique understanding of reality. Finally, teachers adopting a *New Rhetorical* philosophy believe that knowledge is contextual and social in nature. When writing, one must understand how language shapes and changes ones understanding of the world. Berlin's emphasis on the social nature of language, knowledge, and learning reflected a shift of emphasis in composition studies that is still felt today.

As a TA, understanding these various philosophies of composition is important. First, because you are a member of the teaching staff, you will be expected to work within the philosophy of composition that guides your department's writing program. The more you know about that philosophy, the better your chances of developing effective teaching techniques. Second, if your department asks you to adhere to a philosophy of composition you disagree with, having a firm grounding in composition theory will enable you to join in discussions needed to change the direction of the writing program.

If you have the opportunity to develop your class syllabus, make sure all aspects of the course adhere theoretically—that the assignments you employ, the textbook you use, the evaluation methods you adopt, and the classroom pedagogy you favor all complement one another and work toward the same goal. Yet how do you choose a unifying philosophy of composition for your class? Assuming you have studied several philosophies of composition in some depth, these questions might help you make an informed choice:

1. *What is the purpose of the course? What are the course goals?*

The approach you take to a class should help you achieve the stated course goals. This is an especially important consideration if you are teaching an introductory composition class. The director of composition will want to be assured that teachers in every section of the course are working to achieve the same or a similar set of goals.

2. *What type of student will you be working with?*

Will the philosophy of composition you choose benefit the students you will be teaching? Will it help meet their needs? Will it challenge them in ways they need to be challenged—educationally, politically, culturally? Will it support them in ways they need to be supported? Will it complement or challenge the type of instruction they are receiving in their other college classes?

3. *What approaches to the course have been successful in the past?*

If you are teaching a class for the first time, ask teachers who have taught the class what theoretical approach they employed and whether it was successful. If you are revising a course you have taught before, consider your prior experience. What approach did you use earlier? Was it successful? What response did the students give you on their course evaluations? What changes do you need to consider to better educate your students?

4. *What philosophy of composition best matches your interests and values as a writing teacher?*

You will find it difficult to teach a class built around a philosophy you do not personally value. Granted, as a new TA you may find yourself in that position—you may have no choice in the matter, simply teaching the course the way your department or program requires you to teach it. If this is the case, you need to find some way to teach around, through, or against the dominant ideology of the department without violating your responsibilities to the program. When you do have a choice, make an effort to balance your interests, priorities, and values against those of your students. Choose a philosophy of composition you value, but one that also serves the best interests of your students.

You cannot adopt an "atheoretical" or "nonphilosophical" approach to a course, as every act of teaching arises from some set of assumptions about what teachers should teach and how students learn. As a TA, you can improve the quality of your teaching by taking courses in composition theory, reading widely in the field, and discussing these issues with your professors, advisors, and peers.

Selecting Course Textbooks

Composition teachers face a series of difficult decisions when choosing a rhetoric, reader, or handbook for a writing class. As a new TA, you may have no choice when it comes to picking texts—the director of composition may make that decision for you. Other programs may let you choose texts from a departmentally approved list. As you gain more experience, you may be able to choose your own textbooks. Here are some guidelines that can help you make good decisions.

Selecting a Rhetoric

A rhetoric offers students instruction in reading and writing. Some are extensive, addressing a wide range of writing assignments; others are much more focused on particular genres, such as argumentation or expressive writing. Although many rhetorics include sample readings or even handbook sections, their primary emphasis is teaching students how to write certain types of texts. When choosing a rhetoric for your writing course, keep these general guidelines in mind.

Is the Rhetoric Appropriate, Given the Philosophy of Composition Guiding Your Course? Every good writing course is built around some philosophy of composition, a set of assumptions concerning the aim of writing instruction and the nature of language and learning. Rhetorics are built around similar sets of assumptions. As you examine a rhetoric, identify the philosophy of composition it adopts and determine how well it matches the philosophy guiding your class. If the philosophy underlying the textbook contradicts the philosophy underlying your course, choose a different book.

Does the Rhetoric Offer Instruction on the Types of Essays You Teach in Your Course? Be sure there is a good match between the types of essays you want to teach in your course and the types of essays covered in the rhetoric. If there is not a good match, you will find yourself ignoring the textbook (and angering students who spent their money to buy it) or actually teaching against the textbook (telling your students to ignore the instruction offered in the textbook you asked them to purchase). As will be discussed below, the syllabi for most writing classes are built around the essays students are asked to write. Be sure the rhetoric you choose offers your students the instruction they need to complete those assignments successfully.

How Suitable Is the Style and Content of the Rhetoric for the Students You Will Be Teaching?   Is the rhetoric too rudimentary or too advanced for the students who will be taking your class? If either is the case, they might not find the textbook helpful. To make this judgment, evaluate the difficulty of the rhetoric's language, the difficulty of the assignments and exercises, the relevancy and accessibility of its readings, and the utility of any charts or illustrations. Also, read the textbook's preface. Here authors often indicate the type of student they had in mind when writing the book.

How Timely Is the Rhetoric?   Does the rhetoric contain the best that is currently known and thought about writing instruction? How long has it been on the market? How many editions has it been through? Although the most current textbook is not necessarily the best, an up-to-date rhetoric can be a real asset to your course. Changes in technology are coming so fast that having an up-to-date rhetoric is becoming increasingly important. For example, examine what the rhetoric has to say about the use of computer technology when writing or about research on the Internet.

How Authoritative Is the Textbook?   Is the textbook written by experts in the field? Is it published by a reputable publisher? Check out the biographies of the rhetoric's authors—do they work with students similar to yours? Examine where the authors have taught—are those schools similar to yours? Read the authors' preface—do they sound informed? Rhetorics usually arise from an author's experience as a classroom teacher. A teacher whose experiences and students are similar to yours may write a textbook you and your students will find useful.

Are the Length and Cost of the Rhetoric Appropriate?   How "big" a rhetoric do you need for the course you will teach? Some rhetorics come with an extensive set of readings. Will you use these readings in class? Others cover a wide range of writing assignments. How many of them will you assign in your course? The longer the textbook, the more it will cost. Consider whether you want your students to purchase an expensive textbook that contains more material than you will ever cover in class (an exception is selecting a rhetoric that a student will use in more than one class, for example in both English 101 and English 102).

How Useful Is the Available Ancillary Material?   Consider the rhetoric's ancillary material. Many textbooks come with teacher's guides, workbooks, computer software, and Web sites. Examine this material before selecting a rhetoric for your class. How helpful might it be, both for you and for your students? Is it available free from the publisher or is there some additional cost to the students if it comes bundled with the textbook? Sometimes the quality of the ancillary material can help you make the final choice between two close texts.

Selecting a Reader

Readers are collections of sample essays, sometimes produced by professional writers, sometimes by students. Writing teachers use readers in a variety of ways. Some use the readings to spur writing, asking their students to summarize, respond to, or synthesize the selections or to write about the same topic themselves. Others use readings as model essays, asking their students to analyze how a selection is structured, for example, and organize their own essays similarly. When choosing a reader for your writing class, you might consider these questions.

Is the Reader Appropriate Theoretically and Thematically?   Like rhetorics, readers are often built around some philosophy of composition. This theory helps the reader's editor select and organize the selections. You want to ensure there is a good match between the philosophical orientation of the reader and the philosophical orientation of your course. Readers are also frequently built around a particular theme: language, the environment, diversity, the American experience, and so on. Make sure the reader's theme suits your course, that it addresses a theme you want your students to investigate at some length.

How Heterogeneous Are the Readings?   When choosing a reader, how important it is that the readings represent a variety of authors, cultures, and rhetorical modes? Look at the table of contents. How many of the selections are written by men and how many by women? Do the readings offer a monocultural or multicultural perspective on the world? How many of the readings are personal reflection pieces, how many are formal essays, how many are research reports? To what degree are the readings "academic"? To what degree do they come from the popular press? How many disciplines are represented? You want to be sure that selections in a reader are various enough to meet the needs of your students.

How Challenging and Interesting Are the Readings?   Examine the topic, content, and language of the text's selections. Will your students find the readings appropriately challenging and interesting? If students find a reader's selections too difficult, too easy, or too boring, they will be less likely to study the material. Because you want the reader to be an asset to your course, you should consider your students' likely responses to the selections. If you are using a reader for the first time, talk to teachers who have used it in the past to find out which selections worked best for them and their students.

How Useful Are the Discussion Questions? Most readers contain discussion questions for each reading, usually following the selection (sometimes additional study questions are contained in the reader's teaching guide). Study these questions carefully if you plan to use them in your class. Will your students find them useful? Will they find the questions too challenging or too easy? Will the questions likely generate class discussion? Will they help the students better understand the readings? Can they build toward some type of writing assignment? The quality and utility of these discussion questions can be deciding factors when choosing a reader.

What Is the Quality of the Available Ancillary Material? Examine any ancillary material that comes with the reader. Readers sometimes come with teachers' guides that offer a discussion of each selection, tips on teaching the selections, and even possible paper topics for students. Increasingly today, readers are also supported by publishing company Web sites that offer the same kind of information and help. Evaluate the quality and utility of this support material before you select a reader.

Selecting a Handbook

The primary purpose of a handbook is to offer instruction on the mechanical aspects of writing: grammar, punctuation, usage, spelling, and so on. Some handbooks may also contain a chapter or two on rhetoric, the writing process, or a particular genre (for example, business writing). It may seem that selecting a handbook is straightforward—after all, how many different ways can authors discuss comma usage? In reality, though, no two handbooks are alike. Choosing the right handbook for your class will be easier if ask yourself these questions.

What Is the Handbook's Attitude Toward Error? As you read the handbook, what is its tone? How strident is its attitude toward error? Does it recognize a range of acceptable usage and punctuation practice or does it posit a single "correct" way to write? Does this attitude match your own understanding of writing and error? These are issues you will be discussing as a classroom teacher—you want to be sure that you and the handbook you choose are not sending your students mixed messages.

How Extensive Is the Handbook's Coverage? Check the table of contents. What aspects of writing does the handbook address? Looking through just a few handbooks will demonstrate how much variety there is in coverage— some handbooks are streamlined, offering only minimal instruction; others are much more extensive, approaching a rhetoric in the amount of coverage. As you consider a handbook for adoption, determine whether it includes all the information you think your students need. Does it cover material already contained in other textbooks your students purchase? Is this overlap useful?

Is the Layout of the Handbook Helpful? Handbook authors pay close attention to layout. Many are now filled with colored charts, tables, tabbed pages, arrows, and pictures. How useful will students find this aspect of the text? Does the layout make the material more accessible or is it distracting? Consider how the layout of the text might influence the way you or you students might use the handbook in class.

What Kinds of Exercises Does the Handbook Contain? Most academic handbooks contain student exercises. Choose one aspect of grammar, punctuation, or usage and compare handbooks in terms of the exercises they offer. How challenging are the exercises? Are the exercises limited to sentence correction? Does the handbook ask students to edit larger units of text? Is collaborative learning encouraged? Are answer keys provided so students can check their own work? These are the types of questions to consider as you review the exercises contained in a handbook you are considering for adoption.

DESIGNING A COURSE SYLLABUS

If you are a first-time teacher, you may not have the opportunity to design your own syllabus. Instead, you may be required to teach from a standard syllabus someone else has prepared. As the term progresses and you gain some experience and confidence, you may be allowed to make some changes to this syllabus, but you will not be in a position to design your own class. For many new TAs, this is not a problem—they lack the experience and knowledge to design a class and are happy to follow someone else's syllabus the first time they teach.

However, if you have some teaching experience, you may be allowed to design your own syllabus so long as it adheres to certain departmental guidelines (usually concerning the number and type of assignments you have to include). Below is a set of step-by-step directions you can follow as you put together your own syllabus for a writing course. These instructions assume you have already chosen your textbooks.

Step 1: List, in Order, the Writing Assignments You Will Cover in Your Class

Your syllabus will be structured around the due dates of these required papers, so give considerable time to this decision. You need to decide (1) how many papers you will require students to write, (2) what those assignments will be, and (3) how you will sequence them. Some assignment sequences are based on length: briefer assignments early in the course giving way to longer assignments later. Some sequences are based on difficulty: easier assignments building to harder assignments. Some sequences are based on the accumulation of skills: early assignments helping students develop skills they need to complete later assignments. In every case, though, your choice of assignments and their sequence should be based on a coherent, unifying philosophy of composition (see above).

Once you make your decisions, list the specific assignments you will require in the order you will teach them. (Chapter 4 offers more advice on designing writing assignments.)

Step 2: Make a List of all the Days the Class Will Meet

Get out a calendar and your university's bulletin. Find out when the semester begins and list all the days your class will meet through the end of the term. The beginning of your syllabus might look like this if you are teaching a fall class that meets on Monday, Wednesday, and Friday:

Syllabus

		Date	Class Activity	Readings Due
Week 1	M	September 1		
	W	September 3		
	F	September 5		
Week 2	M	September 8		
	W	September 10		
	F	September 12		
Week 3	M	September 15		

Step 3: Fill in all the Days that Class Will *Not* Meet

Note on your syllabus when classes will be canceled for holidays, vacations, study days, and so on. These are days you will not teach. The first part of your syllabus may look like this now:

Syllabus

		Date	Class Activity	Readings Due
Week 1	M	September 1		
	W	September 3		
	F	September 5		
Week 2	M	September 8	No class, Labor Day	
	W	September 10		
	F	September 12		
Week 3	M	September 15		

Step 4: Fill in the Due Dates for Your Major Papers

Decide when you will collect the papers you are going to assign and write in the due date for each one. Your main concern here is spacing out the due dates, leaving enough time for students to complete each assignment. The first few weeks of your syllabus may look like this now:

		Syllabus	
	Date	*Class Activity*	*Readings Due*
Week 1	M September 1		
	W September 3		
	F September 5		
Week 2	M September 8	No class, Labor Day	
	W September 10		
	F September 12		
Week 3	M September 15		Paper #1 Due—Summary

Step 5: From Day to Day, Fill in any Class Activities and Readings You Will Use to Help Students Complete each Assignment and Improve as Readers and Writers

As you think about the material you want to cover in class, the readings you would like to assign and the activities and exercises you would like to employ, fill in:

a. Activities that are directly related to the assignment the students are working on. Indicate, for example, when you will assign the paper, discuss sample or model essays, collect rough drafts, or engage in peer editing sessions.

b. Activities that are related to the writing process. Indicate when you will address prewriting, drafting, and revising skills.

c. Activities designed to promote active learning and critical thinking. For example, indicate days you might stage classroom debates, show films, have the students engage in group work, or meet in the library to research their topics.

d. Days you will discuss material from the textbooks. Indicate the pages the students should have read for that class meeting.

The first part of your syllabus might now look like this:

	Date		Class Activity	Readings Due
			Syllabus	
	Date		*Class Activity*	*Readings Due*
Week 1	M	September 1	Introduce Class	
	W	September 3	Assign Paper #1 —Summary Discuss Paper #1 —Content	10–19, 44–47
	F	September 5	Discuss Reading for Paper #1 Discuss "Prewriting"	1–9
Week 2	M	September 8	No class, Labor Day	
	W	September 10	Handout Discuss Writing "Myths"	Collect Rough Drafts Paper #1
	F	September 12	Return Rough Drafts Review Sample Rough Drafts Peer Editing Session	
Week 3	M	September 15	Assign Paper #2 —Response	Paper #1 Due — Summary

According to this syllabus, on September 3, I will assign paper #1, the summary of a reading from my course text. By that day the students should have read pages 10–19 of the textbook (the section that describes how to write summaries) and pages 44–47 (the reading they will be summarizing). On the 3rd, we will discuss what the students should and should not include in their summaries. On the 5th, we will continue our discussion of the reading the students are summarizing and talk about "prewriting" as part of the writing process (drawing information from pages 1–9 of the textbook). Class will not meet on the 8th (Labor Day), so on the 10th, the students will turn in the rough drafts of their summaries, and I will review them outside of class. That day I will distribute a list of writing "myths" for class discussion so we can continue to explore the students' individual composing processes. On the 12th, I will return the rough drafts of the summaries with my comments and place on an overhead projector a few sample passages for class discussion, pointing out strengths and weaknesses. The students will then form groups to read each other's papers and my comments. Based on this review, I will ask each group to form a final revision "checklist," things to look for as they prepare their final drafts for the 15th. On that day I will collect the students' papers and distribute the assignment for paper #2.

As you plan your syllabus, you might want to leave some open days where nothing is planned. Open days allow you wiggle room in case teaching some aspect of the course takes longer than you had anticipated. Also plan on distributing your syllabus to students in units, not all at once. The first day of class, I give my students a syllabus that outlines the course up to the first paper's due date. When they turn in that paper, I distribute a syllabus that covers class until the next paper's due date. Distributing the syllabus in units throughout the course allows you the opportunity to adjust due dates as you get a better sense of the instruction your students need and the time it takes them to complete projects.

PREPARING A CLASS POLICY SHEET

Before the term begins, you also need to prepare your class policy sheet. This document details essential information about your course and establishes your expectations for student conduct in class. You should distribute your policy sheet the first day of class and thoroughly review it with your students. During the term, any changes in these policies should be spelled out in writing and distributed to your students. Your policy sheet should include the following:

Course Information

Include the name and section number of the courses you are teaching as well as the meeting times, days, and location of the class. Also list the texts you will use in the course. Listing the texts is especially important if students in different sections of the course use different books (as is often the case with introductory composition classes). Your students need to know which texts to buy for the sections you teach.

Teacher Information

Make sure your policy sheet includes your name, office number, telephone number, and e-mail address. Some TAs also like to list their home telephone numbers, but if you do so, understand that you will get calls there. Some TAs like being accessible to their students in this way; others like to get away from work when they are home. If you decide to give out your home telephone number, indicate when students should and should not call— you may not want late night or early morning calls.

Required Work for the Course and Grade Information

List all the work that will figure into the course grade and its weight (how many points it is worth or what percentage of the course grade it represents). In addition to listing the major graded papers, be sure to include any other aspect of the class you will use to determine the course grade, including quizzes, participation, oral reports, rough drafts, peer editing, or group work.

Late Paper Policy

Clearly explain your policy toward late work. First—and this may sound silly—you should define what you mean by "late." Is work not turned in at the beginning of class on the due date late, even if the student comes to class with the paper before the period is over? What if the student is waiting for you in the hallway after class and wants to turn in the paper then? What if the student fails to come to class, but leaves the paper in your mailbox or slides it under your office door while you are teaching? What if the student turns in the paper sometime later the day it is due?

Once you define what "late" means, consider what penalty you will impose on late work. One option is to impose no penalty—students are free to turn in work as late as they like with no consequences. However, such a policy makes due dates meaningless and could result in students falling hopelessly behind in their work (not to mention the huge backlog of papers you will have to grade when students turn in all their late work that last week of classes!). If you decide to penalize late work, spell out the consequences: how many points you will deduct from the work for each day it is late or how you will adjust the paper's grade.

Plagiarism Policy

Plagiarism is an unfortunate fact of college writing classes—at some point every teacher has to deal with students who plagiarize their work (see Chapter 9 for a full discussion of how to address this problem in your classes). On your policy sheet, you need to indicate the penalty you will impose on plagiarized work. Sometimes you need only refer students to a university or department policy on plagiarism or simply reproduce that policy on your sheet. If such a policy does not exist, you need to state how you plan to handle instances of plagiarism in your class.

Again, you have many options. Some TAs will give plagiarized work an "F" with no chance to rewrite the piece. Some will give it an "F" and allow the student to correct the problem, averaging the "F" with the grade on the rewrite. Still others will not grade the plagiarized draft; they simply return the work with instructions to correct the error and resubmit the manuscript. The teacher's response often depends on whether the plagiarism seemed to be purposeful or accidental (again, see Chapter 9). Be sure to discuss your plagiarism policy with your teaching supervisor before you include it on your policy sheet.

Essay Format

If you have preferences, tell your students how you would like them to format the work they turn in for a grade, whether it should be typed, what font size or face your prefer (if any), what margins they should use, what types of headings they should employ, whether to include title pages, and so on. Some teachers put this information on the individual assignment sheets they distribute in class.

Daily Procedures

Will every class begin with five minutes of journal writing? Will one or two students be required to make an oral presentation of some sort to open each class? Will the last five minutes of every class be reserved for questions? Will students be expected to work in groups every Friday? Many teachers like to perform certain tasks on a regular basis in class, always opening class the same way or requiring students to routinely complete certain exercises. Establishing these procedures as an expected part of your course by placing them on your policy sheet helps students know what to expect each day and saves you time, enabling students to get right to work.

Missing Class

If class attendance is tied to the course grade in some way, be sure to explain the policy clearly. If you make a distinction between "excused" and "unexcused" absences, define those terms as well. Many teachers like to distribute in class a list of all of the students' telephone numbers and e-mail addresses so students can contact classmates when they are absent and find out what they missed. If you distribute such a list, get permission from all of the students first; some students might not want their telephone number or e-mail address made public and you should respect their request. Finally, many teachers like to include on their policy sheet a statement explaining that students remain responsible for material covered on days they are absent.

Tardiness

Decide how you will handle students coming late to class (especially if you teach early in the morning) and whether you want to place that policy in writing. Many new TAs do not establish a tardiness policy, believing that it sounds too "high schoolish." A few weeks into the term, however, they find themselves telling students to stop coming late to class. Including a statement concerning tardiness on your policy sheet establishes from the first day of class how important you think it is that students be punctual.

Returning Work

After my first semester of teaching, I started including a statement on my policy sheet letting my students know that I needed at least a week to grade their work, and that if it would take longer, I would tell them. I also stated that they would never have to write an essay without having a chance to review the previous paper they wrote—no paper would be due until I had graded or responded to the previous paper. If you respond to rather than grade individual papers, let your students know how long it will usually take you to return their work.

Conferences

You might also include on your policy sheet information concerning out-of-class conferences. Some TAs like to include a statement encouraging students to see them during office hours. Others like to make conferences mandatory—at some point in the term, every student is required to see them in their office at least once. Many TAs, though, prefer not to put these policies in writing, announcing them in class instead. However, if attending or not attending conferences will affect the students' course grade in any way, put that policy in writing.

Other

Over the years, many TAs have established other policy statements concerning student conduct in class. For example, consider whether you want to establish a policy concerning food and drink in class. Some teachers prohibit food and drink; others allow it so long as the students do not distract their peers. Lately a number of TAs have prohibited cell phones and pagers in class; others establish policies concerning the use of tape recorders and computers in class.

You can find a sample class policy sheet at the end of this chapter, Figure 2.2, which is the one I distributed to students the last time I taught English 102, a course in argumentative writing and research.

SEEING YOURSELF AS A TEACHER

If you are a first-time TA, one of the biggest adjustments you have to make is learning to think of yourself as a teacher. For years you have been a student (and you are *still* a student). But now, you will have to view the classroom from the teacher's perspective. This new role brings with it a new set of responsibilities. However, you received your teaching assistantship because your department believes in your ability to be a good instructor. Although you do have a lot to learn about teaching, you should enter the job with confidence. Your years of experience as a student and writer have taught you more about good teaching than you might know. With some help and guidance, you can learn how to draw on this knowledge in the classroom.

All prospective teachers imagine standing in front of a classroom for the first time, picturing what they will do, what they will say, maybe even what they will wear. Most new TAs model their behavior on a teacher they admire who had an impact on them. This type of imitation can serve as a good starting point for you as a classroom teacher, but it also has some serious limitations. To succeed as an instructor, you need to be yourself and find your own teaching style. Instead of imitating this teacher, analyze the teacher's behavior, identifying what made him or her a good instructor. For example, perhaps you liked a particular professor because she was organized, thorough, and relaxed. Find your own way to embody these traits in the classroom. Your years as a teaching assistant should be filled with experimentation. By employing a variety of teaching techniques, you will discover which methods of instruction you and your students find most comfortable and productive. All good teachers develop and refine their "style" over time with a lot of trial and error. Beginning this process while you are a TA makes sense.

Besides imitating their favorite teachers, new TAs also have a tendency to teach their students how to read and write the way they themselves read and write, which again has certain strengths and limitations. For example, when they talk with students about writing a paper, new TAs often describe a process that works for them. Such advice is certainly sensible—why not share with students techniques that have served you well? Problems occur, however, when teachers fail to realize that their particular way of writing may not be good for *all* of their students —what works for them may not work for others. TAs who insist that their students compose essays the way they themselves write often run into problems because no two writers follow the exact same composing process. Your job as a teacher is to help your students develop their own reading, writing, and thinking skills. As they complete their assignments, you can share with them strategies and techniques that work for you but also help them develop productive strategies of their own.

As a new TA, you also need to develop realistic expectations about your job and your students. Most new TAs are extremely idealistic and enthusiastic; though anxious, they are excited about making a difference in their students' lives. Excellent teachers are able to keep both the idealism and enthusiasm throughout their careers, but they usually learn to temper both with reality. Experienced teachers know that they will not reach every student. Some students simply will not respond to their instruction. Some students simply will not put enough effort into their work to succeed. Some students will waste their talents and gifts. But—and this is crucial—good teachers still try to reach every student.

Teacher burnout results from instructors expecting too much of themselves, their students, or the job: the reality of their occupation cannot match their expectations. What, then, are reasonable expectations for teachers to hold? Here is one: if you do your job well, you can help your students become better readers and writers, but only if the students also work hard to improve. To avoid disappointment and burnout, you need to maintain high but reasonable goals for yourself and for your students.

Another major concern for many new TAs is authority—they wonder whether their students will take them seriously as instructors. Because many new TAs are just a few years older than their students, they worry that their students will not see them as "real" teachers. Others worry that their students may discount their authority because they are not professors. These concerns are natural and understandable. However, also understand that classroom authority is not just a function of age or degree status. Your students will respect your authority as a teacher if you conduct class in a professional, caring manner and help them improve as readers and writers.

Your most important source of authority is knowledge. As a talented reader and writer, you can help your students master many of the skills they need to succeed in college and beyond. Teachers tend to lose authority and credibility if their students feel that the class is a waste of their time, that the teacher lacks expertise, or that the teacher cares little about them as individual learners. You can establish and maintain your authority in the classroom, therefore, by thoughtfully planning and preparing for each class meeting, addressing the individual needs of your students, solving problems quickly when they arise, and conducting class in a professional, mature manner.

Over the years, I have seen TAs lose their authority in the classroom and come close to losing control of their students. Most of these TAs found themselves in this position because they took their teaching and their students for granted. Instead of working hard to develop productive lesson plans, activities, and presentations, they preferred to wing it in class. Instead of offering helpful, thoughtful responses to student work, they rushed though sets of papers, returning student work with little comment. Instead of carefully evaluating student papers, they applied grades arbitrarily. Instead of addressing problems that arose in class, they ignored the situations, hoping things would work themselves out. Over time, however, these actions alienated most of their students and compromised their authority in the classroom.

Other TAs lose their authority in the classroom by trying too hard to relate to their students. Instead of being their students' teachers, they want to be their students' friends. First and foremost, your students want you to be their teacher. This does not mean that you should be cold and distant in the classroom. Over the years, I have developed real, lasting friendships with many of my students, and I think most of my students feel they can approach me with problems or concerns and receive a sympathetic hearing. It does mean, however, that a line exists between you and your students. As a TA, you are your students' teacher, not their peer. Learning this distinction is important for every TA.

THE PRESERVICE WORKSHOP

Before you teach your first class, you will probably be required to attend a department or university preservice workshop. This workshop is extremely important: you will learn about your department and writing program, your specific job requirements, and your course texts and syllabus. You will also be introduced to a variety of teaching techniques and the support services available on campus. Finally, during the workshop, you will meet your fellow TAs and begin to form a new community of teachers.

Taking a few steps can help you get the most out of these preservice workshops. First, prepare. Prior to the workshop, read all the material you have been sent, study the textbooks you will be using in class, and examine any sample course syllabi or assignment sheets you have. Second, participate. The workshop is no time to be silent and passive. Even if you have not taught before, participate fully in the workshop—never hesitate to ask questions or to offer suggestions. Your frank, enthusiastic participation will make the workshop more helpful and enjoyable for everyone. Finally, practice. During the few days or weeks of the workshop, practice what you are learning. If you discuss how to design assignment sheets, try writing up a few and share them with your peers. If you discuss effective lecturing techniques, give a brief presentation or two to your family or friends and ask them to critique your performance. The more practice you get before you teach for the first time, the more comfortable you will be when the term begins. Faculty and experienced TAs running these workshops may also employ small group work, role-playing exercises, and videos to help you reflect on the job at hand and collaborate with your colleagues to improve your teaching. Participating fully in these activities will help you get the most out of your preservice workshop.

WORKS CITED

Berlin, James. "Contemporary Composition: The Major Pedagogical Theories." *College English* 44 (1982): 765–77.

Fulkerson, Richard. "Four Philosophies of Composition." *College Composition and Communication* 30 (1979): 343–48.

ADDITIONAL READINGS

Eckhart, Caroline D., and David H. Stewart. "Towards a Functional Taxonomy of Composition." *College Composition and Communication* 30 (1979): 338–42.

Faigley, Lester. "Competing Theories of Process: A Critique and a Proposal." *College English* 48 (1986): 527–42.

Fulkerson, Richard. "Composition Theory in the Eighties: Axiological Consensus and Paradigmatic Diversity." *College Composition and Communication* 41 (1990): 409–29.

Lindemann, Erika, and Gary Tate, ed. *An Introduction to Composition Studies.* New York: Oxford University Press, 1991.

Tate, Gary, Amy Rupiper, and Kurt Schick. *A Guide to Composition Pedagogies.* New York: Oxford University Press, 2001.

Tate, Gary, Edward P. J. Corbett, and Nancy Meyers. *The Writing Teacher's Sourcebook.* 3rd ed. New York: Oxford University Press, 1994.

Villanueva, Victor, Jr. *Cross Talk in Comp Theory: A Reader.* Urbana, IL: NCTE, 1997.

Wiley, Mark, Barbara Gleason, and Louise Wetherbee Phelps. *Composition in Four Keys: Inquiring into the Field.* Mountain View, CA: Mayfield, 1996.

CHECKLIST 2.1
Tasks to Complete Before You Begin Taking Graduate Courses

Materials You Need to Obtain
- ☐ University Bulletin
- ☐ Course Catalogue
- ☐ Department Course Descriptions

Whom you need to Contact

Department Chair

Name _____

Telephone Number _____

E–mail Address _____

Director of Graduate Study

Name _____

Telephone Number _____

E–mail Address _____

Academic Advisor

Name _____

Telephone Number _____

E–mail Address _____

Director of Human Resources

Name _____

Telephone Number _____

E–mail Address _____

Tasks to Complete
- ☐ Study degree requirements
- ☐ Choose classes you want to take
- ☐ Contact your academic advisor to discuss program and classes
- ☐ Check on housing
- ☐ Check on pay schedule
- ☐ Check on parking
- ☐ Check on computer accounts
- ☐ Check on access to athletic facilities

CHECKLIST 2.2
Preparing to Teach

❑ Read Course Descriptions
❑ Read Textbooks (if assigned to you)
❑ Identify Program's Guiding Philosophy of Composition
❑ Choose a Philosophy of Composition (if you get a choice)
❑ Select Textbooks (if you get to choose)
❑ Rhetoric
❑ Reader
❑ Handbook
❑ Review Required Course Syllabus
❑ Design Course Syllabus (if you have that option)
❑ Design Class Policy Sheet
❑ Review Sample Assignment Sheets
❑ Discuss Course with Faculty and Experienced TAs

FIGURE 2.2   Sample Course Policy Sheet

English 102—College Composition II
Winter, 2000
Dr. Stephen Wilhoit
wilhoit@notes.udayton.edu

Class	**Office**
HM 207	HM 244 X–3405
MWF 9:00–9:50	MWF 10:00–11:30,
	T 9:00–10:30

Texts
Writing Arguments, Ramage and Bean
Bedford Handbook, Hacker
Frankenstein, Shelley

Policies

1.   All essays are due at the beginning of class on the announced due date. Essays not turned in then will be considered late. Late papers are penalized a grade per day (a "B"paper becomes a "C" if it is late).

2.   Unless arrangements are made with me beforehand, you will be expected to turn in all your papers to me personally. When this does not happen, the paper will be counted at least one day late.

3.   If you know you will not be able to turn in a paper on the announced due date, see me *before* the paper is due. We will arrange a new due date.

4.   Missed quizzes cannot be "made up."

continued

continued from page 47

5.   **All essays are to be typed.**
6.   **Keep all of your graded work in a manila folder. I will collect this folder at the end of the term.**
7.   **All first-year students remain subject to the University requirements concerning class attendance.**
8.   **Plagiarized work will receive a failing grade and may constitute grounds for further penalties.**

Grading

Analysis	10% of course grade
Critique	15%
Definition Argument	20%
Proposal Argument	25%
Literary Analysis	20%
Quizzes and Exercises	10%

CHAPTER 3

Teaching that First Class

INTRODUCTION

Many TAs find teaching class for the first time an exciting but scary experience. With planning and preparation, though, that initial class can be more exhilarating than it is nerve wracking. You have important business to conduct that first day: you need to introduce your students to the course, introduce yourself to your students, and begin the process of teaching the class. This chapter suggests how you can get ready to teach that first day, what to do in class the first time you meet with your students, and how to get your course off to a good start.

BEFORE THE TERM STARTS: A FEW TIPS

At least a few days before you teach that first class, have someone review and proofread the final draft of your class policy sheet and the first unit of your course syllabus (see Chapter 2). Make any final changes, then run off enough copies for your students. (Actually, run off a few extra copies in case a student or two adds your class after the term begins.) Do not wait until the first day of class to duplicate this material. If you do, you can count on problems—broken copy machines, crashing computers, inkless printers. Place the copies in your office along with the other material you will need the first day of class, including a packet of index cards, departmental or university policy sheets, the class roster, and your course textbooks.

Before classes start, visit the room where you will be teaching and take a few minutes to look around. Note the location of the light switch, the chalkboard, the overhead projector, the screen, and the electrical plugs. You do not want to be wandering around lost in front of your students the first time you need to flip off a light switch or plug in a projector. Next—and this advice will sound funny—talk out loud in the room and listen to your voice. One of your strangest experiences that first day will be hearing your own voice in class. In fact, some TAs start listening to the sound of their voice and forget what they are saying! Some TAs like to have a friend or officemate sit in the back of the room, listen to them talk, and tell them if their voice is too soft or too loud. Also, write something on the chalkboard and then go to the back of the room and see if you can read it (having a friend in the back of the room can help here too). If there is an overhead projector, turn it on, focus an image, and turn it off. If there are shades on the windows, learn how to work them. All of these preparations, rehearsals, and dry runs will help you get used to your new surroundings and the new perspective you will assume as a teacher.

THE FIRST DAY OF CLASS

The night before you teach that first class, be sure you set your alarm clock and check it twice! Plan to arrive at your office at least a half hour before you are scheduled to teach. When you reach your office, make sure one last time you have all the material you need to take with you to class, listed in Figure 3.1 below. Leave your office in plenty of time to reach your classroom. Take your books, your teaching material, and something to drink—if you are nervous, you will want some coffee, tea, or water before the class is over. When you reach the classroom, arrange your material on the desk and put your name, course number, and section number on the board (give students who are in the wrong room a chance to exit gracefully). If students are in the room

FIGURE 3.1

What to Take to Class with You the First Day

❏ Class Syllabus
❏ Class Policy Sheet
❏ Department Policy Sheet
❏ A Copy of Each Required Textbook
❏ Class Roster
❏ Note Cards
❏ Ideas for Icebreakers
❏ Impromptu Writing Assignments
❏ Pen or Pencil
❏ Beverage

when you arrive, chat with them informally until class begins or say hello as they enter the room. Once the period begins, welcome the students, tell them your name, and again announce the course and section number.

If you have a class roster, call roll. I tell the students to let me know if they prefer to be called something other than the name I have on the list (my oddest experience was a student who went by the nickname Killer, putting a little extra pressure on me when I graded his papers!) An alternative is to ask your students to introduce themselves, telling you their names and a few things about themselves—where they grew up, where they live now, what their plans are for the future, and so on. Letting your students talk even briefly in class that first day makes everyone less nervous, takes some of the attention off of you, and helps you remember your students' names. Next, distribute the note cards you brought and ask your students to write down some information about themselves. Here is what I usually ask for:

Name	Year in School
Campus Address	Major
Campus Telephone Number	Hometown
E-mail Address	High School

On the back of the index card, I ask the students to indicate what high school or college English classes they have taken, what they hope to gain from this course, and what concerns they have about writing. Recently, I have added another question: "Is there anything you would like to tell me about your ability to write papers, any problems you might face, that you think I should know?" This question gives my students the chance to let me know of any disabilities that might impact their ability to write papers. With this information, I can be sure all of my students get the support they need.

Once you collect the index cards, tell the students a little about yourself. I usually talk briefly about my educational background, the classes I teach at the university, my research and writing interests, and my family. How much they tell their students about themselves is problematic for many TAs, especially those in M.A. programs, because of their status in the department: "Do I tell my students I'm *only* a TA?" TAs who ask this question fear that acknowledging their status will damage their authority and credibility in the classroom—students may not see them as "real" teachers. How to handle this situation is really up to you. Do what makes you comfortable. Some TAs tell their students that they are graduate teaching assistants completing their masters or doctorate degrees. Others wait until their students ask, then let them know. Under no circumstances should you lie about your status—never claim a degree or a position in the department you do not have.

Another issue for TAs involves how students should address them in class: should students call them by their last name or their first name? Again, the choice is yours; do what makes you and your students comfortable. Some TAs prefer to be on a first name basis with their students.

Others, concerned about their authority in the classroom, prefer to be called by their last names. In all likelihood, whatever you call yourself that first day—the name you put on the board or on your handouts—will dictate how your students refer to you. Check with your director of composition to see if your department has a policy or a preference on this issue.

After you introduce yourself, distribute and read though your course policy sheet and the first unit of your class syllabus. Pause frequently and invite questions. As you review your policy sheet, assume a businesslike tone—do not apologize for any of the ground rules you set. Make sure your students understand how you will determine their course grade and how you will evaluate any tasks they are required to complete outside the classroom, such as participating in on-line discussion lists or attending evening lectures or films. Finally, make sure your students know how to read your class syllabus and understand when papers, readings, and homework assignments are due.

Reviewing this material will take about twenty-five to thirty minutes, leaving you time for some other activities before you dismiss class. Because this is the first day of the course, you might want to plan some icebreaking activities that will help you get to know your students and help the students get to know each other. One icebreaker was described above—ask the students to introduce themselves in class. An alternative is for the students to pair up, interview each other for five minutes, and then introduce their partner to the rest of the class. You might go around the room and have the students talk about their favorite movies or ideal vacation spots. Other TAs ask their students to describe their favorite high school teachers or talk about the way they like to write papers, using the Writing Process Survey found at the end of this chapter as a starting point (see Figure 3.2). This survey asks students to comment briefly on their writing practices and preferences. The students could complete the survey in class and then discuss the results, including your answers with theirs. This discussion helps you understand how your students write their papers and combats one of the most commonly held myths about composition: that there is only one correct way to write papers.

Other icebreakers may involve writing. For example, the first student in each row takes out a piece of paper and completes this sentence, "The thing that has surprised me the most about college life so far is [[blank]]." This student hands the paper to the next person in the row, who has to add a second sentence that develops the first. This student passes it on, and the next person adds a sentence. The last person in the row brings the paper to the first student in the row, who adds a final sentence and then reads the paragraph out loud to class. The class then votes on the best paragraph. One TA I know likes to have his students write a brief descriptive essay that first day: in one paragraph, the students have to describe someone sitting in the

FIGURE 3.2   Writing Process Survey

1. Briefly describe your writing "rituals," the steps or actions you need to take before you begin to write (e.g., change into comfortable clothes, get something to drink, find a quiet place to work).

2. Do you generally write one draft of a paper before you turn it in or more than one draft? If you do more than one draft, what do you concentrate on in each version?

3. How much planning do you do before you begin to write a paper? What form does this planning take?

4. As you write your paper, do you stop to make corrections, to look up words in a dictionary, to look up rules on grammar, or do you just press on and take care of these matters later?

5. When do you let someone else read your paper? Who usually reads it? Why?

6. When you revise a paper, how extensive are the changes you tend to make? How do you know what to change?

7. What kinds of response do you like to receive about your writing? What kinds of response best help you improve as a writer?

8. What kinds of writing assignments do you prefer to work on? Why?

9. Do you begin working on an assignment right away or do you delay?

10. Do you prefer to work on writing projects alone or with other people?

11. What are your greatest strengths as a writer?
    What are your greatest weaknesses as a writer?

room (but not the teacher!). Students then read their descriptions aloud, and the class tries to identify the person the writer had in mind.

Other teachers like to get a formal writing sample from their students the first day of class, asking their students to write a brief essay in response to a prompt they place on the board. The best prompts are those that interest students and result in essays that are several paragraphs long. If the essay topic is personal, the essay can serve several purposes: it can tell you something about your students' writing skills and help you get to know them. A list of possible prompts is provided in Figure 3.3 at the end of this chapter.

At the end of class, give your students one last chance to ask questions, collect any writing you had them complete, and remind them of any assignments due the next class. After class, review your class roster and the index cards, examine your students' writing samples, and begin preparing for the next class.

GETTING DOWN TO BUSINESS:
THE REST OF THE WEEK

Over the first few class meetings, establish a rhythm and tone for both the class and your teaching. To get the course off to a good start, come to each class prepared and organized, making steady progress on the first unit of your syllabus. Work hard early in the term to engage your students in the class. Using a variety of instructional techniques (see Chapter 7), promote active learning in class. A little creative thought can help you develop class activities that encourage students to invest themselves in the course and understand that you want and expect their participation.

You may also want to schedule brief conferences with your students the first few weeks of class (see Chapter 10). These brief conferences help you become acquainted with your students and make everyone feel more comfortable in class. During the conference, you can talk to your students informally about their families, education, or career goals, and ask them if they have any questions or concerns about the course or their writing. Your goal is to get to know your students as individuals and to form a better understanding of their educational needs.

COMMON CONCERNS

First impressions are important. Rightly or wrongly, most people form their opinions about others based on their first interactions with them. Negative first impressions can be especially hard to change—despite a lot of later evidence that those impressions were wrong. That is one reason so many new TAs worry so much about the first day of class. However, if you have prepared yourself well, there is no good reason to be nervous. The first class meeting does not define the entire course or determine your students' attitude toward you. Teaching is a profession defined by beginnings and endings, growth and change. What you think of your students—and what they think of you—will not be the same at the end of the course as it was at the beginning. Also, realize that on the first day of class, your students are probably more nervous than you are, especially if they are first-year students. You may find yourself having to calm and reassure them.

Other TAs worry about the "disaster" that might befall them that first day, the unexpected event that throws and befuddles them. Such events do occur, but they are never the disaster the TAs tend to think they are. Over the years, I have worked with many TAs who thought their semester was over because they ran into problems that first day. One TA found his classroom doors locked when he arrived to teach at 8:00 a.m. He did not have a key and did not know where to get one, so he conducted that first class in a hallway. Another TA spilled a huge cup of coffee down the front of her dress on the way to class. There was no way to hide the enormous stain. Another tried to use an overhead projector in class the first day and had the screen fall from the ceiling when she pulled it down, shrouding her head and chest. All of these TAs ended up doing well as teachers and later laughed about those first day disasters. These experiences are exceptional. Most TAs know from that first day that they have found their career—being in front of the classroom feels so natural and enjoyable, they know that they will be teaching the rest of their lives.

Rather than focusing on what might go wrong that first day, take steps to lessen your anxiety and make the most of that initial class. With a little preparation and rehearsal, you can make a good impression and get your class off to a strong start. First, be prepared. Mentally rehearse what you will say and do in class and bring all the books and material you need. Second, be organized. You have some important business to accomplish that first day, so you need to go into class with a detailed, clear agenda *in writing*. Third, be confident and relaxed. A big part of teaching a writing class is trust—your students need to believe that you can and will help them improve as writers. You can begin to establish this confidence that first day. Talk to your students, begin to learn their names, answer their questions, smile. Your positive attitude and confidence will help your students learn.

CONCLUSION

The first class meeting and first days of a course are important, especially for new TAs. During this period, you have several goals: to set the tone you want in your class, to get your students off to a good start, and to establish yourself as a teacher. It will be a time of firsts for you. Do not expect perfection; as a teacher, you learn as much from your failures as you do from your successes. Just remember that you are not working alone. Rely on your teaching supervisor and fellow TAs for support and guidance. Do not hesitate to ask for advice or to discuss your teaching plans with others. With good planning and preparation, your first class meeting and the first few days of the course will be exciting and rewarding.

FIGURE 3.3

Possible Impromptu Writing Assignments
for the First Day of Class

1. In what ways has being in college lived up to your expectations so far? In what ways has it failed to live up to your expectations?

2. Who was the best teacher you had in high school? What made this person the best? Be sure to support your claims with specific examples.

3. Write out your "educational biography." Where have you gone to school? What have been the educational highlights of your life and what have been the educational low points?

4. What are your career goals? What occupation would you like when you finish college? Why?

5. Choose three words that best describe you. Why did you choose each one? Support your choice with specific examples and clear explanations.

6. Describe the process you followed when choosing a college. What were you looking for in a school? Why did you choose this school?

7. Who has been the most important person in your life, the person most responsible for making you who you are? How so?

8. If a younger brother or sister asked you about the best major to pursue in college, what advice would you give him or her? Why?

9. Suppose your high school guidance counselor asked you to write a brief essay that could be given to high school freshmen that offered advice on getting the most out of their high school education. Write the first draft of that essay.

10. What is your favorite (movie, television show, singer, band, book, etc.)? Why?

CHAPTER 4

Designing Writing Assignments

INTRODUCTION

As you begin to teach, you will quickly learn the importance of designing effective writing assignments: poorly constructed or ill-conceived assignments are hard for instructors to teach and hard for students to write. Every time you teach a course, you need to decide which writing assignments to include, how to put those assignments in writing, how to help your students write them, and how to evaluate their work. Designing effective writing takes time and practice, but the guidelines in this chapter will help you get started.

PURPOSEFUL WRITING ASSIGNMENTS

An axiom: effective writing assignments are purposeful. Teachers design assignments to serve some purpose or achieve some goal. In most cases, assignments are epistemic; their intent is to help the students learn something about themselves, the course material, or the world beyond their own experience. Most effective assignments also pose a significant problem for students to solve—an intellectual problem, an ethical problem, or a rhetorical problem. They stimulate the students' curiosity and challenge them to grow as readers, writers, and thinkers.

Below are some of the more common goals teachers have for the assignments they design. Consider carefully which of these goals might have a place in your writing class—which seem most appropriate given your students' needs and your program's philosophical orientation (see Chapter 2). Keep in mind that most teachers attempt to achieve several related goals in a composition class, which is why they employ a range of carefully sequenced assignments. Also, any single assignment might serve several purposes in a course and help teachers achieve several related goals.

Goal 1: To Help Students Understand Material Covered in Class

Teachers interested in this goal typically assign papers that require students to restate, critique, or apply material covered in the course to demonstrate that they understand it. The papers may ask students to summarize or paraphrase information; to evaluate readings, lectures, or demonstrations; or to develop novel applications of theories or principles. Commonly employed assignments include summaries, response essays, comparison–contrast papers, critiques, role-playing essays, case studies, journals, and lab or field notes.

Goal 2: To Help Students Learn about Themselves

Teachers interested in this goal want their students to examine their lives, thoughts, and feelings carefully and critically. These assignments often ask students to examine their past experiences, drawing conclusions about their family or cultural background. Other assignments ask them to reflect on their current experiences, both inside and outside the classroom. Still others ask students to speculate on their future lives, critically examining their plans, dreams, and life goals. These assignments are often deeply personal—the students write about their own lives to understand themselves more fully. Other times they are fundamentally political—the students address significant cultural or societal issues related to their lives. To accomplish any of these related goals, teachers may assign graded or ungraded exploratory and reflective essays, field journals, personal narratives, reports, research papers, or creative essays.

Goal 3: To Help Students Learn More about the World Outside their Own Experience

Teachers interested in this goal want their students to investigate a topic beyond their own experience and write about what they learn. Sometimes the papers will be informative—students convey their findings and conclusions to their readers as clearly as possible. Sometimes the papers will be argumentative—

students take a stand on an issue and defend it using the information they have gathered. Still other times they will be persuasive—students attempt to convince their readers to change their beliefs or behaviors using the information they have gathered and various rhetorical appeals. All of these assignments require research: students must thoroughly investigate a topic, evaluate the information they gather, form a position of their own, and perhaps persuade others of that position's soundness or preferability. To accomplish this goal, teachers may ask students to write reports, research papers, interviews, case studies, summaries, comparison–contrast essays, or reviews.

Goal 4: To Help Students Develop Particular Skills

Sometimes teachers use writing assignments to help their students develop particular reading, writing, or thinking skills. For example, by varying the source texts—literary texts, academic reports, advertisements, charts and graphs—required to write a particular paper, teachers can help their students develop certain critical reading skills. Asking students to compose specific types of papers (literary analysis essays, resumes), write to different audiences (expert readers, novice readers), employ a variety of styles (formal, informal), or work in certain media (creating Web sites, presenting oral reports with visual aids) can help them develop a range of writing skills. Requiring students to form and defend assertions, analyze assumptions, critique various perspectives on an issue, or identify logical fallacies can help them develop important critical thinking skills.

CHOOSING WHICH WRITING ASSIGNMENTS TO INCLUDE IN YOUR COURSE: A HEURISTIC

Once you clarify the goals for your writing assignments to achieve, decide which assignments to include on your class syllabus. Which are most appropriate given your students' needs, talents, and interests? Which are best given the theoretical orientation of your writing program? To help you make these decisions, consider the following questions:

1. What departmental guidelines do I have to follow?
Most writing programs establish guidelines every instructor must follow when designing a syllabus and choosing assignments. These guidelines can include:

- the number of papers students must write
- the types of papers students must write
- the types of source texts students must employ
- the research or documentation skills students must learn
- the audiences students must address
- the rhetorical skills students must learn

Make sure you understand the guidelines in place at your institution. If you have the freedom to choose which assignments you will teach, your teaching supervisor and department chair trust your ability to work within these guidelines and expectations. Teachers in every section of an introductory composition course have to pursue a similar set of goals if the writing program is to have any consistency and integrity. As one of the teachers in the program, you should develop assignments that follow these guidelines.

2. What philosophy of composition serves as the basis for the course?
The philosophical orientation of your course will significantly impact the kinds of papers you decide to teach. As a TA, you often have little say in the matter—the writing program is built around a particular philosophy of composition and you are required to work with it. If, however, you are free to design your own course, make sure you base all of your decisions on some coherent, unified theory of composition. Otherwise, you may design a class that contains conflicting elements: your selection of reading and writing assignments may appear random and haphazard, your evaluation methods can conflict with your assignment selection, and your pedagogy may contradict your textbook's instruction. Chapter 2 offers an overview of several current philosophies of composition, but if you are designing a writing course on your own for the first time, work closely with a faculty member who knows the discipline.

3. What are my course goals?
You should understand your overall course goals and the role each assignment plays in helping you achieve them. What do you want each assignment to acomplish? How will the assignment serve the students' needs? How will it serve the goals of the course? Without this understanding, you cannot develop a coherent rationale for the assignment, clear instructions for your students to follow, or effective criteria for evaluating the finished product.

4. How can I build on my students' interests?
Students tend to write better papers if they are interested in the topic. Assignments that build on the students' interests are generally more successful than those that do not. How, though, can you determine your students' interests? What interests you might not interest them. Also, how do you balance this concern with other goals you might have for your assignments, for example, helping the students develop particular skills or learn about topics beyond their own experience? To accomplish these other goals, you might have to require students to write about topics or work with material they do not, at least initially, find interesting. As will be discussed below, you might consider offering your students a choice of topics on each assignment, improving the chances that every student will be able to work on a topic that sparks his or her imagination.

5. What is the current level of my students' writing skills?
Good teachers manage to find the right mixture of challenge and support in their writing assignments. Assignments that are too easy can bore students;

ones that are too difficult can frustrate them. Writing assignments should challenge your students' current abilities and help them develop new skills. Most students can successfully complete writing assignments that are just beyond their current abilities if you support and guide their efforts. The trick, of course, is to design assignments that are developmentally appropriate and to provide instruction that is pedagogically sound.

PUTTING IT IN WRITING: HOW TO DESIGN EFFECTIVE ASSIGNMENT SHEETS

Once you decide which assignments you want to include on your syllabus, put them into writing so you can share them with your students. As composition theorist Linda Flower and others have pointed out, students complete the assignment they think they are being asked to write. If they misunderstand or misinterpret the assignment, their work will not meet your expectations. Putting all assignments in writing and discussing them thoroughly with your students helps reduce the likelihood of misunderstanding and misinterpretation.

The challenge is to keep assignment sheets concise and clear—no more than a page long if possible. Although some information should be on every assignment sheet you distribute, other material is optional. You may want to supplement your assignment sheet with other handouts as you teach your students how to write their essays. Two sample assignment sheets from an introductory course in argumentative writing and library research are included at the end of this chapter (Figure 4.6 and Figure 4.7 at the end of this chapter). Note how layout and graphics—spacing, centering, boldfacing, and underlining—are used to both condense and highlight important aspects of the assignment.

Every assignment sheet should contain the following information:

1. *The type of essay you are asking your students to write.*

Identify the type of essay you want your students to write—summary, comparison–contrast paper, reflective essay, research paper, and so on. Researchers Linda Flower and John Hayes have pointed out that when successful writers face a new task, they search their long-term memories for instances when they completed similar assignments. If asked to write a summary, for example, good writers recall the process they employed to write summaries in the past. As they write the current paper, they draw on strategies they previously found successful. Clearly identifying the type of paper you want your students to write can help them recall times they completed similar projects and remember the writing strategies they found helpful.

2. *The due date of the assignment.*

Stating the paper's due date will help your students organize their time as they complete the project and will reduce the number of arguments you have with your students over late work. More importantly, though, due dates help reinforce a process approach to writing, especially if you also indicate when any preliminary work on the paper is due. For example, for long projects you may want to indicate due dates for the students' choice of topics, scratch outlines, preliminary bibliographies, or rough drafts. These due dates help keep the students on task and reduce the number of students who wait until the last minute to do all of the work (usually with predictably poor results).

3. *The desired length of the assignment.*

Not every teacher likes to indicate how long final drafts should be. They fear that students write to that length even if doing so results in a weaker paper: if a teacher says that a paper should be five pages long, some students will stop at five pages when, given the paper's thesis, it should be longer, whereas other students will pad their paper with fluff to reach five pages.

When it comes to specifying length, you have several options. First, you can leave off any length requirement. If you do, understand that your students will ask, so have a response ready. Teachers who do specify a length requirement tend to establish a minimum length ("at least two pages or three hundred words"), a maximum length ("no more than four pages or six hundred words"), or an acceptable range of lengths (" three to four pages long or 450–600 words"). You may want to check with your students to see which option they prefer. If you do not specify a length on your assignment sheet, you will likely receive a variety of long and short papers, so decide if you would be comfortable responding to or evaluating such a range of responses.

4. *The writing task.*

What, *exactly*, do you want the students to accomplish in their papers? What, *exactly*, is their task? Spell out the assignment as clearly and as unambiguously as possible. Pay special attention to your verbs here and choose the ones that best describe the assignment. Read through it with the eyes of a skeptic. How might the language be misinterpreted? How can it be made clearer? An effective way to clarify the writing task is to point out how it fits into the sequence of assignments students are completing in the course—how does this particular assignment build on previous assignments or build toward future ones?

5. *The rhetorical situation of the assignment.*

At the heart of every assignment is the rhetorical situation—someone writing to someone about something for some purpose. In articulating the rhetorical situation of the assignment, let the students know what role they are to assume as writers, who they are writing to, what subject they should address, and what purpose the essay should serve. Four important elements of all written communication are involved here: the writer, the audience, the topic, and the purpose of the assignment.

The writer. What stance do you expect the students to assume in relation to their audience and topic? What role should they play? What persona should they assume? These are all questions to consider as you put together any assignment sheet. Sometimes you may want them to assume roles close to their own experience: "As a first-semester college student, write a letter to your hometown newspaper identifying what you think is the most important issue facing higher education today." Other times you may ask them to assume a more academic role: "Explain your interpretation of this poem as one literary critic speaking to other critics." Still other times you may want them to assume imaginary roles: "Suppose you are a citizen living in Virginia in 1775. What arguments would you pose to your neighbors to convince them to remain united with Great Britain?" If you say nothing on your assignment sheet about the role you want the students to assume, most students will assume the role of "college student writer." If you expect them to assume a perspective other than this, you need to indicate that on your assignment sheet.

The audience. To whom is the writer writing? If you say nothing about audience on your assignment sheet, your students will likely assume that they are writing to you, their teacher, a representative of the academic community. You can vary the audience of your students' papers in several interesting and challenging ways. For example, early in the term, ask students to write for themselves (notes, reflection pieces, free writing); as the term progresses, ask them to write to people they know well (family members, classmates, friends), and finally to people they do not know and have not met (the readers of a newspaper, the college board of trustees). You may ask them to address imaginary audiences: "Suppose you are writing to the people of nineteenth-century America. Explain one or two aspects of our current political system they might have the hardest time understanding." (A caution: do not be *too* creative when designing imaginary audiences— your students might spend too much time analyzing the audience and slight the other elements of the rhetorical situation.) You can also vary audience in terms of expertise and knowledge, asking your students to write some papers for readers who know something about the topic they are addressing and other papers for readers who know nothing about it. You might vary the audience by level of formality, asking your students to write some papers for readers who would expect formal prose and others for readers who expect informal prose.

The key is to specify on the assignment sheet the audience you intend the students to address and to discuss with them how this aspect of the rhetorical situation might influence their writing. As numerous composition theorists have pointed out, an audience is always a "fiction": writers address their prose not to actual readers but to their interpretation or understanding of those readers. For example, when asked to write a letter to the president of a school board, students imagine what a school board president might be like—what he or she might think or believe. When writing, they construct this audience in their minds and compose their essays accordingly. No two students may interpret the audience the exact same way, which can explain some of the differences in their final drafts. When you specify an audience on an assignment sheet, spend some time talking about it in class, helping each student construct an effective, productive understanding of his or her intended reader.

The topic. You can also vary the topics of your writing assignments in interesting ways. First, though, consider what topics are appropriate given the requirements of your writing program and the philosophy of composition underlying your course. Second, decide whether you want all of your students to write on the same topic: whether you want to offer them a choice of topics or whether you want to have your students choose their own topic. If you offer students a choice of topics, have them commit to one fairly early in the writing process so they can get started with their prewriting activities. Also, reserve the right to veto topics if you think they are inappropriate or unmanageable.

You might ask your students to write about topics directly related to their own lives, topics beyond their own experiences, or some combination of the two. Also consider how you might sequence several assignments around a single topic: through a series of assignments, the students investigate a single topic in some depth and from a variety of perspectives. In fact, many teachers like to design their entire class around a single topic or theme that unites all the assignments.

The purpose. Why are the students writing this assignment? What is their goal? Be sure to spell this out for the students. For example, if they are summarizing an article for someone who has not read the piece, why are they doing it? What is the summary supposed to accomplish? Many traditional writing textbooks tell students that every piece of writing serves one of three purposes: to inform, to persuade, or to entertain. Assignment sheets should do more. What is the *specific* purpose of the writing task you are asking your students to complete? The more fully you explain the goal of the assignment, the easier it will be for students to meet your expectations.

Spelling out the rhetorical situation of the assignment—the intended role of the writer, the intended audience, the topic, and the purpose—will help your students produce more effective essays and also help you grade their work. Teachers evaluate most papers in terms of the assignment's rhetorical situation: how well does the essay accomplish what it is supposed to accomplish given the intended role of the writer, the intended audience, the topic, and the purpose?

6. *The grading criteria.*

Indicate what you will be looking for when you respond to or grade the assignment. In a sentence or two or in a short list, let the students know what aspects of their writing will figure in your evaluation of their work. Some teachers even like to affix a value to different elements of the work, indicating, for example, the number of points the paper's argument will be worth, or its thesis, or its structure, or its use of transitions. (Chapters 5 and 6 offer additional advice on how to respond to and grade student work.)

7. *The format.*

Is there any particular way the students should format their essay? Some instructors offer detailed format guidelines on their course policy sheet—guidelines that apply to every essay the students write in class—whereas other teachers want their students to experiment with format throughout the semester and offer assignment-specific guidelines. In either case, if you believe an assignment ought to be structured in a particular way, share this information with your students. Do not expect your students to "guess" the structure you have in mind. Either specify the format you prefer on your assignment sheet or lead them to this structure by analyzing model essays in class.

8. *The relationship between this assignment and prior assignments.*

As mentioned previously, explain how this assignment builds on skills the students developed when completing previous assignments or builds toward future assignments. When you planned your course, you sequenced the writing assignments in a particular order for specific reasons. Explain those reasons to your students on the assignment sheet. The course will seem more cohesive and organized to students if they understand how the writing assignments are related to one another.

9. *Collaboration guidelines.*

Do you want your students to collaborate on their papers? If they are to work with others, how do you want the groups structured? How do you expect the students in each group to divide the work? How do you plan to evaluate their efforts? If you expect your students to collaborate on an essay, to work in pairs or in groups, let them know on the assignment sheet. (See Chapter 7 for more specific guidelines and advice on collaborative teaching activities.)

10. *Documentation guidelines.*

If applicable, indicate what documentation style you expect the students to follow. Again, some teachers have their students employ only one documentation style the entire term, commonly either the system developed by the Modern Language Association (MLA) or the American Psychological Association (APA). Stating this requirement on the course policy sheet distributed at the beginning of the term is usually sufficient, though including a brief reminder about documentation on an assignment sheet can never hurt. However, if you vary the documentation style you ask your students to follow throughout the term or even on occasion, be sure to specify on the assignment sheet which set of guidelines you want your students to employ.

11. *Options.*

You may offer students several options on a particular assignment—a choice of topics, perhaps, or a choice of formats. Spell out these options as clearly as you can on the assignment sheet. To help your students get started on the project, make sure they tell you which option they choose as soon as possible. Putting off these choices too long can make it impossible for the students to finish their projects on time.

12. *The weight of the paper.*

You may want to remind your students how much each paper is "worth" if you grade individual assignments. Teaches who do not put the weight of the paper on the assignment sheet usually include that information on the class policy sheet they hand out at the beginning of the term. Yet even if this information is on your policy sheet, you may want to repeat it on your individual assignment sheets as well.

13. *Pointers or reminders.*

Based on your experience as a student, teacher, or writer, share any pointers or hints that might help your students write the paper. Also, remind your students to apply the lessons they have been learning in class when writing the essay. These pointers and reminders might concern the students' composing process, format, style, grammar—any aspect of writing you think students should keep in mind as they complete the project.

14. *Warnings.*

Finally, warn your students of any problems that typically occur when writing this type of paper. Share this information with your students so they can avoid the problems themselves.

Figure 4.1 summarizes the information that should be included on an assignment sheet. As most of this information can be conveyed in a sentence or two through careful editing and effective layout, you should be able to keep every assignment sheet around a page long. In her influential book *A Rhetoric for Writing Teachers*, Erika Lindemann lists a series of decisions teachers should make concerning the assignment's task, the process students should follow when composing the essay, the audience they will address, the time line they should

FIGURE 4.1

Vital Information to Include on Every Assignment Sheet

❏ The type of essay you are asking your students to write
❏ The due date of the assignment
❏ The desired length of the assignment
❏ The writing task
❏ The rhetorical situation of the assignment
❏ The grading criteria
❏ The format
❏ The relationship between this assignment and prior assignments
❏ Collaboration guidelines
❏ Documentation guidelines
❏ Options
❏ The weight of the paper
❏ Pointers or reminders
❏ Warnings

---

follow, and the assessment techniques the teacher will employ. The following checklist is based on her ideas and can serve as a useful guide when drafting and revising assignment sheets.

The Task
> *Have you considered:*

❏ what the students are being asked to write
❏ how the assignment fits larger course goals
❏ what students are supposed to learn by completing the assignment
❏ what you will learn about your students as they complete the assignment

The Writing Process
> *Have you considered:*

❏ how students will go about completing the assignment
❏ whether students will work alone or collaborate
❏ how much time students will need to complete the assignment
❏ how students will gather the information they need to complete the assignment
❏ how students will choose among available options

The Audience
> *Have you considered:*

❏ who the students are addressing in their papers
❏ whether the students know how to assess the needs of their audience

The Timetable
> *Have you considered:*

❏ when students will write the paper
❏ what parts of the paper the students will turn in for response
❏ when students will get response to their papers
❏ what deadlines will be specified
❏ how much time students will need to complete the project

Assessment
> *Have you considered:*

❏ how the papers will be evaluated
❏ when the papers will be evaluated
❏ who will evaluate the papers
❏ how revisions or rewrites will be addressed
❏ whether the papers will be graded
❏ what problems the students are likely to encounter
❏ when and how to share the evaluation criteria

SEQUENCING WRITING ASSIGNMENTS

As you plan your course, you should devote a great deal of attention to sequencing your writing assignments. Ideally, the assignments should build on one another in some productive way. One simple plan is to sequence assignments by their length: shorter papers giving way to longer papers. This approach is based on the premise that shorter essays are easier to write than longer essays and that by completing these easier, shorter essays, students develop skills they need to complete longer, more difficult projects. Teachers using this approach typically give students more time to write longer assignments and weigh them more heavily when determining the course grade.

Other teachers, drawing on the work of rhetorical theorists James Moffett and James Britton, sequence their assignments by audience. Through a series of assignments, students are asked to write for audiences that grow increasingly more distant from them. Early in the course, for example, students write for an audience they know well—perhaps themselves or their family. Next, they write for their friends or their classmates, people they may not know quite so well. Students then are asked to address a broader, though still relatively homogenous group, such as a church congregation or members of a particular political party. By the end of the course, they are writing for a vast, relatively unknowable audience—"college educated readers" or "the general public." From assignment to assignment, the students learn how to adjust their prose to meet the needs of these various readers. Figure 4.2 offers a sample writing assignment sequence based on these principles. Some teachers try to sequence assignments according to their "difficulty," a nebulous standard but one that usually refers to the assignment's rhetorical complexity. "Easy" assignments posit a fairly straightforward relationship among the elements of any communicative act: writer, reader, subject, and purpose. As the course progresses, teachers make the relationship among these elements in the assignments increasingly more complex. A typical set of assignments might ask students to address the same topic in several papers, each aimed at reaching a different audience or achieving a different goal. The idea behind this type of sequence is to challenge and gradually stretch the students' rhetorical skills.

FIGURE 4.2   Sequencing Assignments Based on Audience

Audience	Possible Assignment
Self	Reflective essay
Family	Letters home
Friends	Summary of a reading
Classmates	Report or argument
Students at the school	Letter to the school newspaper
School administrators	Proposal concerning the school
Members of the community	Letter to a local newspaper
Academic readers	Formal academic paper
General readers	Magazine article

A more traditional way of sequencing assignments is to employ the modes of discourse: description, narration, exposition, and argumentation. Teachers who adopt this sequence tend to assign descriptive and narrative essays first. They then move to expository (informative) and argumentative papers. Because most students find it easier to write descriptive and narrative essays, teachers begin with these modes, hoping to build on the students' interests and to motivate them with some early success. However, the shift to exposition and argumentation can be problematic. Researchers have found that the skills students develop on earlier descriptive and narrative papers do not transfer easily to expository and argumentative assignments. Many writing programs today only focus on two of the modes, exposition and argumentation, perhaps covering each in its own required composition course.

As mentioned earlier, some teachers like to structure their course around a central theme. In paper after paper, students investigate that theme from a variety of perspectives, using the information they gather when writing one paper to help them complete the next. Over the semester, students develop an expertise that helps them compose more knowledgeable, critical, reflective essays. If everyone in the course is investigating the same theme, collaborative writing projects are easier to manage and students can offer more informed, substantive responses to their peers' papers.

Finally, some writing teachers sequence assignments around a set of skills they want their students to develop. For example, improving the students' ability to write from readings by requiring their students to write summaries (which develop the students' ability to read a text closely and accurately), response essays (which develop their ability to form and defend judgments about a reading), critiques (which develop their ability to assess the quality of a text according to a standard set of criteria), and synthesis essays (which develop their ability to combine information from multiple sources to support a more comprehensive thesis) (see Figure 4. 3)

FIGURE 4.3   Writing from Readings Assignment Sequence

Assignment	Skills Emphasized
Paraphrase	The ability to understand the literal meaning of a source text
Summary	The ability to identify the key points of a source text
Analysis	The ability to identify how a source text is structured
Response	The ability to articulate one's reaction to a source text
Critique	The ability to evaluate the relative quality of a source text
Synthesis	The ability to combine information from source texts

Another common assignment sequence is designed to improve the students' argumentation skills. Early in the term, students learn how to summarize, analyze, and evaluate arguments. They are then asked to write increasingly more sophisticated arguments of their own (see Figure 4.4). An alternative sequence asks students to write arguments based on increasingly more academic source texts: early assignments require students to base their arguments on personal experience, later ones ask them to employ material from the popular press, and the final ones require them to work with academic source texts or interviews.

REDESIGNING WRITING ASSIGNMENTS: LEARNING FROM EXPERIENCE

Once you begin to teach, always try to improve the assignments you use. As you respond to and grade your students' papers, make note of any trends or problems you notice. Is there something students consistently do well? If so, you may want to note this as a "reminder" the next time you write up the assignment. Is there something students tend to have problems with? Again, make a note to include this in the "warning" section of the assignment sheet when you revise it. Finally, be sure to keep copies of good and weak student essays to add to your files. The next time you teach this course, you can use these samples in class as model essays, offering students examples of successful and not so successful papers. (Remember to obtain your students' permission before you use their work this way in your classes.)

Also ask your students what they think of each assignment. Some end-of-the-semester course evaluation forms ask students to comment on the quality of the assignments, but these questions are usually too broad to be helpful and come too late to affect the course you are currently teaching. One way to avoid this problem is to ask the students for their response to the assignments as they complete each paper. On the day the students turn in their essays, ask them to answer a few questions about the assignment and their writing process, jotting down their answers on the back page of their papers. Figure 4.5 offers some of the questions TAs have found help-

FIGURE 4.4   Argument Assignment Sequence

Assignment	Skills Emphasized
Summary	The ability to identify the key elements of an argument
Analysis	The ability to describe how an argument is structured
Critique	The ability to evaluate the quality of an argument
Arguments	The ability to construct an argument

FIGURE 4.5   Questions to Ask Students When They Complete a Paper

---

1. Did you find the assignment interesting?
2. What did you find most difficult about writing the essay?
3. What did you find easiest about completing the project?
4. What do you wish you had spent more time on when completing this essay?
5. What instruction proved most helpful to you when completing this paper?
6. What did you need more help with when completing this paper?
7. What are the strengths of this paper, as you see it?
8. What are the weaknesses of this paper, as you see it?
9. What will you do differently the next time you write a paper like this? What advice would you would give a friend who is about to write the same assignment?

---

ful in the past. If you like the idea of anonymous responses, ask your students to answer these questions on index cards you pass out and then collect. Whatever method you employ, take your students' comments seriously as you reconsider and revise your assignments. Their responses are crucial if you are committed to improving the quality and utility of your assignments.

WORKS CITED

Britton, James, et al. *The Development of Writing Abilities* (11–18). London: Macmillan, 1975

Flower, Linda. "Writer-Based Prose: A Cognitive Basis for Problems in Writing." *College English* 41 (1979): 19–37.

Flower, Linda, and John Hayes. "A Cognitive Process Theory of Writing." *College Composition and Communication* 32 (1981): 365–87.

Lindemann, Erika. *A Rhetoric for Writing Teachers*. New York: Oxford University Press, 1987.

Moffett, James. *Teaching the Universe of Discourse*. Boston: Houghton Mifflin, 1968.

ADDITIONAL READINGS

Anson, Chris, M., Joan Graham, David A. Jolliffe, Nancy S. Shapiro, and Carolyn H. Smith. "Creating Effective Writing Assignments." *Scenarios for Teaching Writing*. Urbana, IL: NCTE, 1993. 1–17.

Bean, John. *Engaging Ideas: The Professor's Guide to Integrating Writing, Critical Thinking, and Active Learning in the Classroom*. San Francisco: Jossey-Bass, 1996.

Brent, Rebecca, and Richard M. Felder. "Writing Assignments: Pathways to Connections, Clarity, Creativity." *College Teaching* 40.2 (1992): 43–7.

Capossela, Toni-Lee, ed. *The Critical Writing Workshop: Designing Writing Assignments to Foster Critical Thinking*. Portsmouth, NH: Boyton/Cook, 1992.

Cox, Gerald H. "Designing Writing Assignments." *Teaching Prose: A Guide for Writing Assignments*. Ed. Fredric Bogel, et al. New York: Norton, 1984. 87–113.

Kiniry, Malcolm, and Ellen Strenski. "Sequencing Expository Writing: A Recursive Approach." *College Composition and Communication* 36 (1985): 191–202.

Raign, Kathryn Rossner. "Writing Assignments." The *Harcourt Brace Guide to Teaching First-Year Composition*. Fort Worth: Harcourt, 1998. 69–81.

Starkey, David, ed. *Teaching Writing Creatively*. Portsmouth, NH: Boyton/Cook, 1998.

Throckmorton, Helen J. "Do Your Writing Assignments Work?" *English Journal* 69.8 (1980): 56–9.

Weese, Katherine L. "'Only Connect': Sequencing Assignments in the Beginning Writing Classroom." *Teaching Academic Literacy: The Uses of Teacher-Research in Developing a Writing Program*. Ed. Katherine L. Weese, Stephen L. Fox, and Stuart Greene. Mahwah, NJ: Lawrence Erlbaum, 1999. 45–64

Weiser, Irwin. "Better Writing Through Rhetorically Based Assignments." *Journal of Teaching Writing* 6 (1987): 41–7.

White, Edward M. "Writing Assignments and Essay Topics." *Assigning, Responding, Evaluating: A Writing Teacher's Guide*. 3rd ed. New York: St. Martin's Press, 1995. 1–24.

Williams, James D. "Writing Assignments." *Preparing to Teach Writing: Research, Theory, and Practice*. Mahwah, NJ: Lawrence Erlbaum, 1998: 242–57.

FIGURE 4.6   Sample Assignment Sheet

Analysis

Length:	**3–4 pages**
Percentage of Grade:	**10%**
Due Date:	**January 24**

Introduction

In this paper, you will analyze an argument, locating and describing its essential elements. "Analysis" involves breaking something down into its parts. When writing this assignment, you will learn how to work with two essential elements of an argument: claims and grounds. We will also discuss a third element, warrants. Completing this assignment will prepare you for the next step in our class, learning how to evaluate the effectiveness of arguments.

Assignment

Compose an argument analysis of "Why Married Mothers Work" by Victor Fuchs (*Writing Arguments*, 259–262). In your analysis, identify the primary claims Fuchs makes and the evidence he uses to support each of those claims.

Organization

The opening of your paper should introduce the topic of the source text, provide its complete title, and identify its author. You will also offer your readers a *brief* summary of the source text (no longer than a paragraph) and provide your thesis. Your thesis will offer an overview of the analysis that follows in the body of your essay.

You can employ one of two organizational schemes for the body of your analysis: block or alternating. Under a block format, you will discuss all of the claims, then all of the evidence. Under an alternating format, you will discuss a claim and its evidence, then another claim and its evidence, then another claim and its evidence, and so on.

Your conclusion will offer a summary of your analysis.

Format and Grading Criteria

Producing a good analysis paper requires care and diligence. You must fully understand the source text and critically analyze its structure. When writing up the results of your study, you must use precise language, fully explaining your conclusions. You will also have to employ good topic sentences and clear transitions to help guide your reader through your essay. Finally, when drafting and revising your paper, you will need to quote and document material properly.

FIGURE 4.7   Sample Assignment Sheet

Critique

Length:	4–5 pages	**Rough Draft Due:**	**February 4**
Percentage of Grade:	15%	**Final Due Date:**	**February 11**

Introduction

When you wrote your analysis paper, you isolated for examination the claims and grounds of an argument. With this assignment, you will support a position of your own–you will assess the quality of the argument Charles Krauthammer presents in his article "How to Save the Homeless Mentally Ill" (WA 221–227), then explain and defend your judgment.

Assignment

Critique the argument Charles Krauthammer presents in "How to Save the Homeless Mentally Ill." In your thesis, you will state your overall assessment of the argument Krauthammer presents, letting your reader know whether you found his argument weak or strong, good or bad. You will base this judgment on a careful evaluation of the various parts of Krauthammer's arguments: his claims, grounds, and warrants.

Preparation

When completing the prewriting for your last paper, you had to identify an author's grounds and claims. Now you need to judge the quality of these elements: does Krauthammer present good claims and good evidence? In addition, you will need to assess the quality of the warrants Krauthammer employs when presenting his case.

You will evaluate these various elements of the source text against the standards we discuss in class. Using these standards, you will determine the strength of Krauthammer's grounds, claims, and warrants. Based on this evaluation, you will form your thesis. If Krauthammer offers solid grounds, claims, and warrants, you will have to argue that he presents a good argument. If, however, you see weaknesses in Krauthammer's claims, grounds, or warrants, your thesis will offer a less positive assessment of the piece.

Organization

In the opening of your essay, you need to summarize the source text and set the context of your essay (indicate the topic of the reading, its author's name, its complete title, and your thesis). In the body of your essay, you will develop and defend your thesis with clear reasoning, full explanations, and material from the source text.

Reminders

For this paper, you must use MLA documentation for all quotations. Though you've used it in earlier essays, do not use first person in this paper ("I," "we," "us," "our," and so on) and do not use contractions. We will discuss why in class.

CHAPTER 5

Responding to Student Writing

RESPONDING VS. GRADING: DIFFERENT GOALS, DIFFERENT PURPOSES

Experienced writing teachers understand that responding to and grading student writing are closely related but separate tasks, each with an important evaluative role to play. When you respond to a student's text, you enter into a dialogue with both the writing and the writer, commenting on a range of issues: the text's ideas and arguments, its format and organization, its voice and style. You can praise the writer's efforts, question his or her judgments, or ask questions. Your responses indicate your reactions to and evaluation of your students' writing and guide your students' efforts to revise their work. A grade, on the other hand, is typically a definitive statement of the work's overall effectiveness according to the standards you establish for the class—a holistic, comprehensive assessment of the text's quality.

Although grades can help your students gauge the quality of their work in relation to the standards you establish for a course, responses can serve a wider range of functions: instruction, praise, censure, inquiry. As you evaluate a set of student papers, you should keep these two forms of evaluation separate in your mind—your responses to a text should do more than justify or explain the grade. The challenge is to find productive ways to combine grades and responses, letting your students know through the grade where their work stands in relation to the desired outcomes for the course and through your comments where their papers are working well and where they need to be improved.

As a teacher, you will devote a tremendous amount of time to evaluating your students' work. The more thought you give to this important aspect of teaching and the more options you have at your disposal, the more effective an instructor you will be.

PURPOSES OF RESPONSE

When you respond to your students' work, keep in mind your primary goal: to help your students become better writers. At their best, responses extend your voice beyond the classroom and help you individualize instruction by speaking directly to your students. Your responses to your students' work can serve any number of the purposes outlined below, but they should always advance your primary goal.

To Point Out Strengths and Weaknesses in Your Student's Writing or Thinking

For most new TAs, responding to a student's paper means marking errors: circling and identifying mistakes, filling the margins with critical commentary, or bracketing sections of text and referring students to certain sections of the course handbook. Commenting on a text's weaknesses is important—it can help students learn to identify and correct mistakes. However, this type of commentary can be counterproductive as well. Instead of improving student writing, too many negative responses can overwhelm or dispirit students. Instead of motivating or guiding revision, it can cause students to abandon their papers in confusion or anger. Teachers also need to point out strengths. Responses should help students identify what is working well in their writing so they can build on these strengths as they revise their work. False praise is not helpful, but honestly commenting on those aspects of a student's paper that work well—or that have the potential of working well—can motivate students toward deeper, fuller revisions.

To Respond to Your Student's Writing

Composition theorist and rhetorician Joe Williams points out in his article, "The Phenomenology of Error," that when teachers read student work, they often get so caught up in looking for errors that they forget to actually *read* the paper to see what the student has to say. When you read a student's paper and respond to it as a reader, you indicate which aspects of the student's paper you found interesting, informative, thought-provoking, humorous, moving, exciting, or boring. When done well and consistently, this type of response can help your students form a clearer sense of what it means to write for "real" readers, not just for teachers who grade their work.

To Encourage Students to Reflect on Their Writing or Thinking

Good responses can help students think more deeply about their writing, encouraging them to reconsider positions they assume, investigate perspectives they ignore, or reassess the accuracy and clarity of their prose. One way to encourage this sort of reflection is to ask questions:

question a student's meaning:

"I'm not sure what you're saying here—do you mean X or Y?"

question a student's interpretation of a source text:

"Are you sure this is really the author's position? Check the last paragraph of her article again."

the consistency of a student's argument:

"Does this really *match what you said about the topic on page two? How can you reconcile the two positions?"*

the depth of a student's thinking on the topic:

"Have you considered the implications of your stand here? If this course of action is taken, how might the public react?"

the student's analysis of his or her audience:

"Have you considered how your readers might react to your choice of words here? What wording might be clearer and less controversial?"

Questions such as these help your students reconsider their ideas and language, promoting more thoughtful, reflective revision.

Pointing out counterpositions can also promote reflection. Raising issues or arguments your students have ignored or slighted helps them address these deficiencies in future drafts. Bring up evidence students don't mention (especially when that evidence casts doubt on their position) or offer alternative interpretations of evidence or examples they do include. Your goal here is to complicate your students' thinking by assuming the stance of a skeptical reader, raising problems the students have to resolve in future drafts. Thinking through the counterpositions you raise helps students develop their critical thinking skills and teaches them how to produce more rhetorically sophisticated papers.

A third response technique that promotes reflection is to remind students of relevant material you covered in class. Suppose, for example, you spent time discussing the importance of offering specific, concrete examples to support assertions. If students turn in papers without this type of support, remind them of what you discussed in class:

> *"Look back at your notes and at the instructions in Chapter 6 of the textbook—what specific examples could go here?"*

This type of response helps students draw connections between their writing and your classroom instruction. Too often students fail to understand the link between what you teach in class and what they write in their papers. Responses that encourage students to reflect on these connections can be productive.

A final way to promote reflection is to paraphrase what your students have written. This is an especially helpful technique when the writing is vague or ambiguous. These responses often read something like this:

> *"You seem to be saying X here. Is that correct?"*

> *"Do you mean to be saying Y? Because that's how this passage reads."*

> *"Here you are saying X, but in the previous paragraph, you said Y—why the difference?"*

Responses such as these encourage students to reread and evaluate what they have written. Many times student writers do not fully realize what they are saying in their papers—through carelessness or lack of skill, they misrepresent their own thoughts on the page. Because they lack good revision skills (and may not even reread what they have written before turning it in), they submit work that does not accurately reflect their thoughts, positions, or experiences. By paraphrasing their words, you urge them to read and reflect on their language and then decide whether they will stand behind what they have written or revise it.

To Guide Your Students' Revision Process

Good responses help students revise their work in productive ways, identifying what needs their attention on particular drafts. For example, when responding to early drafts, focus most of your commentary on the content and structure of your students' papers: it makes little sense to line-edit rough drafts when some of that material may be cut in future versions. When responding to later drafts of the paper, focus your comments on its syntax, word choice, tone, or style. Your responses can guide your students' revision process, drawing their attention to the changes they need to make to each draft of their work. More importantly, though, your responses can offer your students a strategy for addressing these issues, suggesting which changes to make first and what aspects of their writing to address later.

To Help Your Students Look Toward Future Papers

When you respond to the final drafts of your students' papers, you should have future assignments in mind. Good final responses have transfer value: they help your students understand how the lessons they learned when writing the current paper can help them complete upcoming assignments. In a well-planned writing course, students build their writing skills sequentially as they move from assignment to assignment. Your responses can help them see these connections and to think more consciously about their growth and development as writers.

GUIDELINES FOR WRITING
EFFECTIVE RESPONSES

Regardless of their purpose, effective responses exhibit certain characteristics. In addition to being specific and clear, they guide the students' revision efforts and balance criticism with praise. Below are some guidelines you can follow to write more effective responses to your students' work.

Make Your Comments Specific and Clear

When conducting research for her influential essay, "Responding to Student Writing," Nancy Sommers analyzed the responses thirty-five college instructors wrote on their students' papers. Sommers reached several disturbing conclusions. First, she found that most of the teachers' comments were not clear and specific—they tended to use abstract generalizations that could be rubber-stamped on almost any paper. Consider, for example, the teacher who writes "Good" next to a paragraph in a student paper. When reviewing the teacher's comments, a student cannot know which aspect of her writing is being praised: her argument, her examples, her syntax, her word choice, or her punctuation. The same problem applies to comments such as "awk" placed next to an underlined word. What, exactly, is "awkward" about that word—is it a problem with diction, voice, style? The student likely will not be able to tell.

Does that mean that every response has to be fully explained, that you are obligated to offer extensive running commentary on every student paper? No. Sommers's work, however, points out the need for comments to be *more* clear and specific than teachers usually make them. Writing the marginal comment "Good use of quoted material" next to a paragraph is better than just writing "Good." "Awkward word—diction" is better than "awk." When possible, tie your responses to *specific* words, sentences, or paragraphs in the text; link your commentary to the text by circling words, bracketing sentences, drawing lines to paragraphs, whatever it takes. Also, provide enough explanation in your comment to make the intent of your response clear. Clear, specific commentary will best guide your students' efforts to improve their work.

Minimize Your Comments

Many writing teachers overwhelm their students' papers with commentary, often with the best of intentions: these teachers believe that if they do not mark every mistake, their students will not know what to correct when they revise their work. However, such overwhelming commentary may cause more harm than the teacher thinks, and there are alternatives. Several studies have shown that most students find extensive commentary bewildering—it actually inhibits their ability to revise their writing because they often do not know where to start. Consider, for example, how you might react if you were a student getting back a paper with the amount and kind of commentary found in Figure 5.1 below.

When papers are marked this extensively, students usually do not know how to sort through and work with the teacher's comments when they revise. Not knowing where to start their revisions, they give up in frustration. Other students willingly accept every suggestion the teacher makes and revise their

FIGURE 5.1 Teacher Commentary on the Opening Paragraphs of a Student Paper

cliché spl too general an opening

In society today, their are many problems people face. Some of them vague

choppy involve jobs. Some involve family. Others involve politics. One of the most

? again, very general

important is the environment. The enviromnet faces may problems today. Cars transition?

are the major source of air pollution. Something has to be done about the problem

?

vague with cars. Experts say we can make cars less pollutig so they do not do so much

tone?

damage to the environment. Yes, we need too have cars, but cars do not have to

be so damaging to the environment. In this paper I will suggest ways that the awk. thesis

vague problem with cars can be addressed. PV

Cars hurt the environmnet in many ways. But the major problem involves —wordy

who?

air pollution from the exhaust pipes of cars. One expert says, "Automobiles are

the major source of air pollution in most U.S. cities today. They contibute more to

documentation? logic?

pollution than do factories" Therefore, cars pollution is a major threat. A Cars'

exhaust fills the environment with deadly fumes such as carbon dioxide. CO_2 is a

frag ?

known pollutant that causes health problems. Including cancer and emphusema.

how?

In major cities, cars contribute to smog. Smog kills kids and elderly people. If we ?

¶ focus? were able to cut back on the amout of exhause from cars we would be able to clean

up the enviromnet. Especially in our larger cities. frag

paper accordingly, even if they do not understand why they are making the changes. In the end, they have learned little about improving their own writing, only how to make the revisions the teacher tells them to make.

If you adopt a strategy of marking most of the errors you find in a student's paper, you need to take several steps to ensure that your students get the greatest benefit from your hard work. First, try to praise as well as criticize—a little encouragement can sometimes be more productive than a lot of criticism. Notice how the teacher commentary in Figure 5.1 is all negative. Second, help the student make sense of your comments. For example, suppose a student turned in a paper that does not address the assignment, contains twenty-two spelling mistakes, and commits fourteen mechanical errors, all of which you dutifully mark before returning the essay to the student to revise. Without guidance, most students determine where to start their revisions by counting the errors their teacher marks. If you marked twenty-two spelling errors and fourteen mechanical mistakes, most inexperienced students will assume that they should start there: clean up the spelling and mechanical errors, and they are well on their way. Of course, the rewrite may be free of spelling or mechanical errors and still receive an "F" if it again fails to address the assignment—the *primary* problem with the draft. When you mark a lot of errors in a student's paper, your end comments should rank the mistakes in terms of their importance. Let the student know what steps to take in what order when revising. Such guidance can be invaluable.

An alternative to marking every error in a paper is to mark only a few— the most important, the most significant, or the most troublesome. Teachers employing this approach to response—termed "minimal marking" by Richard Haswell—read the paper without marking anything, decide on two or three changes the writer needs to make, then comment on these aspects of the text as they reread the paper. From paper to paper or draft to draft throughout the course, the teacher asks each student to address just one or two problems at a time until, by the end of the term, each student is producing relatively error-free prose.

Minimal marking makes some teachers nervous. They wonder how their students can improve as writers if they do not note every error in every draft of a paper. However, minimal marking encourages students to focus their attention on a few specific aspects of their writing at a time, correcting those weaknesses or building on those strengths.

In the end, though, whether you respond to every error you find in your students' papers or respond to a few patterns of errors in each essay, you goal is the same: to help your students learn how to compose more effective papers.

Do Not Take over the Student's Text

Another problem that Sommers noted in her study was the tendency of some teachers to "appropriate" their students' texts. Through their extensive comments, teachers essentially rewrite the student's paper—substituting their thoughts and language for the student's. If a student incorporates all of these changes when revising, the final draft would be more the teacher's than the student's. To avoid this problem, you need to develop a sensitivity to student intent. As you respond to a paper, determine as clearly as you can what the student is trying to say and offer advice on how to say it more effectively. Your comments should help your students clarify their thinking and writing, to say in their papers what *they* want to say as effectively as possible. Sometimes this entails challenging what the student has written or offering alternative points of view to consider.

Leave Some Work for the Student To Do

You do not need to *correct* all the errors you note in a students' paper. In fact, correcting errors may be the wrong type of response if it does not promote learning. As mentioned above, students will incorporate teacher-suggested changes to their papers even if they do not understand why the changes are needed. When you correct errors, you may be doing work the student needs to do to learn.

Here are a few ways to avoid this problem. First, if you perceive a recurrent problem in a draft—a problem with possessive case, for example—mark the error the first few times it appears and show the student how to punctuate the passages correctly. From that point on, just circle and label the error without fixing it and require the student to submit a corrected copy. Alternatively, you might place an "X" at the end of a line that contains the error and then have the student find and correct the mistake. In either case, you avoid doing work students should do when they revise their papers.

Balance Criticism with Praise

Researcher Ernest Smith studied the way students react to the comments teachers write on their papers and found that the most helpful, productive responses were ones that mixed criticism and praise. In fact, students were much more willing to accept the criticism and heed the advice their teachers offered when it was balanced by praise. In their minds, such a balance suggested that the teacher was being fair and open-minded when responding to their work. Yet Sommers found that few teachers wrote positive comments on papers—most comments were negative, pointing out only weaknesses and errors.

As they revise their work, students need to build on their strengths, not just correct errors. I have found that students understand their weaknesses as writers more clearly than they do their strengths. They actually need less help from their teachers in finding out what is wrong with their writing than they do finding out what is right with it. Try this: ask your students to tell you their greatest weakness as a writer. In almost all cases, they will quickly offer you a specific list. After all, for years teachers have told them what they do wrong. Now, ask them to tell you what they do well as writers. Chances are, you will be met with silence or comments such as, "Getting my work in on time" or "Following directions." With such an attitude, students write defensively—keep the essay short to minimize the chances for error, use only simple sentences (never even try to use a semicolon correctly!), take no risks. Yet students also have certain gifts as writers that they can develop, which is where your responses can help. Point out what the students do well, explain why it is good, and suggest how they might build on that success in other parts of their paper or in future assignments. You will find that even a little praise can go a long way to motivate your students and help them become better, more enthusiastic writers.

WHAT TO RESPOND TO IN STUDENT PAPERS: A HEURISTIC

What should you comment on when responding to student work? Unfortunately, the answer is, it depends. Several factors will influence which aspects of the text you respond to: the particular assignment the students are working on, which draft of the paper you are examining, when in the course you collect the work, what you have covered in class, who the student is, and what you have discussed with the student outside of class. Comments on papers tend to be context-specific: as a teacher, you decide on the most appropriate and instructive comments for this student and this draft of the paper at this point in the course.

To help you make these decisions, consider the questions provided below in Figure 5.2. As you respond to an individual paper, you will not comment on every aspect of writing listed below, but when responding to an entire set of papers, you may address each one at some point. Your guiding principle: comment on those elements of the paper that will help this student produce a better essay or improve as a writer.

FIGURE 5.2   What to Respond to in Student Papers: A Heuristic

Assignment
- Has the student adequately addressed the assignment?
- Are some aspects of the assignment more effectively addressed than others?
- What aspects of the assignment has the writer overlooked or oversimplified?
- How can the writer better address the assignment?
- How has the writer misinterpreted the assignment?

Content
- Is the content of the paper effective?
- Are the claims clearly stated and adequately qualified?
- Are the claims adequately supported by textual references?
- Are the claims adequately supported by facts, evidence, expert testimony, and so on?
- Has the writer adequately explained the link between his or her claims and support?
- Are some areas of the paper more effectively developed than others?
- Which is the most effective section of the paper in terms of content? Which is the weakest?

continued

continued from page 83

- Are the claims and support adequate and appropriate given the rhetorical context of the assignment?
- What changes in content would you suggest?

Organization

- Are there any problems with the organization of the essay?
- Is the structure of the essay clear?
- Is the structure of the essay effective?
- Is the thesis statement clear?
- Does the thesis statement guide the development of the essay?
- Do topic sentences help guide the reader through the essay?
- Is there a clear relationship among the essay's topic sentences and thesis?
- Are there adequate and appropriate transitional devices?
- Where, exactly, does the structure break down?
- Where are topic sentences or transitions especially effective?
- Do any sections of the essay seem out of place? Where might they be relocated?
- Does the essay have an effective opening and closing?
- Is the structure too mechanical and predictable? How might that be fixed?

Paragraphs

- Are the paragraph breaks appropriate and effective?
- Are the paragraphs developed well?
- Do all of the sentences in the paragraphs address or develop the same topic or idea?
- Are there clear links between the sentences in the paragraph?
- Do the paragraphs contain appropriate transitional devices?
- Is it clear how one paragraph leads into the next?
- Which paragraphs are especially effective?
- Which paragraphs need more revision?

Coherence

- Does the paper flow well? Does it read smoothly?
- What sections of the paper read especially well?
- Where does coherence break down? What sections of the paper are especially difficult to follow?
- Is the presentation of ideas or arguments logical?
- Is it clear how each section of the paper relates to the other sections?
- Is the opening and closing satisfying to readers?

Diction, Voice, and Point of View

- Is the diction appropriate for the assignment?
- Are there any lapses or inappropriate shifts in diction?
- Has the student developed an effective voice in the essay?
- What might be a more effective voice to assume?
- How effective is the point of view assumed in the essay?
- What might be a more effective point of view to employ?

Sentences

- Are the sentences grammatically correct?
- Are the sentences punctuated correctly?

- Are the sentences clear?
- Do the sentences vary in length?
- Do the sentences vary in grammatical type: simple, compound, complex, complex–compound?
- Are there too many short, choppy sentences?
- Where can sentences be combined effectively?
- Which sentences are wordy? How might they be made more concise and clear?
- Where are there lapses with parallel structure?
- Which are the most effective sentences?

Word Choice
- Is the student's language precise and clear?
- Where has the student used the wrong word in a sentence?
- Where has the student failed to choose the best word possible?
- Are there problems with jargon?
- Are there problems with euphemisms?
- Are there problems with slang?
- Are certain words too technical, given the assignment and audience?
- Where has the student found just the right word to use?

Mechanics, Grammar, and Punctuation
- Where does the student inappropriately or ineffectively violate the rules of standard written English?
- Where are there problems with mechanics, grammar, or punctuation?
- Which passages in the student's paper make the most effective use of mechanics, grammar, or punctuation?

Documentation
- Has the student documented all material that needs to be documented?
- Has the student successfully avoided plagiarism?
- Is the documentation formally correct?

Appearance
- Has the student followed the format guidelines you established?
- Is the essay presented in a way appropriate for the intended audience?
- Is the appearance of the writing neat and orderly?

Process
- Was the paper turned in on time?
- Were all required deadlines met as the student completed the essay?
- Were all required parts of the essay turned in for evaluation?
- Did the student make it to all required conferences or workshops?
- Did the student actively participate in required peer-writing or editing activities?

Rhetorical Situation
- Does the piece effectively meet the needs of the intended audience?
- Does the piece accomplish its goal?
- Does the piece adequately address the topic?
- Is there a sense of the writer's presence or voice in the piece?
- Is the language appropriate, given the writer's purpose, audience, and voice?

As you work your way through a set of essays, individualize your responses: if one student has a problem with content, focus on that; if another student has trouble with word choice and organization, respond to that. Over time you will also establish a systematic way of examining student papers. For example, you may start by checking whether the student answers the assignment and then comment on the paper's content, structure, style, or mechanics as needed. Establishing this routine helps you respond to papers quickly and comprehensively.

TYPES OF RESPONSES TO STUDENT WORK: A TAXONOMY

Once you determine which aspects of a student's paper you will respond to, decide what form those responses will take. Will you simply circle, label, and correct sentence-level errors? Will you ask a series of questions? Will you tell the student exactly what changes to make in the content and structure of the next draft? What are your options?

In "Evaluating Student Writing," Elaine Lees lays out seven types of responses teachers can use to achieve different ends. Here are the types of responses Lees itemizes, along with an overview of their uses and limitations.

1. Correcting
When correcting, the teacher fixes mistakes in the student's writing—punctuation errors, misspelled words, ungrammatical sentences, and so forth. When revising, students just insert the teacher's corrections. As noted previously, students will incorporate their teacher's corrections even if they do not understand the reasons for the corrections.

2. Emoting
Here the teacher expresses his or her personal responses to the piece. Usually placed in the margin of the paper, these emotional comments reflect the teacher's reactions to the student's writing. Although these comments can be vague (for example, writing *"Nice!"* or *"What?"* next to a paragraph without indicating what language in the paragraph elicited the response) and sometimes hurtful if they are sarcastic or caustic, emoting lets students know how readers might respond to their work.

3. Describing
In unemotional language, the teacher describes his or her reading of the student's text. Such comments might include, *"You seem to shift your argument here without providing a transition"* or *"Your paragraph is straying from your topic sentence here."* These comments imply a course of action to take when revising, leaving room for interpretation. Describing encourages students to reread and reconsider their work and helps to make them responsible for their own revisions.

4. Suggesting
The teacher suggests specific steps the student can take to improve the essay. When "correcting" student papers, the teacher makes the changes; when "sug-

gesting," the teacher leaves the corrections up to the student. For example, the teacher might write, *"You can expand this section of the paper by considering what Smith has to say about Jones,"* or *"You might shorten this section of the essay by combining sentences and eliminating one of the examples you use."* This type of response proves ineffective, however, when the teacher's suggestions are too vague or when the student misinterprets what the teacher has written.

5. Questioning

Writing questions on the students' papers can serve several purposes. Sometimes they point out problems involving clarity or word choice:

> *"What does this sentence mean?"*
>
> *"Would this statement be clear to the target audience?"*

Other times they focus on content or structure:

> *"Are there other experts you could cite here to bolster your argument?"*
>
> *"Would this paragraph be more effective if it were placed earlier in the essay?"*

Still other questions focus on larger rhetorical issues:

> *"Have you really addressed the assignment in this essay? How does this essay address the specific question the assignment asks?"*
>
> *"Given your target audience, is this the best argument to use? How might your readers counter the argument you make here? Would your point here be easy to refute?"*

Questions can prompt reflective revisions. They urge students to reconsider what they have written and to develop their own solutions to problems. The questions teachers ask, though, need to match the student's level of understanding—some questions may be too difficult, abstract, or advanced for a student to answer. When this happens, the questions do not facilitate revision and may, in fact, result in a weaker essay: based on a misunderstanding of a question, a student may make changes that result in a less effective piece of writing.

6. Reminding

With these comments, the teacher draws direct connections between the students' texts and material covered in class. These comments prompt students to recall the lessons they learned in class as they revise their work.

> *"Problems with documentation in this paragraph—remember what we said about documenting all quoted material."*
>
> *"Include here some of the comments students made during our class debate last week."*
>
> *"Look at your notes from class last Tuesday and reorganize this section of the paper so it better matches the required format."*

This type of commentary extends the teacher's voice beyond the classroom and reinforces the importance of what you cover in class.

7. Assigning

These comments typically appear at the end of the students' papers, though they can appear in the margins as well. With assignments, the teacher gives students specific tasks to complete in the next draft of their essay:

> *"Rewrite the opening of the paper to better capture your readers' interest."*
>
> *"Cut the last paragraph in your paper, but find another place to put the last sentence of that paragraph—that comment was effective."*
>
> *"Proofread for problems with comma use—lots of introductory phrases and clauses are missing commas."*

Assignments are more specific and directive than suggestions, questions, or reminders. They tell students specifically what they need to do in the next draft of the paper but leave the work up to the students. Teachers sometimes include assignments at the end of a paper as well to help their students write future essays.

"Try to get started much earlier on the next paper—you need the time to revise."

"On the next paper, move your thesis to the beginning of your paper and employ more references to the course readings."

Students will not take these assignments seriously, however, unless teachers hold them accountable for completing the work.

Experimentation will help you find the most effective modes of response for you and your students. In practice, you will likely employ a variety of responses on every paper you review: corrections and questions and assignments, suggestions and reminders and descriptions. As you hold conferences with your students (see Chapter 9), on occasion ask them which types of comments they find most and least helpful. In my experience, most students will give you an honest answer, enabling you to fine-tune and individualize the commentary you offer their work.

ASSUMING AN ATTITUDE: ROLES TO PLAY WHEN YOU RESPOND TO STUDENT WORK

As you sit down to comment on a student paper, how do you define your task? Do you consider yourself a proofreader responsible for finding and correcting every error? Do you see yourself as a member of the academic community indicating which aspects of the paper meet disciplinary standards and which do not? Do you see yourself as a more experienced writer in a classroom full of writers trying to pass along tricks of the trade that will result in more effective prose?

Below are some of the roles teachers typically assume as they respond to student papers. Defining your role is important because it will help you clarify why you are responding to your students' work, what you hope your comments will accomplish, what aspects of the paper you respond to, what modes of response you employ, and what tone you assume in your comments.

Editor

As an editor, you will spend much of your time marking, commenting on, and correcting sentence-level errors. You will focus much of your attention on grammar, punctuation, word choice, and syntax—helping students recraft sentences and correct errors. Editing is time-consuming, demanding work; you need to be conversant in the rules and conventions of standard written English and pay close attention to every word and every punctuation mark in the student's essay. You also need to consider how to balance praise and censure in your commentary, how to guide the student's revision efforts, and how to address other, more holistic aspects of the paper, such as content, structure, and rhetorical appeals.

Average Reader

In this role, you read a student's paper the way you would read a newspaper or a magazine— to see what the writer has to say. Through your questions, reactions, and descriptions of the text, you let the writer know how you are responding to his or her work as an average reader. You note sentence-level errors that inhibit your understanding of the text or that annoy you as a reader, and let the writer know what sections of the paper interest you, which ones need further development, which ones are hard to follow, and which ones work well.

Academic Reader

This is a more specialized role —your main questions are: how well does this paper meet the standards of academic discourse? Does it do what academic papers are supposed to do, sound like they are supposed to sound, and look the way they are supposed to look? If not, what changes does the writer need to make? To assume this role, you need to be familiar with the standards of academic writing and must be able to explain those standards to your students. Your commentary points out where students have met those standards and where they have not.

Coach

Teachers who assume to role of a coach often see themselves as the more experienced writer in a classroom full of writers, all of whom have something important to contribute to the course. They frequently establish writing workshops in class during which students work collaboratively to draft and revise manuscripts. These teachers generally believe that praise works better than censure and like to offer practical, experience-based advice to their students. While not overlooking sentence-level errors, they generally withhold commentary on those elements of the manuscript until late in the revision process. To play the role of coach successfully, though, teachers need students who are willing to see themselves as writers and who are ready to take upon themselves a large part of the responsibility for improving their work.

As you evaluate a set of papers, you may well find yourself shifting roles, sometimes responding to the text like an academic reader, sometimes like an editor. Most teachers work this way. However, most teachers also have a dominant role in mind. As a TA, you should experiment with the roles you assume to discover which you find most comfortable and which your students find most beneficial.

WHO RESPONDS TO YOUR STUDENTS' WRITING AND WHEN

Two other important questions to consider: who will respond to your students' work and at what point during the composing process will they do it? You have more options here than you might at first suspect. While you will respond to much or most of your students' writing, consider these alternatives: not responding to the writing at all or having the students' peers respond to it.

No Response

You do not need to respond to everything your students write for class. In fact, much of the writing your students do can be for their eyes only, exploratory or reflective writing intended to help them clarify their thoughts, develop material for more formal essays, or explore course readings.

Of course, skeptics always ask, "But if no one responds to (or grades) this writing, will students take the assignments seriously?" If you worry about students not completing these assignments, explain why they are important, how completing these assignments will help them understand the course material and write better papers. In class, use the assignments to prompt class discussion—select students to read aloud what they have written and ask other students to respond. If all else fails, collect the assignments and give students credit for completing the work responding to it. (On my syllabus, I reserve around ten percent of the course grade for ungraded assignments such as these. If students complete ninety percent or more of them satisfactorily, they get an "A" for that ten percent of the grade; eighty to eighty-nine percent earns a "B," and so on.) Do not fall into the trap of believing that students only learn in class if they have the benefit of your commentary on their work: they will learn quite a bit on their own if you design writing assignments that challenge their thinking or require them to apply course material in interesting ways.

Peer Response

Many teachers do not trust peer response—they believe that students who are not accomplished writers themselves can offer little help to other inexperienced writers. That position makes some sense, especially if you simply ask your students to exchange papers and "respond" to each other's work. However, with proper instruction and guidance, peer response can help your students become better writers.

When teaching students how to be effective peer editors, I borrow heavily from the suggestions composition theorist Kenneth Bruffee offers in his essay, "The Brooklyn Plan: Attaining Intellectual Growth through Peer-Group Tutoring." Adopting Bruffee's advice, the first time students exchange rough drafts in my class, I ask them to approach the text as average readers, indicating in their written comments what they found interesting, boring, or confusing about the essay. The next time they review a peer's manuscript, I ask them to again respond as average readers but also to make a few suggestions for improving the piece, acting more as coaches or academic readers. On later papers, I ask the peer reviewers to edit the manuscripts, making both suggestions and corrections. As Bruffee maintains, students do not know how to respond to their peers' papers without this type of training, structure, and guidance.

You may also guide your students' efforts by using peer edit or peer response sheets in class. These worksheets lead the students through the process of responding to their peers' papers by asking them to answer a series of questions, provide certain information, or perform certain tasks (see Figure 5.3, Figure 5.4, and Figure 5.5 at the end of this chapter for sample peer response sheets). At the end of the peer response session, the student returns the peer's paper and the response sheet. Some teachers like the writer to turn in the response sheet with the paper's final draft to give the peer respondent credit for his or her work.

If so much training and guidance is needed, why would any teacher use peer response? There are several reasons. First, as the teacher, you may not be able to respond to the rough drafts of every paper your students write—there just might not be enough time. With peer responses, every student has the opportunity to get some response to every paper he or she writes. Second, many of your students will be better readers and respondents than they are writers. They have more experience as readers than they do as writers and with some instruction can be taught how to use their textual knowledge to offer constructive peer response. In doing so, they will develop critical reading skills that should, over time, help them write better papers themselves. Third, peer response helps your students learn how to write for real readers. Peers can help students learn which aspects of their writing are clear or confused, interesting or boring, well developed or vague. Fourth, responding to their peers' papers teaches students important editing skills they can apply to their own writing: by responding to and editing their peers' work, they learn how to revise and edit their own work more effectively. Finally, peer response is flexible. Students can respond to each others' work in class, outside of class, or on the Web.

In their classrooms, teachers set up peer response sessions in a variety of ways. Sometimes they have students work in pairs, randomly exchanging their work with each other in class. Other times teachers like to set up peer response groups, three or four students who share their work with each other. Sometimes group membership remains stable throughout the term; other times teachers vary group membership throughout the term so students get to write for a wider variety of readers. Increasingly, teachers expect students to post their work on a Web site so their peers can log on and offer their response outside of class.

Finally, as a teacher you need to decide when this response will occur. In his article, "Teamwork and Feedback: Broadening the Base of Collaborative Writing," writer and editor Richard Gebhardt points out that most teachers ask peers to respond only to completed rough drafts. He argues that response can benefit students throughout the writing process. Accepting his argument, here are a few ways you can ensure your students receive responses throughout the composing process, from either you or peers:

- Students bring a list of paper topics to class, discuss it with their peers, and make a preliminary choice of topic for their papers.

- Working in pairs or in small groups, students discuss their paper topics with their peers. This exercise helps student writers better understand their audience's interests and needs.

- Students write out their paper topic and turn it in. You respond to their topic and suggest how they might proceed with the paper.

- Students bring to class a preliminary list of ideas for the body of their essay and discuss their ideas with their peers, who ask questions or help them narrow the list to the most interesting or promising possibilities.

- Students give you a rough outline of what they plan to include in their paper. You respond to it outside of class and return it with your comments.

- Students bring a rough draft of their thesis statement to class, and you or their peers respond to or critique it.

- Students bring a rough draft of their opening paragraph to class, and you or their peers respond to or critique it.

- Students bring a rough draft of their essay to class and exchange it with a peer for response.

- Students give you a rough draft of their essay for response. You respond to it outside of class and return it with your comments.

- Students give every member of their peer response group a copy of their rough draft. Their peers take the rough drafts home, respond to them, and then discuss them in their groups the next time the class meets.

- Students read their rough drafts aloud to just one other student or to a small group of students. If their peers have a copy of the essay, they read along and note on the manuscript any changes the writer makes while reading it aloud. They then discuss the paper with the writer.

- Students bring a rough draft of their paper to class and a peer reads it aloud.

Finding effective ways to combine teacher and peer response throughout the writing process will be one of the real challenges you face as an instructor.

DIFFERENT MEDIUMS OF RESPONSE

The most traditional way of responding to student work is to write your comments on the student's essay. However, many teachers do not like to do this: they feel that it takes too long, that students rarely read and often do not understand the comments, or that their commentary may overwhelm the student. Other options, described below, might be more effective.

Writing Responses on Student Papers

If you chose to write your comments directly on your students' papers through a combination of marginal notes and end notes, taking certain steps can make this type of response more efficient and effective. First, as you respond to your students' work, draw a distinction between marginal and end comments. Marginal comments usually address specific aspects of the manuscript—particular passages, sentences, or words—whereas end comments usually address more global aspects of the paper. Teachers typically use the end comments to offer comprehensive assessments of the manuscript, suggest the direction future drafts of essays should take, offer advice on future papers, or motivate the student. You can save some time when writing responses by avoiding the temptation to repeat in your end comments what you have written in your marginal comments. If your comments include abbreviations or proofreading marks, be sure your students understand them. Do not assume that your students will approach you if they find your comments confusing—often they will not.

Response Sheets

Instead of writing on the students' papers, some teachers prefer to use response sheets. These sheets often include general headings, such as "Content," "Structure," or "Mechanics," under which teachers write their comments. If the teacher awards points or a grade for certain aspects of the paper, the sheet often includes space for that information as well (see Figure 5.6 at the end of the chapter). Other response sheets are much more specific, itemizing in some detail the elements of the essay the teacher evaluates. These sheets often have blank spaces next to each item where the teacher can comment on, evaluate, or "score" that particular aspect of the essay (see Figure 5.7 at the end of the chapter). Teachers using response sheets usually read through a student's paper, getting a sense of its strengths and weaknesses, and writing only a few comments on the essay itself. They then fill out a response sheet, referring back to the paper as often as needed, and attach the sheet when they return the paper.

Many students like response sheets. They believe the commentary is more focused and clear than marginal and end notes. Revising is easier, they think, because the comments address specific aspects of their paper, helping them understand exactly what they did well and what still needs work. Many students also like having the response sheet in hand as they plan and draft their papers—the sheet lets them know exactly what the teacher will be looking for when evaluating the essay. Some teachers, though, avoid using response sheets because they feel it limits the range and nature of the response they offer students, too narrowly restricting it to predetermined categories.

Oral Responses

You may decide to provide oral responses to your students' work. The most common procedure is to meet with students individually in your office and either read through the paper with your student at that time, offering commentary as you go, or review with the student the comments you have already written on the paper or on a response sheet.

Oral responses give you the opportunity to answer your students' questions directly, explain what they do not understand, and ask them questions about the meaning or intent of their essay. These conferences can be uncomfortable, however, if the student writing is especially weak or if the student challenges your judgment or authority. If you choose this option, ask your students to take notes during the conference for later review. (See Chapter 10 for a fuller discussion of student conferences.)

Taped Responses

Some teachers like to tape record their responses to student work. Students turn in a cassette tape with their papers. The teacher reads the student's paper, perhaps writing a few comments on the manuscript, then turns on a tape recorder and goes back through the paper, recording his or her comments on the cassette tape. The teacher then returns the paper and the tape. Students listen to the tape with the paper in front of them, referring to the manuscript as needed.

Teachers who use this method of response like it because they can talk much faster than they can write, offering more detailed response in less time than writing would require. Many students also like taped responses because they find the amount of commentary the teacher offers helpful when they revise and believe the responses are clearer and more detailed than the written comments they are used to receiving. Some students, however, do not like this method of response. They have a hard time following the teacher's comments on tape and sometimes complain about the tone of the teacher's comments—some teachers sound too sarcastic or frustrated on tape.

FINAL TIPS

Here are a few final suggestions that might help you respond to your students' work more effectively.

1. Respond in pencil.

I find responding in pencil beneficial for several reasons. First, many students have told me they find comments written in pencil less intimidating that those written in ink. More importantly though, responding in pencil allows you to erase comments easily. Sometimes my comments are wrong, and I have to change them before returning the papers. Sometimes, on further reflection, I want to change the comments to make them more clear or more helpful. Sometimes my comments are too caustic—I am tired or frustrated when I write them—and I need to edit them before I return the papers. Responding in pencil makes it much easier for me to go back and change my comments.

2. Set time limits.

Generally speaking, try to spend no more than twenty minutes responding to a paper. If you spend more time than this, you may be writing too many comments or spending too much time second guessing your judgment. Setting time limits helps you keep a good pace and comment on a set of papers without exhausting yourself. Many TAs I know even set timers on their desk so the buzzer will let them know when it is time to move on.

3. Remember why you are responding to your students' writing.
No matter what type of response you offer your students' writing or when you offer it, always keep in mind the primary purposes of response: your comments should always teach your students how to be better, more effective readers, writers, and thinkers.

WORKS CITED

Bruffee, Kenneth. "The Brooklyn Plan: Attaining Intellectual Growth through Peer-Group Tutoring." *Liberal Education* 64 (1978): 447–68.

Gebhardt, Richard. "Teamwork and Feedback: Broadening the Base of Collaborative Writing." *College English* 42 (1980): 69–74.

Haswell, Richard H. "Minimal Marking." *College English* 45 (1983): 600–04.

Lees, Elaine. "Evaluating Student Writing." *College Composition and Communication* 30 (1979): 370–74.

Smith, Ernest "'It Doesn't Bother Me, But Sometimes It's Discouraging': Students Respond to Teachers' Written Responses." *Journal of Teaching Writing* 8 (1989): 253–65.

Sommers, Nancy. "Responding to Student Writing." *College Composition and Communication* 33 (1982): 148–56.

Williams, Joseph M. "The Phenomenology of Error." *College Composition and Communication* 32 (1981): 152–68.

ADDITIONAL READINGS

Auten, Janet Gebhart. "How Students Read Us: Audience Awareness and Teacher Commentary on Writing." *The Writing Instructor* 11 (Winter, 1992): 83–94.

Doher, Gary. "Do Teachers' Comments on Students' Papers Help?" *College Teaching* 39.2 (1991): 48–54.

Moxley, Joseph M. "Responding to Student Writing: Goals, Methods, Alternatives." *Freshman English News* 17 (1992): 3–11.

———. "Teacher's Goals and Methods of Responding to Student Writing." *Composition Studies* 20.1 (1992): 17–33.

Rubin, Lois, and Mary Lou Ellena-Wygonik. "'I Still Think It Was a Good Paper': A Study of Students' Evaluations of Their Own Writing." *Journal of Teaching Writing* 12.2 (1994): 199–215.

Sorcinelli, Mary Deane, and Peter Elbow, ed. *Writing to Learn: Strategies for Assignment and Responding to Writing Across the Disciplines*. San Francisco: Jossey-Bass, 1997.

Straub, Richard, ed. *A Sourcebook for Responding to Student Writing*. Cresskill, NJ: Hampton, P, 1999.

Walvoord, Barbara E. Fassler. "Principles of Effective Response." *Helping Students Write Well*. 2nd ed. New York: MLA, 1986. 141–53.

Ziv, Nina D. "The Effect of Teacher Comments on the Writing of Four College Freshmen." *New Directions in Composition Research*. Ed. Richard Beach and Lillian Bridwell. New York: Guilford, 1984. 362–80.

FIGURE 5.3   Peer Response Sheet (for an early draft)

Exchange drafts with a peer and then answer the following questions. When you are finished, return this sheet and the draft to the writer and then discuss your responses.

1. What is the writer's topic? Is the topic made clear by the title?

2. What is the main claim being made by the writer in this draft? Paraphrase it below:

3. Do you find the topic interesting? What questions do you have about the topic? What, as a reader, would you like to learn about the topic? Place your responses below:

4. Right now, what are the major strengths of this draft?

5. How might the draft be improved to make it more effective? Offer 3 to 4 **specific** suggestions below:

FIGURE 5.4   Peer Response Sheet (for a later draft)

In the margin of the paper, number all of the paragraphs. Read all the way through your peer's paper and then answer these questions:

1. Is each assertion in the paper supported by material drawn from the readings (as the assignment requires)? If not, which paragraphs need more textual support (list the numbers of the paragraphs):

2. Does the writer explain, in his or her own words, how the support material does, in fact, support his or her assertion? If not, which paragraphs need more explanation?

3. Which assertion is the least convincing in this draft? What can the writer do to improve it?

4. After reading this paper, what questions do you have? Write them on the back of this sheet.

5. Copy the writer's thesis statement below (if there is no thesis statement, let the writer know and write below what you think the main argument is):

6. Is the paper developed in the order you would expect, based on the writer's thesis? If not, what seems out of order?

7. Are the paragraph breaks logical and clear? Where in the paper do you note any problems?

8. Does the writer employ effective transitions between and within the paragraphs? Where in the paper do you note any problems?

9. Note any grammatical or punctuation errors you find. Just circle them.

10. Does the paper have a title? If so, does it give you a good sense of the paper's content and direction? If not, suggest a title.

FIGURE 5.5   Peer Response Sheet

Writer's Name

Editor's Name _____

Editor: Read through this essay and number all of the paragraphs. Make any needed comments, suggestions, or corrections directly on the essay.

1. Check to make sure the paper has:
   a. a title
   b. a thesis statement
      If either is missing, write a note on the paper letting the writer know.

2. Check to make sure the introduction:
   a. captures your interest
   b. introduces the topic of the essay
   c. leads smoothly to the thesis

3. Check to make sure the "background" section of the essay:
   a. gives you enough information to understand the argument presented in the rest of the paper
   b. is clearly written
   c. is documented where necessary

4. Look at each section of the body one at a time. Make sure:
   a. each assertion is clearly and effectively introduced
   b. each assertion is supported by textual evidence

continued

continued from page 97

    c. all support material is linked to the assertion through effective explanations and examples

    d. possible objections are noted and dealt with effectively

5. Help the writer improve the quality of his or her sentences. Going through the essay one paragraph at a time:

    a. note any sentences or words you do not understand or have a hard time reading

    b. note any problems with punctuation

    c. note any problems with word choice

    d. note any problems with documentation

6. On the back of this sheet, summarize the writer's essay. What have you learned from the paper? What do you still have questions about?

FIGURE 5.6   Teacher Response Sheet

Name _____

Content

Points: _____

Comments:

Organization

Points: _____

Comments:

Mechanics

Points: _____

Comments:

Paper Grade: _____

FIGURE 5.7   Teacher Response Sheet

Content	Excellent	Adequate	Weak	See ¶
Clear Assertions	_____	_____	_____	_____
Textual Support	_____	_____	_____	_____
Reasoning	_____	_____	_____	_____
Addressing Opposing Views	_____	_____	_____	_____
Organization				
Thesis Statement	_____	_____	_____	_____
Topic Sentences	_____	_____	_____	_____
Transitions between Paragraphs	_____	_____	_____	_____
Transitions within Paragraphs	_____	_____	_____	_____
Paragraphs				
Focus	_____	_____	_____	_____
Unity	_____	_____	_____	_____
Development	_____	_____	_____	_____
Sentences				
Variety	_____	_____	_____	_____
Clarity	_____	_____	_____	_____
Grammar	_____	_____	_____	_____
Word Choice				
Diction	_____	_____	_____	_____
Tone	_____	_____	_____	_____
Clarity	_____	_____	_____	_____
Mechanics				
Punctuation	_____	_____	_____	_____
Spelling	_____	_____	_____	_____
Conventions	_____	_____	_____	_____

Overall Assessment:

CHAPTER 6

Grading Student Writing

PURPOSES OF GRADING

As pointed out in the previous chapter, when evaluating student work, you should draw a distinction between responding and grading. Responses generally point the way to future work, explaining how students can build on strengths and address problems. And while writing teachers stress the process of writing and the importance of revision, at some point, students have to turn in final drafts of their papers, drafts that represent the best work they can currently produce. The grade offers them a final, summative assessment of that work. A series of graded papers gives students a sense of trajectory in the course: is the quality of work getting better, remaining stable, or growing worse? Grades can also let students know how their work fares in comparison with work produced by other students in the class. Though some teachers and students reject the notion of grading papers (see "Arguments against Grading" below), many students want the final judgment that grades provide.

Assigning grades provides teachers with a way to communicate a comprehensive evaluation of a student's work. Although teachers can finesse the comments they write on papers, grades typically offer less ambiguous assessments of the student's writing. Some teachers also use grades to motivate students, though this can be a tricky proposition: low grades challenge some students to try harder, but they cause others to give up. As students' grades rise, many react positively and try even harder to improve; others, however, see that they have reached the level of achievement they hoped to attain and stop trying. Teachers who hope to use grades to motivate students must never sacrifice the first goal of grading, though: to provide students an honest, qualitative assessment of their writing.

Institutionally, grades serve several purposes as well. Directors of composition or department chairs sometimes use course grades to help them evaluate a teacher's effectiveness or to assess how well the writing program is achieving its goals. Universities and departments may also use grades to determine which students get into certain programs, win certain awards, or earn certain scholarships or fellowships.

Understandably, few tasks challenge new TAs more than sitting down to grade that first set of papers. This chapter offers some advice on grading that might lessen some of your anxiety. Like every other aspect of teaching, grading becomes much easier with practice. With some thought and preparation, assigning grades to student work may go more smoothly than you think.

GRADING STANDARDS

Before grading a set of papers, you need to determine your grading criteria—the standards you will use to make qualitative judgments about your students' work. As a new TA, you will likely grade papers the way you think teachers in the past have graded your work. However, you need to give much thought to your goals and practices when grading student work and consider all available options.

In some programs, TAs are expected to develop their own grading standards; in others, TAs are expected to follow departmental or program grading guidelines. If you are expected to follow departmental grading criteria, you will likely be taught how to use them during preservice or in-service training sessions. In most cases, these guidelines describe "A" level papers, "B" level papers, and so on. Your job is to read a student's paper and determine whether it best matches the description of an "A" paper, a "B" paper, and so on. Sometimes additional guidelines are provided for determining pluses and minuses. These grading criteria are often produced by departmental committees and reflect standards the department wants student writers to achieve. If you have a question about any of the descriptions or how to apply them to any of your students' papers, talk with your teaching supervisor. Your supervisor may also arrange several "norming sessions" throughout the semester. During these workshops, you and other instructors will read through a set of student papers and discuss the grades you would give them according to the department rubric. You then discuss the grades you awarded each paper, explaining what aspects of the essay and the rubric led you to that evaluation. These sessions give you the chance to practice applying the rubric and to gauge whether you tend to grade higher or lower than your colleagues. Once the term begins, be sure you have a copy of the department guidelines close at hand each time you grade a set of papers.

In other programs you will establish your own grading standards. Because these standards can vary widely from teacher to teacher, generalizing about them here is difficult. Instead, I will share with you the grading standards I use when I evaluate student work in my first-year writing classes. They may help you develop your own standards.

First, as I explain these standards to my students, I draw a distinction between high school and college writing expectations. Early in the semester and prior to handing back the first set of papers, I ask my students the following question:

> Suppose as a writer in this class, you meet every demand spelled out on an assignment sheet. You've done everything the assignment asked you to do without making very many errors—maybe a misspelled word here or there or a missing comma. You've not gone much beyond what the assignment asked you to do, but you've completed the assignment competently. What grade do you think you should get on that paper?

Uniformly, my students will say that the paper should get an "A" or a "B." That is the grading standard most of them worked under in high school—work done competently got an "A" or a "B." I tell them that in my mind, that paper deserves a "C." At our institution, a "C" is given to "average" student work. *Every* student in class should be able to complete the assignment competently, given their level of ability and the instruction I offer in class. If *every* student should be able to meet that standard, work that does is, in my mind, *average*. "B" level work is "good" (it goes beyond minimum expectations in some way), and "A" level work is "excellent" (it goes well beyond minimum expectations for the assignment). In terms of its content, structure, mechanics, and style, an "A" paper is exceptional and noteworthy. Papers that have serious problems meeting the minimum requirements of the assignment are "poor" and get a "D." Ones that fail to meet those requirements receive an "F." This, then, is the grading standard I employ:

A = exceptional writing that goes well beyond minimum expectations for the assignment

B = good writing that exceeds minimum expectations for the assignment

C = average writing that meets minimum expectations for the assignment

D = poor writing that does not meet all of the minimum expectations for the assignment

F = failing writing that does not meet the minimum expectations for the assignment

I can apply these standards to individual papers that I grade holistically or atomistically (options described below) or to portfolios of student work. If you want to develop a more detailed grading rubric, you can establish evaluative criteria for specific elements of the students' work, such as its organization, development, adherence to conventions, and style.

Whether you follow your department's grading standards or develop standards of your own, your goal is consistency: as you work through a set of papers, essays receiving the same grade ought to be comparable in quality. You also want to have clear reasons for the grades you assign. A grade ought to be based on the quality of a student's writing and reasoning. If a student questions a grade, you should be able to point to specific places in the text where the writing is strong or weak, and you should be able to explain how those passages helped you determine the essay's grade.

APPROACHES TO GRADING: HOLISTIC, ATOMISTIC, AND PORTFOLIO EVALUATION

Simply having grading standards, however, does not tell you how to apply them. Today most teachers employ one of three approaches to grading: holistic, atomistic, and portfolio evaluation. Placement and exit examinations are typically evaluated holistically—the procedure enables administrators to grade a large number of essays quickly and reliably. Teachers who grade papers holistically in their classes first develop a grading rubric, a description of an "A" paper, a "B" paper, and so on (see Figure 6.1 at the end of this chapter for a sample holistic evaluation guide). They then read through a student's essay, decide which description it best matches, and give the paper that grade. They do not comment on the student's paper; they just read it through once or twice, match it to a description, give it a grade, and move on. Holistic grading enables teachers to grade papers quickly, but it offers little instruction to students when they get the papers back, even if teachers distribute the grading rubric. Because each grade description addresses several elements of writing, a student getting a "C" on his essay may not know why it received that grade, only that, all things considered, the teacher thought his essay best matched the description of a "C" paper on the rubric.

Atomistic grading practices are much more common. Here teachers base their grade on separate evaluations of distinct elements in the essay. As they read an essay, they assess the quality of these elements and then combine or average these evaluations to determine the paper's grade. Teachers grading this way commonly write comments on the student's essay or employ a response sheet that lists the elements of the essay the teacher will evaluate when grading student work. Beside each element is an open space where the teacher writes comments, awards points, or assigns a grade to each element (see Figure 6.2 at the end of this chapter for a sample response sheet and Chapter 5 for other examples).

Another option available to teachers involves moving the process of awarding grades to the end of the course through portfolio evaluation. Portfolio evaluation procedures can vary from teacher to teacher, but many follow the process described here. Throughout the course, as students complete their papers, the teacher collects and comments on the essays but does not grade them. The students get the papers back and have the opportunity to revise them in light of the teacher's comments. At the end of the term, the student submits clean, revised "final" copies of the papers for a grade. This collection of revised essays makes up their portfolio. Some teachers let students choose which papers to include in the portfolio, allowing them to drop their weakest work. Some require students to include particular papers in the portfolio (for example, a research paper or a literary analysis essay). Many teachers also like their students to include a reflective essay with their portfolio in which they comment on the work they have included in the collection and reflect on their experiences in the course.

When grading the portfolio, teachers again have several options. Some teachers give the portfolio a single, collective grade, in essence stating that, as a whole, the papers in the portfolio represent "A" level work or "B" level work, and so on. Other teachers prefer to grade each paper in the portfolio individually. Under either system, the papers are typically graded holistically or atomistically using a response sheet. Few teachers write comments on the papers in the portfolio because they have commented so extensively on the drafts.

Many teachers like portfolio evaluation because it encourages students to revise their work and deemphasizes grades early in the course when students should be focusing on skill development. Many students also like this approach to grading—they feel it gives them more time to revise their work, a better opportunity to produce higher quality essays, and more control over their grade. Students who do not like portfolio evaluation usually object to it because they want to know their paper grades as they complete assignments throughout the course. If students are adamant about wanting to know their grades, teachers can tell them what their grades would have been had the essays been graded. However, teachers using portfolio evaluation should deemphasize grades as much as they can during the term, focusing on revision instead.

As a TA, if you are interested in using portfolio evaluation in your courses, check with your teaching supervisor first. Some leading experts in portfolio evaluation disagree about whether it is appropriate for inexperienced TAs. Kathleen Yancey at Clemson University questions whether new TAs have sufficiently internalized grading standards to evaluate portfolios effectively. How can TAs award a portfolio an "A" or a "B," she wonders, if they have little experience determining whether individual papers merit an "A" or a "B"? Irwin Weiser at Purdue University claims that inexperienced TAs can be taught how to develop adequate grading standards for portfolios, even if they have not spent the term assigning grades to individual papers.

GRADING INDIVIDUAL PAPERS: SUGGESTED PROCEDURES

Here are some procedures that can help make grading more effective, efficient, and fair.

Review the Assignment Before You Grade any Papers

Even if you wrote the assignment yourself, read it again before you start grading. Remind yourself what you asked the students to do. You will then be in a better position to determine if the students have met or exceeded your expectations when you grade their work. If you are grading papers for a professor who wrote the assignment, be sure you understand what the professor intended the assignment to achieve before you evaluate any student work. If you have any questions about the assignment, ask the professor for clarifications.

Read a Few Papers Before You Start Assigning Grades

Read through a few papers quickly to get a sense of how well the students are answering the assignment. Your expectations might be too high or too low for those first few papers if you do not have a sense of how well the class did as a whole. In fact, some teachers like to read the entire set of papers quickly before they respond to or grade any essays. This way their comments and grades will be based on a fuller sense of how well all of the students handled the assignment.

Grade in Pencil

Even as an experienced grader, I find myself needing to change grades as I work my way through a set of papers. You may find yourself in the same position—when you first start grading a set of essays, what looks like an "A" paper at the top of the stack may not look like an "A" by the time you reach the bottom of the stack. Your standards become more clear and certain the more you read your students' work. Grading in pencil makes it easier to change your grade if necessary.

Grade in Batches

If you have a lot of papers to evaluate, divide them into groups of five or six and grade them one batch at a time. After each batch, take a break and reward yourself—listen to some music, get something to eat, take a brief walk. Grading in batches gives you a sense of progress as you make your way through a set of papers. Sitting in front of a huge stack of papers can be intimidating— a small stack does not look so bad. This tip may sound silly, but it works—it does speed up grading for most teachers.

When in Doubt, Set the Paper Aside and Get Help

If you are not sure what grade to give a paper, set it aside and ask your office-mate or teaching supervisor to read it and offer an opinion. Such uncertainty is common. You may have read so many papers that sound alike that you find it hard to draw distinctions. You may have had problems with a particular student in class and do not know if you are being fair with your grade. You may just be uncertain about a grade—some features make it a "C" paper, others make it a "B." Whatever the reason for your doubts, ask for an outside opinion. Do not tell your officemate or teaching supervisor what grade you were thinking of giving the paper; just have the person read it and tell you what grade it deserves. Use the response to help you make up your own mind.

Review the Grades Before You Return the Papers

After you evaluate all the papers, if possible set them aside for a day or two and then sort them into piles by grade—all the "A" papers together, all the "B+" papers together, and so on. Then quickly review the papers, pile by pile. Are all the papers in each pile really comparable in quality? Do any of the papers belong in a different pile? If so, move the papers to that pile and adjust your grade. I find that this last review increases the confidence I have in the grades I give. It serves as a form of quality control, helping me be sure I applied the same set of standards throughout the grading process. This review also gives me one last chance to review the comments I wrote on the students' papers and make sure they are clear and correct.

Do Not Delay

As a rule, try to have papers returned to students in a week. If that is not possible, get them back to the students as soon as you can and certainly before the next paper is due. For a graduate student, putting off work can cause problems. You may begin to feel enormous pressure if you have stacks of ungraded student papers. If the demands of your graduate course work cause you to fall behind in your grading, finish your course work first. Just tell your students when they can expect to get their papers back.

Explain Your Grading Procedures to Your Students

Always explain to your students the process you follow to grade their work—what you look for when you evaluate their papers, how often you read their essays when determining a grade, how much time you spend determining grades, and so on. Students have fewer questions about their grades when they understand your grading standards and procedures. They also more readily accept your judgment of their work when they understand how fair and thorough you are as a grader. In my own classes, I explain my grading procedures early in the semester and review them in class before I return each set of papers.

REWRITES OF GRADED WORK

Many TAs ask whether students should be able to rewrite papers that have been graded. Among experienced writing teachers, you will find a wide range of positions on this question. Some teachers say absolutely not: students are free to revise a paper as many times as they wish before turning it in for a grade, but when they turn it in, that is the final draft. These teachers will work with students as much as the students like as they draft each paper, but once the paper is graded, it is time to move on to the next assignment. Other teachers let students rewrite one or two graded papers a term, ones the students choose or ones the teacher chooses. Teachers who adopt this policy have to decide if the final grade for the paper is the rewrite grade or an average of the original grade and the rewrite grade. Other teachers allow students to rewrite as many graded papers as they like as often as they like. The teacher grades and comments on each revised draft and the student decides when to end the process. Again, though, the teacher has to determine how to calculate the ultimate grade for the paper.

As you decide whether to allow students to rewrite graded papers, talk to your teaching supervisor—your department may have a policy on this matter. Consider what is fair to your students and what is manageable for you. Letting students rewrite any paper they like sounds immanently fair, but can you grade all those papers? What happens at the end of the term when you have to complete your own seminar papers and a wave of rewrites comes in for you to read and grade? If you allow students to rewrite graded papers, you may need to set limits on how many they can rewrite, how often they can rewrite them, and when rewrites are due (stipulating, for example, that no rewrites are allowed after a certain date at the end of the term). Your rewrite policy needs to be fair to all of your students, educationally sound, and practical.

AN ARGUMENT AGAINST GRADING

Although grading student writing remains the norm in writing programs across the country, not everyone agrees that it is a good idea. Over the years, many educators have spoken against grading student work, but probably the most well-respected and effective advocate of this position is Peter Elbow. In several publications, Elbow has argued that grading student work does little to improve their writing skills and may, in fact, hamper their education. For example, in "Getting Along without Grades—and Getting Along with Them Too," Elbow outlines five arguments against awarding letter grades to student work:

- Grades are not trustworthy: grading is too subjective and too unreliable.
- Grades have no inherent meaning: students may not know what an "A" or a "B + " actually means.
- Grading contributes little to the students' growth as writers: a letter grade does not tell a student what he or she did well or badly or how to improve.

- Grading undermines the student–teacher relationship and poisons the classroom atmosphere: students work only for the grade, value only the grade, begin to see the teacher as an evaluator more than a coach, and assume an adversarial relationship with their teacher and classmates.

- Grading unnecessarily burdens instructors: determining grades can be difficult and stressful because fairness and consistency are so hard to achieve.

Elbow is not opposed to evaluating student work. In fact, he thinks eliminating grades will result in more evaluation, not less, moving teachers to adopt the kinds of evaluation that truly help students assess the quality of their work and teach them how to improve as writers: more teacher commentary on papers, more student-teacher discussions about writing, and more peer workshops in the classroom.

As an alternative to letter grades, Elbow suggests sorting papers into two categories (pass or fail) or three categories (exceptional, adequate, and inadequate). Under Elbow's plan, teachers respond to drafts of their students' papers until the student produces work at a passing level. Without grades, he argues, the students' attention is focused on continually improving their writing skills and revising their papers.

As a TA, if you choose not to grade your students' papers, clear the procedure with your teaching supervisor first. That option might not be open to you at your school. However, if you do adopt such a policy, explain it clearly to your students. Elbow notes that many students expect their work to be graded and will be upset with you if it is not. Let your students know why you have adopted this policy and how it will affect them and their writing in the course.

WORKS CITED

Elbow, Peter. "Getting Along without Grades—And Getting Along with Them Too." *Everyone Can Write: Essays Toward a Hopeful Theory of Writing and Teaching Writing.* New York: Oxford University Press, 2000. 399–421.

Weiser, Irwin. "Portfolios and the New Teacher of Writing." *New Directions in Portfolios Assessment.* Eds. Laurel Black, Donald A. Daiker, Jeffrey Sommers, and Gail Stygall. Portsmouth: Boyton/Cook, 1994. 219–29.

Yancey, Kathleen Blake. "Make Haste Slowly: Graduate Teaching Assistants and Portfolios." *New Directions in Portfolios Assessment.* Eds. Laurel Black, Donald A. Daiker, Jeffrey Sommers, and Gail Stygall. Portsmouth: Boyton/Cook, 1994. 210–18.

ADDITIONAL READINGS

Bloom, Lynn Z. "Why I (Used to) Hate to Give Grades." *College Composition and Communication* 48 (1997): 360–71.

Cooper, Charles R., and Lee Odell, ed. *Evaluating Writing: Describing, Measuring, Judging.* Urbana: NCTE, 1977.

———. *Evaluating Writing: The Role of Teachers' Knowledge about Text, Learning, and Culture*. Urbana, NCTE, 1999.

Dragga, Sam. "Praiseworthy Grading." *Journal of Teaching Writing* 4 (1985): 264–68.

Elbow, Peter. "Grading Student Writing: Making It Simpler, Fairer, Clearer." *Writing to Learn: Strategies for Assigning and Responding to Writing Across the Curriculum.* Mary Deane Sorcinelli and Peter Elbow, ed. San Francisco: Jossey-Bass, 1997. 127–40.

———. "Ranking, Evaluating, and Liking: Sorting Out Three Forms of Judgment." *College English* 55 (1993): 187–206.

———. "Taking Time Out from Grading and Evaluating Writing While Working in a Conventional System." *Assessing Writing* 4 (1997): 5–27.

Garrison, Roger H. "What Is an 'A' Paper? A 'B'? A 'C'? A 'D'?" *Teaching English in the Two-Year College* 7 (1981): 209–10.

Hipple, Theodore W. and Bruce Bartholomew. "What Beginning Teachers Need to Know about Grading." *English Education* 14 (1982): 95–8.

Hobson, Eric. "Designing and Grading Written Assignments." *Changing the Way We Grade Student Performance.* Rebecca S. Anderson and Bruce W. Speck, ed. San Francisco: Jossey-Bass, 1998. 51–7.

Peckham, Irvin. "Beyond Grades." *Composition Studies/Freshman English News* 21.2 (1993): 16–31.

Tchudi, Stephen, ed. *Alternatives to Grading Student Writing*. Urbana: NCTE, 1997.

White, Edward M. *Assigning, Responding, Evaluating: A Writing Teacher's Guide*. 3rd ed. New York: St. Martin's Press, 1995.

Zak, Francis, and Christopher C. Weaver, ed. *The Theory and Practice of Grading Writing: Problems and Possibilities*. Albany: State University of New York Press, 1998.

FIGURE 6.1

Holistic Grading Rubric
(used to evaluate an impromptu writing sample)

"A" Papers

An "A" impromptu handles writing and reading demands with ease and instructs the reader.
- thesis is clearly stated, addresses the questions, and controls the paper
- paragraphs are on topic; paragraphs are fully developed and develop thesis; effective introductory and concluding paragraphs; some variety in paragrah length and structure
- support is carefully chosen and employed effectively; substantiates all major assertions
- sentences are always clear; middle diction used throughout; effective word choice
- avoids most grammar errors; those present do not confuse meaning

"B" Papers

A "B" impromptu handles writing and reasoning demands competently, but development of the essay is mechanical and unoriginal.
- thesis is clearly stated, addresses the questions, and controls the paper
- paragraphs are on topic; most paragraphs are fully developed and develop thesis; effective introductory and concluding paragraphs are present; little variety in paragrah length and structure
- support is carefully chosen and used to suppodrt assertions; competent, but not original
- sentences are clear but would benefit from greater variety; middle diction used throughout
- some errors present; but errors do not confuse meaning

"C" Papers

An "C" impromptu displays reasoning and writing skills, but weaknesses in application are evident.
- thesis is general, does not focus clearly on the question, does not give paper a clear direction
- most of the paragraphs are on topic and may need restructuring; introduction and conclusion are perfunctory
- summarizes support; some connections between support and assertions not clear; frequent use of generalizations
- most sentences clear; some confusion from substandard diction and grammatical errors
- some careless errors present; errors affect meaning of some passages

"D" Papers

A "D" impromptu displays rudimentary reasoning and writing skills.
- thesis is vague and does not address question
- some units not paragraphs; order and reasoning of paragraphs inconsistent; introduction and conclusion not present or ineffective
- support relies on summary or irrelevant personal experience and reflection; generalizations poorly supported

- sentences often incomplete and unclear; diction imprecise and often substandard
- numerous grammatical errors; affects meaning of many passages

"F" Papers

An "F" impromptu displays confused reasoning and uncontrolled writing skills.
- thesis is vague, missing, or scattered; does not address question
- some units not paragraphs; paragraph breaks not present; paragraphs do not develop topic; introduction and conclusion missing
- support relies on summary or irrelevant personal experience; generalizations not supported
- sentences often incomplete; diction imprecise and substandard
- pattern of significant grammatical errors; writing unclear

FIGURE 6.2

Grading Sheet

	Points Awarded
Content (30 points possible)	
Assertions	_____
Support	_____
Reasoning	_____
Organization (25 points possible)	
Thesis Statement	_____
Topic Sentences	_____
Transitions	_____
Paragraphs (10 points possible)	
Focus	_____
Unity	_____
Development	_____
Sentences (10 points possible)	
Variety	_____
Clarity	_____
Grammar	_____
Word Choice (10 points possible)	
Diction	_____
Tone	_____
Clarity	_____
Mechanics (10 points possible)	
Punctuation	_____
Spelling	_____
Conventions	_____
Other (5 points possible)	
Rough Draft	_____
Peer Response Sheet	_____
Total Points _____	**Grade** _____

CHAPTER 7

Presenting Material in Class

VARIETY: A KEY TO EFFECTIVE TEACHING

There is no one right way to teach—teaching is more of an art than a science. Over time, every teacher develops a unique teaching style, a way of presenting course material and interacting with students he or she finds comfortable and effective. Good teachers, though, know how to adapt their teaching style to suit the size and structure of each class they teach and to address their students' individual needs.

During your years as a TA, take the opportunity to experiment with ways of presenting course material and begin to develop your own teaching style. This chapter will outline different methods of instruction. Discuss them with your teaching supervisor and experienced peers. See what has worked for them. Try a few yourself. Of course, when you try something new, you run the risk of failure—your class may not run as smoothly as you had planned or your students might not respond as enthusiastically as you had hoped. However, remember that bad teaching experiences set the stage for successful teaching experiences later if you take the time to reflect on what worked, what went wrong, and what you will do differently the next time you cover that material.

LECTURING

Although lecturing has long formed the core of most college teaching, research on student learning increasingly has shown that it is not always the best way to teach—it is effective in some circumstances but not in others. As a result, instructors have developed other ways to help their students learn. Lectures still have their place in most classrooms, however, even in a writing class. Good instructors know when to lecture and how to do it effectively.

When to Lecture

Lecturing is one of the most effective ways to provide students a clear, organized overview of new material. Through lectures, teachers can introduce students to different concepts and ideas and lay out the groundwork for future learning. Inductive learning—letting the students learn the material on their own through structured exercises—has its strengths, but lecturing allows teachers to cover more material in a shorter period of time.

At certain points in writing and literature courses, lectures are fairly common. For example, you are likely to deliver a lecture the first day of class, offering your students an overview of and introduction to the course. You will also lecture when you assign a new paper. After you distribute the assignment sheet, you need to tell your students about this particular type of essay, explain the rhetorical context of the assignment, and describe the grading standards you will apply. Whenever you present new information—how to organize, draft, or revise one's work; how to achieve greater sentence variety; how to use semicolons properly; how to write about literary texts—you will likely introduce the material through a brief lecture. Developing a sense of when you need to lecture and when you need to employ other instructional techniques comes with experience.

How to Lecture Effectively

Like any other instructional technique, lectures lose their effectiveness if they are handled badly. Below are some guidelines that will help you improve your skills.

Be Brief

In writing classes especially, good lectures tend to be short. You will rarely need to lecture for an entire class period. In most cases, you will combine lectures with other learning activities. For example, a ten- to fifteen-minute lecture followed by some hands-on student work or class discussion is often the best way to present new material.

Plan and Organize

The best lectures are well planned and organized. Few experienced teachers—and even fewer new instructors—can offer effective extemporaneous lectures. Instead, good lecturers spend considerable time planning and rehearsing what they will say to their students. When planning a lecture, first consider these questions:

1. What is my goal? What do I want my students to learn from my presentation? Decide on the content, length, and structure of your lecture.

2. What background information do my students need to comprehend this new information? The best way for students to absorb new ideas is to relate them to familiar ideas, what they already know and understand. Without an adequate introduction to the topic of your lecture, your students might not be able to grasp the new material.

3. Why is it important for my students to learn this material? Start your lecture by appealing to your students' needs and concerns, letting them know why and how the material you are about to present is important to them.

4. What are the key points I need to cover? Edit your lecture and keep your presentation brief and focused. Jot down all the main points to serve as an outline for your presentation.

5. What is the best way to order this information? Are there logical or chronological connections between the key points I want to cover? If so, how can I highlight these connections in my presentation? Does some material have to come first so the students can understand what comes next? Refine the structure of your lecture so it presents the material in the most coherent order.

6. What examples can I offer to illustrate and explain the material? Too many TAs fail to develop illustrative examples while planning their lectures. Instead, they hope examples will just spring to mind as they talk in class. A better course of action is to develop them ahead of time.

7. What visual aids will I employ as I lecture? How will I use the chalk board or overhead projector? What handouts or outlines can I develop that will help my students understand my presentation? Effective visual aids take time to plan and prepare; you need to start early.

8. When will I pause for questions as I lecture? What questions might my students have? How will I answer them? Many new TAs are afraid that their students will ask them questions they cannot answer. They fear the embarrassment and loss of credibility that might result if they have to stumble for a response. As you plan a lecture, take time to consider the questions your students might ask and the answers you might give; this will considerably lessen your anxiety.

Answering these questions will help you develop and structure your lecture. As you prepare for class, set aside enough time to consider each question carefully.

Speak Clearly, Maintain Good Eye Contact, and Pace Yourself

Remember the fundamentals of good public speaking. First, make sure your voice is loud and clear. As you begin your lecture, ask your students, especially those sitting in the back of the room, whether they can hear you.

Second, do not read your lecture in class Instead, lecture from brief notes you can refer to when necessary. Try to talk *to* or *with* your students, not *at* them. Look your students in the eye as you speak, moving your gaze around the room. Maintaining good eye contact will help keep your students engaged in the lecture and will help you "read" the room—puzzled looks on your students' faces will let you know when you need to pause for questions or to clarify points; bored looks will let you know when to change your delivery or to move on to the next point you plan to cover.

Your lectures also need to be well paced. Too many new TAs rush through their lectures, only pausing at the end for questions. Pacing your lecture means speaking at a comfortable rate and pausing at regular intervals for student questions and comments. In fact, good lecturers pause often to reiterate points, solicit questions, or offer clarifying examples or explanations. If you find yourself talking too quickly as you lecture or sense that you are pausing too infrequently for questions, stop occasionally to write something on the blackboard or on an overhead. As you do, ask your students if they have any questions. At certain points in your lecture, stop and ask your students to write down any questions they have or to summarize in a sentence or two what they have learned. You can collect their responses and read them later or ask a few students to share their questions or summaries in class, answering their questions or clarifying their understanding of the material before you continue with the lecture.

Use Examples

Good lecturers use lots of examples to help explain the material they are covering. In fact, the more abstract the concept, the more important it is to offer illustrative examples. If possible, draw these examples from your students' experience and knowledge—the arts, popular culture, sports, history, current events—anything that can help your students better comprehend the material. Analogy and metaphor are useful too: explain concept A, which the students may not understand, by relating it to concept B, which they likely do. Do not make the mistake, though, of believing that examples speak for themselves or are self-evidently clear. Be sure you explain the relevance of the examples you offer, explicitly demonstrating their connection to the material you are presenting. Finally, many instructors believe that using several short examples to illustrate a point is more effective than using a single, extended example; it increases the likelihood that you will find one that helps every student.

Draw Connections

Point out connections between material you are covering for the first time and material the students have already studied in class, and explain the differences or similarities. Even though you might think that the connection among units in your course is clear, do not expect your students to make those connections on their own. Highlighting these connections is a proven way to improve student learning. It affords students a context for the new material, a way to relate the unknown and new to the known and understood. It also helps unify your course. Students can see how the material they cover in class does not lose its relevance and how one unit builds on the next.

Link Lectures and Exercises

Finally, good lecturers know that students learn more by doing than by listening. Develop in-class or out-of-class exercises and activities that require your students to apply the information or concepts you discuss in your lecture. Follow-up exercises help students master the material and help you determine how much your students learned. Therefore, design exercises that call on more than just the students' ability to memorize and repeat information. If these are the only critical thinking skills the students must use to complete the exercise successfully, you are not helping them learn the material as thoroughly as they can and should. Instead, develop exercises that require students to employ the new material in meaningful ways—to solve problems, for example, or to advance their work on a class assignment.

CLASS DISCUSSIONS

Giving lectures requires you to do most of the talking. To achieve the opposite effect, use class discussions. Preparing for and managing a class discussion takes about the same amount of time and work as preparing for a lecture. However, in class discussions, you employ a different set of teaching skills and achieve goals that are hard to reach through lectures.

The Roles Discussions Can Play in a Course

Class discussions help students explore ideas, develop positions, learn from their peers, and become more involved in the course. Some teachers like to use discussions early in a course as an icebreaker, an opportunity for students to speak their minds and get to know each other. Others use discussions throughout the course as a way for students to develop important critical thinking skills. During discussions, students must present their ideas clearly and convincingly to a sometimes skeptical audience. If they are challenged during the discussion, students have to listen carefully to the questions or objections being raised, assess their merit, and explain or defend their own position, skills that can transfer to their written work.

Sometimes discussions just happen. There are hot topics on campus the students want to talk about or a course reading that pushes the right buttons. When this occurs, teachers have a hard decision to make: cut off discussion and get on with the lesson plan for the day or let the discussion continue and catch up on the lesson plan some other time (truly gifted teachers can combine the two, finding a way to draw connections between the spontaneous discussion and their planned class activities).

Most of the time, though, discussions are planned and purposeful—teachers set aside time on their syllabus for discussions as a way to cover course material, teach particular skills, or achieve certain class goals. For example, teachers may use discussions to help students gain a better understanding of a required reading. If this reading will serve as the basis of a paper the students are writing, the discussions help them understand and interpret the text, acquaint them with alternative interpretations of the reading, and help them develop material for their papers. Often ideas and insights generated by these discussions find their way into the students' papers. Other times the reading may serve as a model for a paper the students are writing. In this case, discussions are often analytical, the class working together to dissect the reading's content, structure, or style. Again, students can use the insights generated by this discussion to plan and draft their own essays. Still other times, the reading may serve only as a prompt for discussion. The teacher has certain rhetorical or argumentative skills he or she wants the students to develop through discussion and asks the students to discuss a reading likely to elicit strong responses.

Sometimes discussions will focus on the topic of the papers the students are writing—single parenting, the presidential election, deforestation, parking on campus. These discussions can help students better understand the issue and develop material for their essays. More importantly, though, they help students determine what they really think about the topic, where they stand on an issue, and how they might best communicate their ideas. During discussions, students can articulate their positions and ideas provisionally to see what kind of reaction they receive. Articulating their ideas during a discussion can serve as a kind of "rough draft" for these students. The responses they receive from their peers will help them develop, refine, or more clearly articulate their ideas when they write them out.

Still other times, teachers use discussions just to energize their students. On a day that the students seem particularly tired or distracted, they may decide to talk about the upcoming Oscar presentations, campus drinking policies, or the career expectations of men and women—any issue the students may find interesting. As they discuss the topic, the teacher may expect the students to employ some of the rhetorical skills they have learned in the class, but usually the goal is simply to have a good discussion. Sometimes even a brief debate can raise the energy level of the class, reignite interest in the course, and motivate the students to learn what the teacher will cover next in class.

Types of Discussions

Some discussions are open and others are structured. Open discussions allow the students to set the agenda. To begin these discussions, teachers may pose a general question to get the students talking (something like *"What did you think about the readings due for today?"* or *"What did you think of the president's speech last night?"*), but they allow the students to dictate the content and direction of the discussion. With structured discussions, teachers set a more definite agenda, perhaps writing on the blackboard a specific question or two they want the students to address (*"Which of the readings due for today made the best use of emotional appeals?"* or *"During his speech last night, the president specifically addressed several people sitting in the audience—how did that help him advance his argument?"*). As the students respond to these questions, the teacher keeps them on topic, not allowing them to drift to unrelated issues. Either type of discussion can be effective, and you ought to experiment with both.

Discussions can also be brief or long. Sometimes you may want your students to discuss a reading for only the first ten minutes of a class before they move on to some other task. At the end of a lecture, you may want to reserve ten or fifteen minutes for questions and a short discussion of the material you presented. Other times you may want to devote an entire class period to discussion. If your students are tackling a difficult reading, for example, you may want to spend the entire class talking about the text and answering their questions. Other times you may want to spend a class period debating the topic of the students' papers. As a teaching tool, class discussions can be very flexible.

Finally, with the widespread use of technology today, you might want to use electronic discussions, both in class and out of class. Electronic discussions—through chat rooms, threaded discussions, and the like—allow students to "meet" and exchange ideas any day of the week, any time of day. If you are not skilled at setting up electronic discussions but would like to use them in your class, ask your teaching supervisor for help locating people on campus who can instruct you. (See Chapter 8 for advice on using on-line threaded discussions.)

The Teacher's Role in Class Discussions

During a class discussion, the teacher has several roles to play. You have to get the discussion started, keep it going, and keep it organized. More importantly, though, you have to be sure the discussion is serving its intended purpose and meeting your students' needs.

Teacher as Prompter

As the prompter, you start the discussion and keep your students active and involved. If the conversation flags at some point, step in and reenergize it. If some students are not participating, draw them in. If important points are being ignored or shortchanged, redirect the conversation.

Teacher as Organizer

This role starts before the class meets. Prepare for a discussion the way you prepare for any other class activity, choosing the topic or question you will ask the students to address, deciding on the format of the discussion, and determining the amount of time you will devote to the activity. During the discussion itself, keep the students on task, point out trends you see in their comments, and redirect the discussion if it moves in unproductive or inappropriate directions. The catch: you need to do all of this without monopolizing class time or commandeering the conversation, a tricky procedure that takes a lot of practice to master.

Teacher as Recorder

As the recorder, you take notes on the blackboard or on an overhead projector, recording the points students raise as impartially and comprehensively as you can. At the end of the discussion, you and your students can sort through these notes to identify trends, weed out errors, or synthesize ideas.

Teacher as Synthesizer

Class discussions should not end in confusion. Instead, when possible and appropriate, help students synthesize their comments, producing a final position or statement most or all can accept. However, when the point of a discussion is not to build a consensus but rather to air ideas and explore possibilities, help your students summarize, as clearly and impartially as they can, what they have heard each other saying and what their final positions seem to be.

Teacher as Instructor

Finally, at the end of any class discussion, point out what the students should have gained or learned from the conversation. Over the years, I have watched TAs lead wonderful discussions, but when the class was over, I wondered whether the students made any connection between the discussion and the course. Did they understand the reason for the discussion? Did they see how it was connected to particular course goals or writing projects? I know from talking to some of these students and reading the evaluation forms they complete at the end of the term that these connections are often unclear. With this in mind, at the end of every discussion, be sure to explain why you chose to devote class time to the activity and how the students might use the ideas and insights they generated in class. As an alternative, ask your students to write a brief, informal essay at the end of the period in which they summarize what they learned in class that day and critique its utility.

Strengths and Weaknesses of Class Discussions

Class discussions can be unpredictable and unwieldy. No amount of planning can help you completely control where a discussion might go. Though that unpredictability might frighten you as an inexperienced teacher, the possibilities should also thrill you. Class discussions can generate a lot of heat, but also a lot of light. Your students will often amaze you with the quality and depth of their thinking. They might also disappoint you with the predictability and shallowness of their comments. Class discussions bring out both kinds of responses from students.

Though class discussions can be time consuming, if you manage them well they can greatly benefit your students. First, students generally like discussions. They often do not get an opportunity to express themselves in their classes. The enthusiasm discussions generate spills over into other aspects of the course. Second, students usually find discussions instructive. They like hearing what other students think, and they learn from their peers in ways they might not learn from you. Do not get fooled into believing that you alone are responsible for educating the students in your class. Third, lessons learned during class discussions often transfer to the students' writing, helping them develop, organize, and present their essays more effectively.

Finally, discussions can help make classes more interesting and exciting for you. Listen carefully to what your students have to say; they will raise questions you have not considered and offer interpretations you find interesting or challenging. Play the role of student yourself and see what you can learn. During almost every discussion I've had in my classes, students make comments that increase my understanding of the material and help me develop new ways of presenting it in class.

ORAL REPORTS

Oral reports increase your students' involvement in their own education. Turning the classroom over to your students puts them center stage while you take a seat. There are many ways to structure oral reports and many uses they can serve in the classroom.

Types of Oral Reports

Oral reports can introduce new material, supplement your own teaching, or showcase the results of student work. In the first case, you ask students to research material you want to cover in class and have them briefly report their findings. This approach can work with even the most mundane topics. For example, I have students report on documentation practices when I have to cover that material. I assign one group of students to study MLA documentation and another to study APA. I give them a list of points I want covered in their reports, such as what material needs to be documented in papers, how to document that material, and how to write up a works cited list, then allow them two weeks to gather their information and develop their presentation. I encourage the students to be as creative as they can be. Presentations have included lectures, films, demonstrations, mock quiz shows, and even a "documentation Olympics."

Oral reports can also supplement instruction you offer in class. For example, suppose you are teaching the novel *Frankenstein*. You may want to offer a brief lecture introducing the book and its author, then ask groups of students to develop more detailed oral reports on Mary Shelley, the Prometheus myth, the rise of modern science, child-rearing practices of nineteenth-century Europe, or any other relevant topics. The students' job is to take your comments as a starting point, investigate the topic more thoroughly, and present the results of their research orally in class. All the students in class will benefit from these informative reports.

Finally, oral reports focus on the student's own writing. Many teachers require oral reports as part of a longer research project. After the students have finished writing their research papers, they report on the topic orally in class, offering a brief abstract of their paper, discussing the research questions they investigated, summarizing their findings, or giving a full account of the steps they followed when completing the project. Oral reports acknowledge publicly the students' hard work and offer them an opportunity to instruct their peers.

Oral Report Guidelines

If you employ oral reports, these guidelines can help you design the task, manage the presentations, and provide your students the guidance they need to complete the assignment successfully.

1. Consider whether you want your students to work individually or with others. Students can work on the projects individually; they can work with others but present their reports individually; or they can work in groups and offer a group presentation. Working in groups on oral presentations offers some real advantages, even if the students will give individual presentations. Members of the group can help with research; offer advice on the content, structure, and style of the presentation; provide moral support for students who might be nervous about speaking in public; and serve as rehearsal audiences.

2. Offer detailed guidelines that specify the topic you expect them to cover, the format you expect them to employ (whether you want individual or group presentations), their goal (what the presentation should accomplish), the appropriate tone and diction (serious or humorous, formal or informal), the time limits for each presentation (minimum and/or maximum time limits), the use of visual aids (such as overheads, charts, pictures, samples, or graphs), and required handouts or other documents (e.g., presentation notes for their peers, a summary of the report for you, or a reflection essay on the process of developing the report). The more detailed and clear the guidelines, the better the presentations are likely to be.

3. Strictly enforce these guidelines. Managing time is often difficult for students giving oral reports, but if a presentation runs long, you need to cut it off and stick to your schedule. Not doing so is unfair to the other presenters.

4. Develop a way to evaluate each presentation, identifying its strengths and weaknesses. Evaluating the presentations lets the students know that you value the oral reports—they are not just "busy work." Develop a checklist for the presentations that indicates which aspects of the reports will be critiqued. You can evaluate the reports yourself or have the students evaluate their peers.

5. Strictly enforce attendance on presentation days. Students sometimes skip class when their peers present material. Let your students know that the presentations are an important part of the class.

6. Offer your students some instruction in public speaking, even though many of them may have taken or are currently taking a course in oral communication. Sample oral report guidelines for students are included at the end of this chapter (Figure 7.1).

Oral Reports in a Writing Class?

If you want to include oral reports in your classes, you might run into some resistance. Many teachers see no value in them; they do not believe students have anything to teach other students and would rather devote class time to other types of instruction. Other teachers may use oral reports in a literature class but not in a writing class. After all, they reason, since a writing class covers writing, what is there to "talk" about? But oral reports can serve several important purposes in a writing class. First, they can get the students more involved in class material they may otherwise find alienating and uninteresting. As they research topics in a writing class and increase their expertise, they may find the material more interesting and challenging than they thought they would. Second, oral reports help students develop important rhetorical skills that can transfer directly to their writing. The rhetorical situation of oral reports matches the rhetorical situation of the students' essays: someone communicating something to someone for some purpose. In the case of oral reports, the audience is real and immediate. In preparing for and delivering their oral reports, students can learn important lessons about effective communication that can lead to more effective writing—how to gather evidence to support a thesis, how to anticipate audience response, how to organize information and employ transitional devices, how to develop successful introductions and conclusions.

GROUP WORK AND COLLABORATIVE LEARNING

Recent research in learning theory has bolstered what experience taught teachers long ago: working with peers helps students learn. In brief, these theories hold that knowledge is social in nature. Over time, people in a society come to agree on what is right and true; as this consensus changes, so do the knowledge claims. In the past, for example, humanity "knew" that the world was flat, "knew" that women could not run marathons, and "knew" that the atom could never be split. Part of a college education, this theory holds, is learning how to take part in this process: how to reason through information and arguments with others, form opinions, address disputes, and form a consensus. This sort of collaborative learning has found a comfortable home in many composition and literature classes.

Organizing Student Groups—Some Options

Teachers tend to organize groups in several ways. They sometimes let the students form groups on their own with the membership changing every time they collaborate. When teachers want their students to work together on a project, they simply ask the students to divide themselves into groups. (It is always best to keep these groups small—no more than five members. In larger groups, not every student gets a chance to participate fully.) These ad hoc groups can be formed quickly in class, allowing students to work with a wide variety of peers.

Other times teachers let students form groups that remain stable for the entire term—since membership does not change, the students are always working with the same set of peers. Some teachers like to place students in particular groups rather than allowing the students to self-select. Some place students into groups based on the students' skills and talents, hoping that stronger students in the group can help weaker students. Others place students into groups based on the students' educational background, gender, personality, or life experience, hoping to get combinations that will enable each group of students to work together productively throughout the course.

Stable groups have some advantages. Over time, the students get to know one another well, developing friendships and trust that can help them work together more effectively and efficiently. However, personality clashes in the group can diminish their effectiveness and teachers sometimes have to step in to negotiate conflicts or change group membership.

Using Group Work in Class

Teachers often use group work to promote and improve class discussion. For example, before discussing a reading in class, they will have the students talk about it in smaller groups. Many students who are reluctant to speak in class are more willing to talk in a smaller group, giving everyone a chance to contribute. Some teachers like each group to take notes on a clear overhead transparency during its discussion. When the groups are finished, the teacher can then place the notes on an overhead projector, asking each group to give an oral report on its deliberations.

Other teachers use collaborative learning groups to help the students complete in-class exercises and assignments. One option is to have the students, as a group, complete an exercise or assignment together, reaching a consensus on their answers or responses. Another option is to have each member of the group complete the exercise or assignment individually but to get help from the other group members when necessary. Students benefit from this sort of exercise when they work together to form an answer or when they help a peer complete the assignment. Most experienced teachers will acknowledge that sometimes a peer instructor succeeds in helping a student understand material in ways a teacher cannot.

Teachers also use peer groups to help students complete more formal writing assignments. As students work on their papers, they can turn to the members of their group for assistance. Their peers can help them develop material for their paper, organize their ideas, strengthen their arguments, or revise their drafts. Some teachers like every student in the group to compose his or her own essay, receiving help along the way from the other group members. Other teachers like the students in each group to produce a single essay together. Teachers typically allow the students to divide the work however they wish. The only guideline is that every student in the group is expected to participate in producing the essay. To facilitate the process, some teachers like to meet with the groups from time to time as they work on the project. Other teachers like the group members to submit brief, periodic progress reports that detail the status of the paper and describe the contributions of each member.

Grading these collaborative projects can be difficult, though. Some teachers give every group member the grade the paper receives: if the paper gets an "A," every group member gets an "A." Other teachers allow the group members to grade each other's contribution to the final paper: each student's grade is an average of the paper grade and the grades he or she receives from the other group members.

Guidelines for Effective Group Work

As with any other teaching technique, learning how to use group work effectively takes time and practice. These guidelines may help.

1. Keep groups small: three to five students is ideal. If the groups are too large, some students might not participate fully.

2. Be sure all of the students in every group understand the assigned task and know what they are supposed to do. If you use groups only occasionally in class, students may waste time trying to get started if they do not understand the assignment. Before and after the students divide into groups, explain the task thoroughly and ask for questions. As the students work on a project, circulate from group to group and see if the students have any questions.

3. Set clear deadlines. Let every member of the group know what is due when. If you are using a brief group assignment in class, set the deadline in terms of minutes: tell each group exactly how much time they have to complete their work. Deadlines help the groups stay focused. If groups are working on long-term projects, establish deadlines for the completed assignments and any preliminary parts of the assignment. For example, set deadlines for turning in topics, bibliographies, preliminary drafts, or progress reports.

4. When necessary, help the students in each group get organized. Most teachers prefer to let the group members decide who does what work. If you feel that your students need more direction, suggest how the students might divide the work, allowing them to decide who will do which job, or assign each group member a specific task to complete.

5. For long projects, have each group submit periodic reports on their progress. These informal reports should summarize what the group has accomplished thus far, what their next steps are, what problems they are encountering, and what questions they have. Some teachers prefer to meet periodically with each group to get the same sort of response. Meeting face-to-face with the students allows the teacher to ask follow-up questions, but getting individual responses in writing gives students the opportunity to raise issues they might not raise in front of the whole group.

6. Devote class time to the projects. Let student groups meet periodically during class to work on their assignment. This is especially helpful for nontraditional students, students who live off campus, students who hold full-time jobs, or students with families. These students may have a hard time meeting with the other group members outside of class.

7. Make yourself available for conferences. Let your students know that if they have any questions or problems, they can meet with you individually or with the other group members. Encourage the students to resolve conflicts themselves, but when necessary, step in and help a struggling group solve its problems.

These guidelines do not guarantee success, but they might help you make group work and collaborative learning a successful part of your course.

IN-CLASS WRITING

In-class writing assignments can accomplish many goals. They can help students develop their critical thinking skills, master course material, reflect on their experiences and education, or complete larger writing projects. They can help you assess student learning and gauge the level of your students' involvement in the course. Whether they are ungraded or graded, informal or formal, brief or long, in-class writing assignments can play an important role in the classes you teach.

Different Uses for In-Class Writing

You can employ ungraded in-class writing activities to promote student learning in several ways. For example, before a class begins, students can summarize or respond to the readings due that day or answer a specific question you ask. This writing can serve as the basis for class discussion or you can collect and read the students' work to see how well they understand the material. During class, pause occasionally and ask your students to summarize or respond to what you have been discussing or to jot down any questions they have. You can collect this writing and read it later or ask several students to read aloud what they have written and then offer your response. At the end of class, ask students to summarize, respond to, or critique the material you covered and then write down any questions they have. Again, you can collect these papers and read them later, perhaps answering the students' questions the next time class meets. All of these brief, ungraded writing assignments promote learning because they give your students the opportunity to reflect on what they are learning and to ask questions.

Other times you may use in-class writing assignments to help students complete larger projects. For example, on the day you hand out an assignment, the students can brainstorm a list of topics they might address. The students then exchange lists and discuss their options. After they have completed some research on the assignment, they might compose a rough outline of their paper in class or draft a preliminary thesis statement. Again, they share this writing with their peers or turn it in for your comments. As they begin to draft their essays, they can write or revise any part of the paper in class—an opening paragraph, a conclusion, a works cited list. Composing these drafts in class allows you to answer specific questions your students have and to give their writing your immediate response.

Finally, you may decide to have your students compose formal, graded essays in class. Some teachers require their students to compose these essays spontaneously—the students are seeing the assignment for the first time and have to plan, draft, and revise their paper in class. Other teaches like to give their students the assignment ahead of time so they have the chance to plan their responses; some teachers even allow them to consult outlines, texts, or notes as they compose their essay in class. While many teachers ask their students to compose their essays in one class period, others devote two or more class sessions to the assignment. The first class session the students get the assignment, plan their response, and perhaps draft an essay. During subsequent class periods, the students get a chance to revise their papers. Outside of class, they are free to discuss their essays with other students and to consider how they will rewrite their papers.

Many instructors like to include in-class essays on their syllabus because it is such a common academic genre—several studies show that students across the curriculum can expect to write graded in-class essays and examinations throughout their college years. These teachers believe that the purpose of an introductory composition course is, at least in part, to prepare students to write the kinds of papers they will encounter in a variety of college classes. Other instructors include in-class essays on their syllabi because these assignments give them a sense of how well their students can write on their own. With papers written outside of class, students can get help from tutors, parents, roommates, or friends. In class, they usually have to write their papers without the same kinds of assistance.

Guidelines for Ungraded In-Class Writing Assignments

Ungraded in-class writing activities work best if they are brief, focused, low pressure, and varied.

1. Keep these assignments short—limit the amount of time students write (perhaps only five minutes) or the length of their response. Make sure the students can complete the assignment in the time available.

2. Keep the assignments focused. Link the writing to a particular question or text you want the students to address. The more focused and specific the assignment, the better. You do not want students spending time trying to narrow the topic of their essay when they should be writing their response.

3. Keep these assignments informal. Informal writing encourages students to be creative and exploratory, which is exactly what you want with this type of assignment.

4. When appropriate, comment on the content of the students' writing but do not grade their work. As the teacher, you may never actually look at much of this writing, but occasionally you may want to collect and read what the students have written. When you do, comment on what the students have written, but do not edit their writing.

5. Vary the writing activities, because certain kinds of writing tasks will help some students more than others. Let some be text-based (summaries of or responses to readings) and others experience-based (reflection or response essays). Tie some to academic genres (summaries or outlines) and others to creative genres (poems or stories). Make some analytical and some exploratory.

Guidelines for Graded In-Class Writing Assignments

The best way you can help your students succeed with graded, in-class essays such as essay exams is to spend time teaching them how to compose this type of paper.

1. Do not assume that your students already know how to write in-class essays—they may have been required to write them throughout high school and college without ever being taught how to do it well.

2. Teach your students how to prepare for in-class essays. Here you can cover several skills: reviewing course material, anticipating possible test questions, considering answers to those questions, and examining past examinations when available. If students have access to the assignment before they have to write their essays, teach them how to plan their responses.

3. Teach your students how to analyze test questions or assignments. When analyzing models, make sure your students know how to identify the purpose of an assignment, the task they must complete, the intended

audience of the piece, and the desired length of the response. Many in-class writing assignments are poorly constructed—students have a hard time identifying exactly what the teacher is asking them to write. You can help your students by giving them several strategies for analyzing the way in-class assignments are worded.

4. Teach your students how to adopt a process approach to composing in-class essays. Even if they are expected to complete the entire essay in one sitting, teach them how to engage in appropriate planning activities, how to draft their response, and how to save time to review and revise their answer.

5. Make sure your students understand good in-class essays have an introduction; a controlling thesis statement; paragraph breaks; appropriate evidence, examples, and support; effective transitions; and a conclusion.

6. Offer your students some tips on time management. For example, tell them to read the entire test question or assignment before they begin to plan and draft their response. Advise them to set aside a few minutes to plan their answer and to compose a scratch outline of their response. Suggest that as they compose their response, they follow that outline and that they save a few minutes at the end of the class to revise and proofread their essay.

If you require your students to write formal in-class essays, be sure you apply appropriate evaluative criteria when you grade their work. Outside of class, students have as much time as they need to plan, draft, revise, and proofread their work; in class, they do not. Your grading standards need to recognize this reality.

Limitations of In-Class Writing

Many teachers find that students do not take ungraded in-class assignments seriously—they either fail to do the work or do it half-heartedly. If you find this to be a problem with your students, talk to them about the importance of the assignments; help them see how these activities develop important reading, writing, and thinking skills. You might also reward students who do good work. For instance, instead of giving this work a letter grade, some teachers evaluate it on a pass-fail basis and dedicate a small portion of the course grade to successfully passing these assignments. Other teachers like to duplicate the best responses and discuss them in class.

Graded in-class writing assignments have drawbacks as well. Many teachers believe that these assignments cannot accurately represent every student's ability to write because they so severely truncate the writing process and bypass collaborative learning. Grading is also an issue: what standards are appropriate and fair? If you can find ways of addressing these limitations, in-class writing activities may play a significant role in your class.

MULTIMEDIA RESOURCES

Showing films in class, playing music, logging onto Web sites—these are just some of the ways you can complement your classroom teaching with multimedia presentations. Employed wisely, these resources can help you present material, enliven the classroom, and boost student interest. As with all the teaching methods discussed in this chapter, though, be sure you have a good reason for using multimedia resources in the classroom—they should augment instruction, not substitute for it.

Over the years, instructors have found many reasons to show films in their writing and literature classes. Some instructors use them as writing prompts, asking their students to respond to or critique the movies they show. Other instructors have students compare films (for example, two versions of *Hamlet*) or compare written and filmed versions of the same work (for example, the play *Hamlet* and a filmed version). Still other teachers show films to stir debate—for example, a class studying the theme of war may watch *Saving Private Ryan* or *Platoon*. Since most students today have grown up in a visual culture, showing films can help them learn. Other students find watching a film a nice break from usual classroom procedures, motivating them to think about the course material in new and productive ways.

One real drawback to using films in class, though, is time. How many class periods will you devote to showing a film? One? Two? Teachers facing this problem have a few options. One, of course, is to show the film outside of class: reserve a classroom one afternoon or evening and have your students come to watch the film. Some students' schedules, though, make it difficult for them to attend these showings. To avoid this problem, some teachers show only parts of a film in class and use the rest of the period for other types of instruction. Still others show the entire film in class, devoting as many class periods to it as needed. If you decide on this final option, be sure you are showing the film for the right reason—to complement and support your teaching, not to be a replacement for it. Too often new TAs show a film to "kill" a class or two, saving them prep time. If this is the only reason you are showing a video, change your plans.

Other visual resources include slides, photographs, paintings, or advertisements. Teachers use these visual aids much the way they use films in class—to serve as the basis for writing assignments or to prompt class discussion. Assignments typically ask students to describe, respond to, interpret, or compare the material.

Teachers who use a lot of visual resources in their classes find the overhead projector to be a valuable tool. Some like to place notes or summaries on the overhead as they lecture to help guide their students through the material. If groups of students are working on an exercise that requires them to report back to the class as a whole, many teachers like to have the students write their responses, or notes on blank overhead sheets. They collect these sheets when the groups are finished and place them on the projector as each group gives its report, sharing that material with the rest of the students.

Many teachers use overheads to present sample texts to their students. If the class is discussing a reading, for example, the teacher makes an overhead transparency of the text, places it on the projector, and points out particular passages for attention. This technique is especially helpful if the instructor is teaching students how to annotate a text—the teacher can mark the text right in front of the students, explaining what she is doing and why, modeling the behavior she expects them to master. Other teachers like to place sample student texts on the overhead for discussion, copying sentences, paragraphs, or whole essays onto transparencies to critique in class (always get the student's permission to use his or her work this way). Still other teachers like to have their students compose, edit, or revise writing in class with the aid of an overhead projector. When teaching grammar and mechanics, for example, they place an exercise on an overhead transparency sheet. Individually or in groups, students work through the passages and volunteers step forward to write their answers on the transparency. The teacher then leads a discussion of the response.

Audio technology can also supplement classroom instruction. For example, some teachers like to play music for their students as they write journal entries in class because they believe that the music aids student writing. Others make music the source text for an assignment, asking students to analyze, compare, or respond to song lyrics. To improve their students' critical listening, note-taking, and summary skills, teachers may audiotape a brief interview and play it back for students, asking them to summarize its content.

CHOOSING AMONG TEACHING TECHNIQUES

As I stated at the beginning of this chapter, effective teachers present course material in a wide variety of ways. During your years as a TA, you will begin to develop your own repertoire of teaching techniques. With experience, you will learn how to match these techniques to your course goals. Figure 7.2 at the end of this chapter lists some of the more common course goals and suggests particular techniques you might use to achieve them.

THE TEACHER AS PERFORMING RHETORICIAN

At its heart, teaching, like writing, is a public rhetorical act: someone (the teacher) talking to someone (a student) to achieve a particular end (the student's education). This turns the teacher into a performer. The importance and power of good classroom performance should not be underestimated: in the classroom, teachers are always "on stage," always performing for an audience, always working to achieve their goals.

Understandably, the performance aspect of teaching is a major concern for new TAs. Many will be standing in front of the classroom as a teacher for the first time, and they are not sure how to perform. Even the basics are a mystery: where do I stand? Should I use the lectern? What should I do with my hands? Will my voice be loud enough? Too loud? How much should I move around the room? Unfortunately, there are no easy answers: every teacher develops his or own performance style in the classroom. Some teachers are most comfortable standing behind a lectern, reading from notes. Others like to move away from the desk, circulate around the room, and interact informally with their students.

While individual performance styles differ, most successful teachers exhibit similar traits. Below are a few suggestions that could make your classroom presentation more successful and engaging.

1. Relax and prepare.

Early in the term, many new TAs find it hard to relax in the classroom because they are afraid: afraid they will not perform well, afraid they do not "know enough" to be good teachers, afraid students will ask them questions they cannot answer, afraid they will embarrass themselves. These fears are understandable, but they are also easily addressed. Experience erases most of them—most TAs find teaching more thrilling than they expected and quickly learn that they have much to offer their students. Other fears can be lessened by thoroughly preparing for every class. As this chapter and others have suggested, if you carefully consider your goals for a course, determine a strategy for addressing them, prepare your material ahead of time, and anticipate problems that might arise, you can go into class more confident and self-assured.

2. Find a comfortable presentation style.

Do you stand or sit in class? If you stand, do you stay in one place or move around? If you sit, do you sit behind a desk, in front of the desk, or with your students? The answer to all of these questions is the same: do what feels comfortable. No choice is inherently better or worse than the alternatives. As a TA, you will likely experiment with all of these options. In fact, you may assume one style when lecturing and another when leading discussions. Again, you should do what makes you comfortable.

Several years ago I worked with a first-year TA who just could not feel at ease standing in front of the classroom. She was a skilled writer and reader and had the potential to be a good teacher, but she could not relax when her students focused all of their attention on her. She felt too much in the spotlight to teach effectively. She also waited too long to get help; by the time she talked to me, she was ready to resign her assistantship. As we discussed the problem, she said she preferred group work to lecturing—moving from group to group and talking to a few students at a time was less stressful for her than delivering course material in front of the entire class. When I suggested structuring the entire class around group work, she seemed incredulous. "You can do that?" she asked. I assured her she could, and in a few hours we had redesigned her syllabus and developed a series of classroom activities that stressed collaborative learning. This change in pedagogy greatly reduced the TA's fears and frustrations, and she finished the program with a strong teaching record.

3. Find ways to connect with your students.

When teaching, make sure you talk *to* your students, not *at* or *past* them. This is one of the major weaknesses TAs exhibit—instead of talking to their students, connecting with them individually, they talk at them, rarely making eye contact or acknowledging their presence some other way. Effective teachers operate on at least two levels in the classroom: part of their attention is focused on the material they are teaching while another part is focused on their students' responses and reactions to that material. This skill comes to some teachers naturally; others have to cultivate it. Even in a crowded classroom, you have to pay attention to individual students, looking them in the eye as you move your attention around the room. When you speak, speak to individual students. Smiling, nodding, pointing your finger—these gestures all help you establish and maintain contact with your students. If you are comfortable moving around the room when you teach, be sure you change where you stand so you do not end up addressing students in only one part of the room. Connecting with your students keeps them interested in the class and helps convey the message that you are concerned about their education. It also helps you assess the effectiveness of your instruction. Puzzled or bored looks let you know when to offer further explanations or change topics.

4. Maintain a professional relationship with your students.

New TAs can fall into several traps as they build a working relationship with their students. For example, some TAs try to establish their authority in the classroom by being authoritarian and autocratic. Modeling themselves on some version of Professor Kingsfield from *The Paper Chase*, they try to intimidate their students. In most cases this is a defensive move: these TAs feel that if they make them cower, the students are less likely to act up in class or to ask challenging questions. Other TAs try too hard to be their students' friend. They spend so much of their time in class being the "cool" teacher, swapping stories with their students about campus life, dating, or drinking that they shortchange the students' instruction. These TAs are frequently reluctant to give bad grades or to criticize their students' work because they want the students to "like" them. Of course, being liked is not in and of itself bad, but sometimes being a teacher means telling your students certain truths about their writing and thinking that will upset them. All of your students may not like you all of the time if you are doing your job well. Being your students' friend and being their teacher are not mutually exclusive, but as a TA, you must realize that you are first and foremost your students' teacher. When you walk into the classroom, you assume that role in their lives. Most of your students have lots of friends; they need you to be their teacher.

5. Vary the way you present material in class.

Finally, alternate the way you present material throughout a course. Routine is both a blessing and a curse for teachers and students. Certain aspects of a course are standard—calling roll, assigning and collecting papers, discussing readings. These routines help teachers plan their courses and help students know what to expect. Routine, though, can also stifle student interest and innovative teaching. Sometimes students learn more when they are outside their "comfort zone," when teachers ask them to think or act in unexpected ways. Mixing up the way you present material in class can keep your students on their toes, help them maintain an interest in the course, and meet the needs of students with different learning styles. Changing the way you present course material can also reinvigorate your teaching. Like students, teachers can get stale as a semester drags along. Sometimes teachers need to challenge themselves to keep their teaching fresh.

CONCLUSION

Good teachers are always teaching. The few hours they spend in class each week succeed because of the many hours they spend outside of class designing activities and assignments that will help their students become better readers, writers, and thinkers. Experience will teach you how to improve as a classroom teacher, how to avoid problems, and how to learn from any mistakes you happen to make. Like other good instructors, you will also come to recognize those "teachable moments" in class when your students are most ready to learn. Mastering a range of pedagogical techniques will give you the tools you need to make the most out of those moments. You also will learn how to read your students' responses in class. You will know which classroom activities they find most helpful if you read their body language, listen to their comments, and respect their opinions. Your best course of action is to care deeply about your students' learning and to work conscientiously in their best interest.

ADDITIONAL READINGS

Brinkley, Alan, et al. *The Chicago Handbook for Teachers: A Practical Guide to the College Classroom*. Chicago: University of Chicago Press, 1999.

Brookfield, Stephen, and Stephen Preskill. *Discussion as a Way of Teaching: Tools and Techniques for Democratic Classrooms*. San Francisco: Jossey-Bass, 1999.

Bruffee, Kenneth A. *Collaborative Learning: Higher Education, Interdependence, and the Authority of Knowledge*. Baltimore: Johns Hopkins University Press, 1999.

Cannon, Robert, and David Newble. *A Handbook for Teachers in Universities and Colleges: A Guide to Improving Teaching Methods*. 4th ed. London: Kogan, 2000.

Dunn, Rita, and Shirley A. Griggs, ed. *Practical Approaches to Using Learning Styles in Higher Education*. Westport, CN: Bergin & Garvey, 2000.

Feldman, Kenneth A., and Michael B. Paulsen, ed. *Teaching and Learning in the College Classroom*. 2nd ed. Needhan Heights, MA: Simon & Shuster, 1998.

Fry, Heather, Steve Ketteridge, and Stephanie Marshall, ed. *A Handbook for Teaching and Learning in Higher Education: Enhancing Academic Practice*. London: Kogan, 1999.

Fry, John, Karen Medsker, and Dede Bonner. "Teaching Methods and Strategies." *The Adjunct Faculty Handbook.* Ed. Virginia Bianco-Mathis and Neal Chalofsky. Thousand Oaks, CA: Sage, 1996. 55–114.

Johnson, Glenn R. *First Steps to Excellence in College Teaching.* Madison: Magna, 1995.

Lambert, Leo M., Stacey Lance Tice, and Patricia H. Featherstone, ed. *University Teaching: A Guide for Graduate Students.* Syracuse: Syracuse University Press, 1996.

McKeachie, Wilbert J. *McKeachie's Teaching Tips: Strategies, Research, and Theory for College and University Teachers.* 10th ed. Boston: Houghton, 1999.

Perry, Raymond P., and John C. Smart, ed. *Effective Teaching in Higher Education: Research and Practice.* New York: Agathon, 1997.

Silverman, Sharon L., and Martha E. Casazza. *Learning and Development: Making Connections to Enhance Teaching.* San Francisco: Jossey-Bass, 2000.

FIGURE 7.1 Oral Report Guidelines for Students

Preparation

1. Research your topic thoroughly. Make sure you know more about your topic than you have time to share in your presentation.
2. Organize your comments through an outline or informal list. Consider:
   a. what information you will include in your oral report
   b. what order you will present the material in
   c. what transitions you will use to lead your listeners comfortably from point to point
   d. how and when you will use visual aids.
3. Write out some notes to follow, but do not write out the entire presentation. Do not "read" your paper to class. Use the notes to guide your presentation.
4. Develop a set of examples you can use to illustrate the points you want to make.
5. Anticipate questions your listeners might ask and develop answers or responses.
6. Rehearse, rehearse, rehearse. Make sure your comments are clear, organized, and thorough. Make sure your presentation conforms to time limits.
7. Prepare any visual aids you plan on using and duplicate any handouts you will distribute.

Delivery

8. As much as possible, relax and speak clearly.
9. Do not "read" your paper. Instead, know your topic well enough to comment on it intelligently and informatively with only occasional references to your notes.
10. Consider distributing an outline of your presentation so your audience can follow along and take notes.
11. Pace yourself—do not speak too quickly or too slowly.
12. Make eye contact with your listeners.
13. Pause occasionally for questions.
14. When appropriate and helpful, use visual aids and handouts.
15. Save time at the end for questions.

FIGURE 7.2   Possible Teaching Techniques

Goal	Possible Approach
To convey factual information	Lecturing
	Using overheads and handouts
To motivate learning	Group work
	Multimedia
To practice particular writing skills	Group work
	In-class writing
	Exercises on overheads
To teach critical reading	Critique sample texts on overhead
	Group work and reports
To encourage collaborative learning	Group work
	Group reports using overheads
To offer peer response to student writing	Group work/peer editing
To model desired skills	Lectures
	Writing on the overhead
To test learning	In-class writing
	Oral reports
To teach critical thinking	Group work
	Debates
	Multimedia

CHAPTER 8

Technology, Teaching, and Learning

INTRODUCTION

Technology is changing the way teachers teach and students learn. Increasingly, teachers communicate with students through e-mail messages, post course material on Web sites, hold class in computer labs, and conduct research on the Internet. As a TA, you have to be technology-savvy. Though you may not be an expert in all of these new technologies, during your years as a graduate teaching assistant you will probably learn how to use most of them. This chapter will outline some of the ways technology can help you teach your classes, communicate with your students, and complete your degree work.

E-MAIL

Moving conversations beyond the classroom and office, e-mail has changed how teachers communicate with their students. Here are just a few of the tasks teachers routinely accomplish through e-mail messages.

1. Answering their students' questions.

E-mail makes it easy for students to ask you questions outside of class. Any time of day, they can send you questions on any topic, ask you to respond to their work, or check on their progress in the course. Being able to communicate this way is especially valuable to students who tend to be quiet in class, who feel insecure about asking questions in front of others, or who cannot meet with you during your regular office hours.

2. Distributing announcements or reminders.

Sending an e-mail message is one of the most effective ways for you to reach your students with important announcements. For example, if you need to change a homework assignment, alter your office hours, or cancel a class, e-mail messages can help ensure that all of your students get the word. However, do not rely on e-mail messages alone to communicate important information to students. Changes in course syllabi, assignments, or policies should be placed in writing and distributed to students in class as well, not just announced via e-mail.

3. Spurring class discussions.

As you prepare to discuss material in class, send your students an e-mail message listing one or two questions you'd like to address. Receiving the questions before a class meets allows your students the opportunity to think through their responses, often making discussions more productive. You might even vary the questions you send, asking some students to consider an issue from one perspective and other students to consider it from an alternative point of view. When the class meets, you can encourage debate by having the students present their opposing conclusions.

4. Forming ever wider communities of learners.

As students e-mail you and each other, they form a growing community of learners who share information, ideas, and opinions. If it suits your course goals, expand this community by encouraging your students to e-mail students in other sections of your course, students taking other classes, even students enrolled at other institutions. These e-mail exchanges can help your students form connections with a variety of people across and beyond your institution.

5. Checking on a student's well-being.

Occasionally you might want to e-mail students who are struggling in your course. This is especially true if particular students stop attending class and you have no other way to contact them. A brief e-mail message can let the students know that you have noticed and are concerned about their absence. Sending and receiving e-mail messages greatly increases the opportunity you have to correspond with students who need special encouragement or support.

E-mail has also changed how graduate students communicate with their professors and other members of the profession. Many of your teachers will communicate with you through e-mail messages and will expect you to correspond with them and others in class the same way.

As a graduate student, you may also find listservs playing an important role in your education. Listservs are essentially distribution lists that allow members to correspond with one another. Most academic listservs focus on a particular area of study, and membership is open to anyone interested in the topic. Listservs give you access to the most current discussions in a field. One word of warning though—some listservs are very active. As a subscriber, you may start receiving dozens of e-mail messages every day. If reading and responding to these messages every day is going to distract you from your work, consider subscribing in digest form so you get all the messages for the week delivered at once, perhaps on the weekend, when you have more time to read them. Figure 8.1 lists some of the listservs you might want to join as a TA.

THREADED DISCUSSIONS

Initially, you may need help setting up threaded discussions on your campus computer system, but once you learn how to design them, you may find them a valuable teaching tool. Threaded discussions allow participants to talk about a topic on-line—responding to a prompt you provide, responding to each other's comments, raising questions, offering answers, asking for clarifications, stating and defending positions. Threaded discussions encourage students to think through issues, reflect on what others have to say, and join public debates.

In establishing a threaded discussion for a class, you have several options. First, consider whether you want the discussion to be open or directed. With open discussions, students raise and comment on any topic they like. Directed discussions are more focused. The teacher typically asks the students to respond to a specific question, topic, or text.

Second, decide when you want your students to join the discussion: before you cover the relevant material in class, after you cover it, or both. For example, suppose you plan to discuss a reading from your textbook on a Monday. Ask your students to read the material and discuss it on-line over the weekend before they come to class. However, if you think the material is particularly difficult, you might prefer to talk about it in class before asking your students to discuss it on their own.

Third, decide who will participate in the threaded discussion. Will everyone in class respond to the same prompt? If you teach multiple sections of a course, would you prefer to set up a separate discussion for each group of students? Would you like the students in different sections of your course to talk only with each other as they consider the topic or with students outside your class?

Finally, decide on your role in the discussion. Will you join in or remain silent? Teachers maintain different positions on this question. Some believe their presence disrupts the discussion: students too willingly defer to the teacher's point of view rather than debate the topic among themselves. Other teachers like to join the discussion and encourage students to question their comments the same way they question their peers' responses.

FIGURE 8.1   A Sampling of Listservs

College Talk
> College Talk
> www.listmgr

Creative Writing Pedagogy
> CREWRT-L
> listerv@mizzou1.missouri.edu

Creative Writing and Composition Pedagogy
> CWOMP
> listmgr@lists.ncte.org

English Education
> NCTE-EE
> listmgr@lists.ncte.org

English Education Research and Pedagogical Methods
> CEE-Methods
> listmgr@lists.ncte.org

Graduate Study in English
> GradTalk
> listmgr@lists.ncte.org

History of Rhetoric
> H-RHETOR
> listserv@uicvm.uic.edu

Labor Practices in Education
> Labor
> listmgr@lists.ncte.org

Language and Learning Across the Curriculum
> LALAC-L
> http://www.sfasu.edu/lalac/#email

Online Writing Center Consortium
> OWCC
> http://owcc.colostate.edu/elist.cfm

RhetNet Listserv
> RHETNT-L
> listerv@mizzou1.missouri.edu

Service Learning
> Service-Learning
> listmgr@lists.ncte.org

Though threaded discussions can facilitate student learning, there are a few drawbacks to using them. First, they take time to set up and to maintain, especially if you are establishing one for the first time. Second, technology breaks down: like any other computer application, threaded discussions can crash, a frustrating experience for you and your students. Third, students sometimes resist joining threaded discussions. Some students may not have ready access to a computer, making it difficult to join the discussion, while others may resent having to devote time to any course activity outside of class. You can mitigate some of these concerns, however, if you carefully explain the purpose of threaded discussions, make the work students do on-line an important part of your course, and offer students the training they need to participate actively in the discussions.

WEB SITES

Every year, more and more teachers are creating course Web sites that include important information and resources. Many also require their students to build Web sites that focus on certain aspects of the course. Below are some suggestions for making teacher- and student-designed Web sites an important part of the writing and literature classes you teach.

Course Web Sites

If you do not know how to design a Web page, in the coming years you will likely learn. Many instructors today find their course Web sites as indispensable as their textbooks and syllabi. Moreover, programs such as Front Page and Dreamweaver have made it relatively easy to design functional, attractive Web pages. Many campus computing and teaching centers also help teachers design and launch course Web pages. With practice and guidance, you should have little trouble building a site of your own.

Why Build a Course Web Site?

Teachers sometimes wonder why they need a course Web site. After all, much of the material a Web site contains can be distributed to students in other ways—by handing out material in class, sending students e-mail messages, or placing course texts on reserve at the campus library. However, a course Web site offers you and your students some real advantages. First, well-designed Web sites offer your students ready access to important course information. While students may lose or misplace material you distribute in class, they can always find a copy on your Web site. Second, having a Web site allows you to update information quickly. For example, if you need to change an assigned reading or rearrange dates for a set of oral reports, you can post a notice on your Web site. Third, with a course Web page, your students can access information when they need it. The material is available on-line twenty-four hours a day. As they compose their papers, students can turn to the Web site for information when it will be of most use to them. Finally, Web sites enable students and teachers to communicate with each other more effectively. With interactive Web sites, students can send messages to their teachers or peers and share their work with others.

What are the *disadvantages* of building a course Web site? For one thing, it takes time and some expertise. If you do not know how to use a Web-building program, you need to learn. Some universities hire students or staff to build Web sites for faculty, but you need to know how to do it yourself if you hope to keep your site up to date. Also, some teachers believe Web sites establish needless barriers between instructors and their students: they fear that instead of turning to their teachers for help, students will turn to their computers, depersonalizing education in truly harmful ways. As you integrate Web technology into your curriculum, you need to decide whether this fear is valid, whether Web technology decreases the personal interaction you have with your students. If you think it does, you may need to reconsider the role Web sites play in your course.

What Does a Course Web Site Contain?

The content of a course Web site will change from class to class; however, the types of material you include on these sites will remain fairly consistent.

1. Course Material

Include on your site the basic course information you distribute to your students in class. Including it on your Web site can save you from late night telephone calls or e-mail messages from panicked students who realize they have misplaced the paperwork you distributed in class. Be sure your Web site includes:

- the class syllabus
- the list of course policies
- the class reading list
- all assignment sheets for the class
- all grading rubrics for the class
- all instructional material you distribute in class
- all in-class exercises and worksheets

Placing this material on your Web site makes it available to your students any time they need it.

2. Course Readings

If you have your students read, discuss, or write about material not contained in your course textbooks, post it on your Web site. Your students can then read the material on-line or print out a copy of their own. Be careful about copyright laws, however. Check with your teaching supervisor or a college librarian before you post copyrighted material. Either should be able to get you a copy of the regulations you need to follow and any permission forms you need to complete.

3. Instructional Material

As students work on a particular writing project, most teachers develop supplemental instructional material—advice on choosing a topic, paradigms to follow when organizing the paper, guidelines on documentation, lists of required elements for the final draft, and so on. Posting this material on your Web site enables students to access it when they need it most. Many teachers also like to post instructional material concerning other aspects of their course, such as paragraph development, sentence variety, word choice, grammar, voice, and style.

4. Supplemental Course Material

Post supplemental material that might interest your students. For example, students at the institution where I teach study Mary Shelley's *Frankenstein* in their introductory writing classes as part of an integrated humanities program. English instructors teaching this course have included on their Web sites supplemental material touching on a wide range of relevant topics, including Mary Shelley's life, the Romantic movement, nineteenth-century medicine, the book of Genesis, Promethean myths, film versions of the novel, alchemy, *Paradise Lost*, and gothic art and architecture. The teachers believe this supplemental material helps their students better understand the novel.

5. Sample Papers

One of the most effective ways to teach students how to write any type of paper is to offer them model essays. These sample papers help students understand how their final products should look and sound. If you choose to post a student's paper on your Web site, first secure that student's written permission.

6. Work in Progress

Some instructors like to reserve a spot on their Web sites for work in progress—in effect creating a space for on-line peer editing. Here's how it typically works. A student posts a rough draft of her essay on the Web site. Members of her peer edit group (or every student in class, depending on how you want to structure the assignment) access the draft and offer commentary. In most cases, students are able to read and respond to the rough draft and the comments other students have offered. After the deadline for response has passed, the student removes the rough draft from the site and downloads all of the commentary. Using the Web site in this way allows students to critique their peers' writing outside of class, when they can devote as much time to the task as they need.

7. Links

One of the greatest advantages of having a course Web site is the ability to include links to a vast range of Internet resources. You can provide links to on-line writing labs, additional readings, sample papers—any sites you think will help or interest your students.

What Are the Qualities of an Effective Web Page?

You will find a range of opinion on how to design an effective Web site. However, most experts agree that effective sites exhibit the following qualities:

1. Web sites should be well organized. In fact, you may spend more time deciding how to organize your site than you spend deciding what to put on it. Planning your site takes attention and care—organize the site in a way that helps students find the information they need quickly and efficiently.

2. Web pages should be easy to navigate. Students should be able to get to the information they need with the fewest clicks possible and be able to get back to the home page easily.

3. Web sites should be comprehensive. Here your students can help. As they use the site, solicit their response. What are they finding helpful? What needs to be changed? What needs to be added? What information, resources, or links would improve the site?

4. Web sites should be concise. Understandably, course Web sites tend to be text heavy—more writing than graphics. Even so, think graphically as you design your site. How can you condense the material on your site? How can you combine links on a page so students do not have to venture deeper and deeper into your site to find the material they need? Make your site as useful, helpful, and user-friendly as you can.

Student Web Sites

Increasingly, teachers are asking students to develop course-related Web sites of their own. In addition to writing essays and taking tests in the class, students (often working in groups) construct course-related Web sites that combine text, graphics, and links. Though there is tremendous variety in the way teachers design these assignments, students typically have to complete the following tasks:

1. Choose a topic

Instructors usually require students to build a Web site around a topic that grows out of a significant course theme or text. For example, teachers interested in building an assignment around *Frankenstein* could ask students to design a Web site offering information on Mary Shelley, nineteenth-century medicine, or alchemy. Some teachers like students to develop appropriate topics on their own, while others like students to choose from a list of topics they distribute in class.

2. Research that topic

Once they have a topic, students have to conduct their research. Unlike doing research for a traditional term paper, though, conducting research for a Web site includes locating the most appropriate texts, graphics, and links.

3. Design and launch the site

As they sift through all the material they gather, students must decide how to format the information: what text to include, which graphics to incorporate, and which links to provide. In addition, they have to decide what to document, how to document it, and how to include a reference list. Finally, they must avoid problems with copyright violation and plagiarism—both tricky issues for anyone building a Web site.

Teachers who ask students to build course Web sites often remark on their students' enthusiasm for the projects and argue that in completing the work, students develop the skills they need to succeed in an increasingly technological academy and society. Detractors, however, question whether these assignments suit the educational needs and learning style of every student, whether individual students learn particular skills if they complete the project as part of a group, and whether the skills students learn while developing Web sites help them write more traditional research papers. These teachers may decide not to have their students build Web pages or may have them write traditional research papers in the course as well.

THE INTERNET

The Internet offers an astonishing variety of resources of interest to TAs related to teaching writing and literature, graduate study, professional development. While a comprehensive review of these resources is beyond the scope of this chapter, below you will find a brief overview of the kinds of material and information the Internet places at your disposal. The best advice? Log on and explore. Here are some starting points.

On-line Writing Labs

Several writing programs, writing centers, and English departments maintain on-line writing labs (OWLs). Most of these sites offer advice on writing academic essays, avoiding common writing problems, conducting research, and employing various documentation formats. Many contain links to other OWLs or to various writing resources, such as on-line encyclopedias and dictionaries. Some even provide sample writing exercises and other course material teachers at that institution have found helpful. In the past, many OWLs allowed anyone logging on to correspond with one of the school's writing tutors. However, today most OWLs limit this service to students attending the host institution. Figure 8.2 lists some of the best OWLs currently available.

Reference Sites

As you write a paper, do you ever need quick access to an encyclopedia, dictionary, atlas, or some other reference work? Increasingly these resources are available on the Internet. Sharing particularly helpful sites with your students is a good idea—the information these sites provide can help your students complete

FIGURE 8.2   OWLs

Colorado State University
   http://writing.colostate.edu/

Dakota State University
   http://www.departments.dsu.edu/owl/

Ferris State University
   http://www.ferris.edu/htmls/academics/departments/writingcenter/
      homepage.htm

George Mason University
   http://writingcenter.gmu.edu/

University of Illinois at Chicago
   http://www.uic.edu/depts/engl/writing/

University of Maine
   http://www.ume.maine.edu/~wcenter/

University of Minnesota
   http://www.owc.umn.edu

University of Missouri
   http://www.missouri.edu/~writery

Purdue University
   http://owl.english.purdue.edu

St. Cloud State University
   http://leo.stcloudstate/edu

Temple University
   http://www.temple.edu/writingctr/cWeb500.htm

Virginia Tech
   http://www.english.ut.edu/%7Eowl.html

Weber State University
   http://catsis.Weber.edu/writingcenter/

University of Wisconsin
   http://www.wisc.edu/writing

their research projects and improve their papers. Be sure, though, to teach your students how to document material drawn from on-line sources. Documenting this material can be complicated, and students often need a great deal of guidance and practice. Figure 8.3 lists some helpful reference sites.

FIGURE 8.3   Reference Sites

Almanacs

Fast Facts
 http://gwu.edu/~gprice/handbook.htm

Global Statistics
 http://www.xist.org

Information Please Almanac
 http://www.infoplease.com/

Dictionaries

The American Heritage Dictionary of the English Language, 4th ed.
 http://bartleby.com/61/

Cambridge Dictionary of American English
 http://cup.cam.ac.uk/esl/dictionary

Dictionary.com
 http://www.dictionary.com/

Merriam-Webster's Collegiate Dictionary
 http://www.m-w.com/netdict.htm

Encyclopedias

Britannica Online
 http://www.britannica.com/

The Columbia Encyclopedia: 6th Edition
 http://www.bartleby.com/65/

Microsoft Encarta Concise Encyclopedia
 http://encarta.msn.com/

Literary Criticism

Cambridge History of English and American Literature
 http://www.bartleby.com/cambridge

The New York Times Book Review
 http://www.nytimes.com/books/

Online Literary Criticism Collection
 http://www.ipl.org/ref/litcrit/

Undergraduate Guide to Critical Theory
 http://omni.cc.purdue.edu/~felluga/theory.html

Writing

Citing Electronic Resources
   http://www.ipl.org/ref.QIE/FARQ/netciteFARQ.html

English Grammar FAQ
   http://www-personal.umich.edu/~jlawler/aue.html

Writer's Handbook
   http://www.wisc.edu/writing/Handbook/handbook.html

Writers' Workshop Online Writing Guide
   http://www.english.uiuc.edu/cws/wworkshop/index.htm

FIGURE 8.4   Style Manual Sites

American Psychological Association (APA)
   http://www.apa.org

Chicago Manual of Style (CMS)
   http://www.press.uchicago.edu

Columbia Guide to Online Style (CGOS)
   http://www.columbia.edu/cu/cup/cgus/idx _ basic.html

Council of Biology Editors (CBE)
   http://cbe.sdsc.edu/

Modern Language Association (MLA)
   http://www.mla.org

Style Manuals

College students are often confused by the wide array of documentation styles they encounter in courses across the curriculum. "Why," they often ask, "can't you just all agree to use MLA or APA?" Until faculty in every department agree on one documentation style—which does not seem likely to occur—students will continue to struggle with this aspect of academic writing. Some help, though, is available on-line. Most of the major style manuals maintain Web sites where students can find advice and sample entries. Figure 8.4 lists the sites of several commonly employed documentation style manuals.

Paper Mills and Plagiarism Detection Sites

Several commercial companies will sell students papers on almost any topic. All a student has to do is log onto the company's Web site, enter a credit card number, and order a paper. As a teacher, you need to know these sites exist, and you should talk about them in class as well. Some may suggest that talking about paper mills in class will only make students more likely to use them. However, these students will learn about the sites quickly enough whether you talk about them or not, and your students need to understand that you know these sites exist.

You should also tell your students about the on-line answer to paper mills—on-line plagiarism detection sites. These sites allow teachers to send in papers they think may have been purchased from a paper mill. The service checks the papers against essays that exist on the Internet and lets the teacher know if matches turn up. Many academic libraries now subscribe to these services; check with your librarian to see if your library does. Though these searches are not completely reliable, they can help you detect many instances of plagiarism. You can also check to see if a paper has been purchased from a paper mill by using a search engine such as Google. All you need to do is to type a suspicious passage in the dialog box, click on Search, and the engine will look for matches on the Internet. If you choose this method of plagiarism detection, run your search on several engines to improve your coverage of the Internet. (For advice on helping students avoid problems with plagiarism, see Chapter 9.)

Figure 8.5 lists some of the commonly employed paper mills and several plagiarism detection services.

Primary Text Sites

Several Internet sites offer full texts of literary works. Some also provide helpful featues like concordances, biographical sketches of the author, and links to relevant criticism. Figure 8.6 lists some of the more commonly employed primary text sites.

Text-, Author-, Genre-, and Period-Specific Sites

Other literary Internet sites focus on specific authors, texts, genres, and literary periods. For example, if your students are reading David Mamet's *American Buffalo*, they will likely find the play discussed on sites devoted to David Mamet, *American Buffalo*, drama, and contemporary American literature. To conduct a comprehensive Internet search on the play, they would have to investigate all of these sites. Part of your job is teaching your students how to employ multiple searches, varying the terms they use.

Course Material

When you teach a course, chances are someone has already taught the same or a similar course. And the chances are getting better every day that the

FIGURE 8.5   Paper Mills and Plagiarism Detection Sites

<u>Paper Mills</u>

Academic Papers.com
   http://www.academicpapers.com/index.asp

College Term Papers.com
   http://www.collegetermpapers.com/

Evil House of Cheat
   http://www.cheathouse.com

Research Papers.net
   http://www.researchpapers.net

Research Papers Online
   http://www.ezwrite.com/

School Sucks
   http://www.schoolsucks.com/

<u>Plagiarism Detection Sites</u>

Plagi Serve
   http://www.plagiserve.com

Plagiarism.com
   http://www.plagiarism.com

Turnitin
   http://www.turnitin.com

course material that person developed is available on-line. However, finding this material can prove difficult because it may not be catalogued or collected in one place. The best strategy for finding the material may be to conduct a search of the course title. You can also ask for course material on a relevant listserve. Most faculty are willing to share.

Faculty Development Sites

As a TA, you may not be too concerned about faculty development, but as I argue in Chapter 12, you probably should be. The information and resources offered on faculty development Web sites can help you grow as a teacher, researcher, and member of the academic community. They typically include material on teaching and research, assessment, publication, student development, and professional growth. Figure 8.7 lists some of the sites you might consult.

FIGURE 8.6   Primary Text Sites

Alex: A Catalogue of Electronic Texts on the Internet
   http://sunsite.berkeley.edu/alex/

Bartleby.com
   http://www.bartleby.com/

Biblomania
   http://www.bibliomania.com

The English Server Fiction Collection
   http://english-www.hss.cmu.edu/fiction/

Internet Classics Archive
   http://classics.mit.edu

On-line Books Page
   http://on-linebooks.library.upenn.edu/

Project Gutenberg
   http://promo.net/pg/

Graduate Program Descriptions

You would be hard pressed to find a graduate program in this country that did not have a Web site. Using any search engine, you can log onto these Web pages and gather information on any graduate program that interests you. Accessing these sites is especially helpful when choosing a graduate program to attend or comparing program requirements at institutions across the country. These sites typically include information on the degrees the school offers, financial assistance, teaching and research assistantships, and the graduate faculty.

On-Line Journals

The number of academic journals available on-line is growing yearly. Some of these journals are published only on-line, while others are also available in print. Sites such as AcademicWriting (⟨http://aw.colostate.edu/⟩) provide links to many of these resources. You can also find them by employing on-line search engines such as the CCCC Bibliography of Composition and Rhetoric (⟨http://www.ibiblio.org/ccc⟩) or CompPile (⟨http://comppile.tamucc.edu/⟩). Figure 8.8 lists some of these on-line journals.

COMPUTER CLASSROOMS

Technology is also changing where teachers teach writing and literature classes today. These courses are moving out of traditional classrooms into computer labs, computer classrooms, and cyberspace. At some point in grad-

FIGURE 8.7   Professional Development Sites

AAHE: The American Association for Higher Education
http://www.aahe.org

Center for Excellence in Learning and Teaching (Pennsylvania State University)
http://www.psu.edu/celt/

Center for Teaching (University of Iowa)
http://www.uiowa.edu/~centeach/

Center for Teaching Effectiveness (University of Texas)
http://www.utexas.edu/academic/cte

Center for Teaching Excellence (Kansas University)
http://falcon.cc.ku.edu/~cte/

Center for Teaching Excellence (University of Maryland)
http://www.inform.umd/edu/EdRes/FacRes/CTE/

POD: Professional and Organizational Development Network in Higher Education
http://lamar.colostate.edu/~ckfgill/

Searle Center for Teaching Excellence
http://president.scfte.northwestern.edu

Society for Teaching and Learning in Higher Education
http://www.tss.voguelph.ca/stlhe

---

uate school, you will likely have the opportunity to teach a class in a computer lab or computer classroom. Take advantage of these opportunities when they come your way; the experience will be invaluable.

Teaching in a computer lab or classroom for the first time can challenge your skills as an instructor. Although it is possible to teach classes in these settings as if you were still in a traditional classroom, learn how to take advantage of the available technology. Once you know you will teach in a computer lab or computer classroom, taking the following steps will help you prepare:

1. Talk to Experienced Instructors.
Before you teach in a computer lab or classroom for the first time, talk to teachers who have taught in a similar setting. Find out how teaching in the computer classroom affected their course content and pedagogy. Ask to look at their paper assignments and exercises. Talk to them about any problems they encountered. Experienced instructors will prove to be one of your best sources of information as you prepare to teach in a computer classroom for the first time.

2. Study the Literature.
The number of books, journal articles, and conference papers that address teaching in a computer lab or classroom is growing rapidly each year. Some

FIGURE 8.8   On-line Journals

BWe: Basic Writing e-Journal
http://www.asu.edu/clas/english/composition/cbw/journal 1.htm

Computers and Composition
http://www.cwrl.utexas.edu/~ccjrnl/

Inventio: Creative Thinking about Learning and Teaching
http://www.doiiit.gmu.edu/inventio/

Journal of Advanced Composition Online
http://jac.gsu.edu/

Journal of Critical Pedagogy
http://www.wmc.edu/academics/library/pub/jcp/jcp.html

Kairos: A Journal for Teaching of Writing in Webbed Environments
http://english.ttu.edu/kairos

PRE/TEXT: Electra(Lite)
http://www.utdallas.edu/pretext/index1a.html

Technical Communication Quarterly
http://english.ttu.edu/attwtest/ATTWpubsTCQ.asp

The Writing Instructor
http://flansburgh.english.purdue.edu/twi/

---

of this work is theoretical (how technology is changing our understanding of what it means to teach and to learn), some is practical (how to develop an effective pedagogy in these settings), and some is testimonial (how various instructors responded to teaching in computerized classrooms or labs). Studying this material before you teach in a computer classroom for the first time can be helpful. You can gain a better understanding of what works and does not work in these classrooms, how to use the available technology to its best advantage, how your students are likely to respond to your instruction, and how you might address the problems that are likely to occur. The "Additional Readings" section included at the end of this chapter lists some resources to consult.

3. Visit the Classroom.

Before you teach in a computer lab or classroom for the first time, visit the room with someone who knows how all the equipment works. During your visit, try to run all the equipment you will use when you teach. Also, be sure you know how to turn on and off the lights in the room, raise and lower screens, and run the software programs your students will use in class. The first day of class is not the time to realize that all the computers in the room are equipped with Microsoft Word and you know how to use only WordPerfect.

4. Find out Who to Call for Help.

Sometimes your students will know more about the hardware and software than you do, and you can ask them for assistance. But do not count on this being the case. Most computer classrooms and labs are staffed by people who know how to work all the equipment, run all the programs, and solve common problems. Before you begin to teach in that classroom or lab, be sure you know who to call for expert assistance. Have a telephone number or e-mail address handy when you teach. If the machines or programs begin to crash in the middle of class, you need to know who can help you.

CONCLUSION

Advances in technology have changed and will continue to change the way you teach and complete your degree work. Staying current with technology requires the ability and willingness to learn and to adapt. In a rapidly changing profession, you need to read widely in the field, welcome the opportunity to work with and master emerging technologies, develop creative classroom applications of technology, work with students in a range of new environments, and foster a reflective attitude toward your work. Technology in and of itself is neither good nor bad. The question you need to ask is this: how can advances in technology help me become a more effective teacher and scholar?

ADDITIONAL READINGS

Collins, James L., and Elizabeth A. Sommers, ed. *Writing On-Line: Using Computers in the Teaching of Writing*. Upper Montclair, NJ: Boyton/Cook, 1895.

DeWitt, Scott Lloyd, and Kip Strasma, ed. *Contexts, Intertexts, and Hypertexts*. Cresskill, NJ: Hampton Press, 1999.

Halpern, Jeanne W., and Sarah Liggett. *Computers & Composing: How the New Technologies Are Changing Writing*. Carbondale, IL: Southern Illinois University Press, 1984.

Handa, Carolyn, ed. *Computers and Community: Teaching Composition in the Twenty-First Century*. Portsmouth, NH: Boyton/Cook, 1990.

Harrington, Susanmarie, Rebecca Rickly, and Michael Day, ed. *The Online Writing Classroom*. Cresskill, NJ: Hampton P, 2000.

Hawisher, Gail E., and Cynthia L. Selfe, ed. *Critical Perspectives on Computers and Composition Instruction*. New York: Teachers College Press, 1989.

———. *Evolving Perspectives on Computers and Composition Studies: Questions for the 1990s*. Urbana, IL: NCTE, 1991.

Hawisher, Gail E., and Paul LeBlanc, ed. *Reimagining Computers and Composition: Teaching and Research in the Virtual Age*. Portsmouth, NH: Boyton/Cook, 1992.

Hawisher, Gail E., Paul LeBlanc, Charles Moran, and Cynthia L. Self. *Computers and the Teaching of Writing in American Higher Education: 1979–1994: A History.* Norwood, NJ: Ablex, 1996.

Holdstein, Deborah H., and Cynthia L. Selfe, ed. *Computers and Writing: Theory, Research, Practice.* New York: MLA, 1990.

Inman, James A., and Donna N. Sewell, ed. *Taking Flight with OWLs: Examining Electronic Writing Center Work.* Mahwah, NJ: Lawrence Erlbaum, 2000.

Myers, Linda, ed.. *Approaches to Computer Writing Classrooms.* Albany: State University of New York Press, 1993.

Selfe, Cynthia L. *Creating a Computer-Supported Writing Facility: A Blueprint for Action.* Houghton, MI: Michigan Technological University Press, 1989.

Williams, Noel, and Patrik Holt. *Computers and Writing: Models and Tools.* Norwood, NJ: Ablex, 1989.

CHAPTER 9

Troubleshooting in the Classroom

INTRODUCTION

Occasionally you will have to deal with problematic students who talk out of turn in class, plagiarize their work, or openly question your authority. As a result of their lack of experience and confidence, many new TAs have a hard time deciding how to respond to these students. Caught off guard, they tend to ignore the situation or react defensively, missing an opportunity to address and solve the problem quickly. The best way to cope with these situations is to think about them ahead of time and prepare appropriate responses.

This chapter discusses different ways to address some of the problems TAs face in introductory-level classes. I will emphasize one point repeatedly: never feel like you have to solve problems on your own. Wherever you teach, there are faculty members who will help—seek them out.

STUDENTS WHO DISRUPT CLASS

You may have students who do not know how to be quiet in class. Although teachers often want their students to participate in class, other times they want students to be quiet and listen. Some students have a hard time learning this lesson, interrupting others and monopolizing discussions by talking out of turn. Unfortunately, even one student like this can ruin a class. His or her actions make it difficult to teach the class and discourage other students from speaking up appropriately. You need to address disruptive students promptly and firmly.

Sometimes students talk with classmates while you are speaking. To stop this behavior, stop talking and stare at the disruptive students until they fall silent, walk toward the disruptive students while you speak until you get their attention, or confront them directly, asking them to be quiet. Sometimes you will have to quiet down every student in class. This situation often occurs at the beginning of class or when the students are working in small groups and you have to call everyone back to order. Get their attention by using a loud, firm voice or begin to write something on the blackboard. As a rule, students will stop talking and start to copy *anything* you place on the board.

If a particular student just will not be quiet in class, try talking to him individually outside of class. Ask the student to stay a moment after the others have left, and talk to him in the empty classroom or in your office. If the student does not have time to talk, set up an appointment. When you talk to students who behave this way, be straightforward. Tell them that you need to discuss their classroom behavior, describe the behavior that you think is disruptive, offer examples of when they have engaged in this behavior, explain why such behavior is unacceptable, and ask for their response. Listen respectfully to their explanations or apologies, then let them know that their disruptive behavior has to stop. If they continue to be disruptive in class, see your supervisor for advice. It may be that an administrator needs to talk to the students or even transfer them out of your class.

Most people want to avoid confrontations. Consequently, they often ignore problems, thinking they will solve themselves. This is how TAs often respond to disruptive students—they think that if they just ignore the situation, it will stop. Usually, though, this is the wrong approach to take. Truly disruptive students will often escalate their behavior until they get a response. They will try to draw other students to their "side," silence anyone who challenges them, and make themselves the center of attention in the classroom. Address the problem quickly so it does not build. Remain calm and judicious. You know such behavior is not acceptable in your class, so operate from that position—let these students know that they must change the way they act.

STUDENTS WHO ARE SILENT IN CLASS

Sometimes the opposite problem occurs—you run into a group of students who never seem willing to speak up in class. No matter what you try, the students just do not care to participate. They would rather sit passively and take notes while you talk. There are times, of course, when this is just what you want, but there are other times when you want your students to discuss a reading, ask questions about an assignment, or just let you know if they are satisfied with the course. Unresponsive students are a problem in these situations, but there are a few things you can do to encourage more class participation.

First, consider the way you respond to your students in class. Sometimes the way teachers interact with students can discourage them from speaking up. For example, a few years ago I had a colleague ask me for help. He said he was having a hard time getting his students to participate in his literature class, and he was tired of lecturing. He asked me to come watch his class and offer advice. I sat in the back of the room the next time the class met and quickly found out why this teacher's students were so quiet. The professor asked a question about the novel the students were reading, and one student offered an answer. The professor's response was so negative and sarcastic that the student's face turned red and he remained silent the rest of the class. Another student tried to answer a follow-up question and received similar treatment. The rest of the professor's questions went unanswered, and the professor grew obviously impatient at the long silences in class. He finally gave up, threw me a "see what I mean" glance, and lectured the rest of the period. I tried to figure out how to tell this professor he needed to change the way he spoke to his students if he expected them to participate in class.

Second, examine your own attitudes and behavior. Some teachers can assume a confrontational relationship with their students and succeed, but not many. Students are more likely to take part in classes where the teacher develops an atmosphere of trust and respect. If students feel their teacher will take their comments seriously and will not intimidate or ridicule them, they are much more likely to participate actively in class. Consider these points: do you value your students' opinions? Do you listen carefully and respectfully to what they have to say? Do you respond in a way that encourages students to elaborate on their views? Do you urge others to join in?

Third, examine whether your students truly have the opportunity to talk in your class. When teaching, how do you encourage participation? What activities do you think will get students talking? Do you just expect it to happen spontaneously? If you do, you will likely be disappointed. Teachers who want their students to take part in class build into their course opportunities for that to happen; several techniques are described below.

1. Ask the right kinds of questions.
During class discussions, asking factual questions such as, "How does the author open his essay?" will generate less response than asking speculative questions such as, "The author opens her essay with a quotation. Why does she do this? Do you think it works?" Ask questions that require your students to think and to solve problems, that cannot be easily answered. Posing the right kinds of questions and responding positively to your students' responses can greatly improve class participation.

2. Link writing and speaking activities.

Writing something first gives students a chance to think about the topic and articulate their opinions, increasing the likelihood that they will speak up in class. For example, ask your students to write briefly about a topic before they discuss it. Ask them to answer a question you write on the board, respond to a quotation from a text, or reflect on their own knowledge and experience. If no one responds when you open the discussion, ask a few students to read aloud what they wrote and see if the other students agree or disagree. Before you or your students know it, the discussion will be going strong.

3. Employ collaborative learning techniques.

Divide your students into small groups to work on projects before reporting to the class as a whole. Sometimes students who are reluctant to speak up in front of the entire class will talk more freely in a small group of students (see Chapter 7 for tips on forming and supervising group work in class). As students converse in their groups, circulate and encourage everyone to join in. Try then to transfer the energy and conversation of the small groups to the entire class by having each group summarize its work. Well-planned group activities can result in debates in which different groups have to assume and defend different positions on an issue or different interpretations of material. Small group work establishes a new dynamic in the classroom that often facilitates participation, especially among shy students.

4. Require oral reports.

Assign individual students to give brief, five- to ten- minute reports on any topic related to the class or ask groups of students to give longer reports (see Chapter 7 for more tips on how to incorporate group reports in a writing class). To promote discussion, ask certain students to serve as respondents for each oral report, summarizing and critiquing what they heard. A series of oral reports and responses followed by class discussions can involve most students.

5. Call on unresponsive students by name.

Calling on students forces their participation. Understand, though, that because many students do not like being called on, this strategy can spur resentment if handled poorly. If a student clearly has no response, do not engage in prolonged public embarrassment. Move on to another student. If this happens frequently with the same student, you may want to speak to him or her outside of class. The student may be having problems with the course.

6. Arrive at your class early.

Engage in informal conversation with a few students before class. Ask them about their weekend plans, their other classes, their favorite television show, anything. When the class starts, just keep the conversation going for a little while. During class, if no one is responding to your questions or prompts, return to those students. Ask them what they think. Continue the discussion by speaking directly to others nearby, eventually pulling more and more students into the conversation.

7. Schedule brief conferences.

If a class remains unresponsive despite your best efforts, schedule a five-to ten-minute conference with each student. During each conference, share your observations about the course and your desire to have everyone participate more fully. Ask your students what would make them feel more comfortable in class and what topics they would like to discuss. These conferences can work wonders and dramatically increase your students' participation in class.

STUDENTS WHO CHALLENGE YOU IN CLASS

Because you are a TA, students may be more willing to question your expertise, fairness, or competence than they would be to question the knowledge and authority of a professor. How you respond depends largely on the nature of the challenge. For example, sometimes it is hard to distinguish between curiosity and confrontation. How would you interpret a student asking, "How old are you anyway?" A TA I worked with thought this question was a challenge to her authority and answered, "Old enough to teach you." The student did not ask again. Other TAs who heard this story thought the question was innocent—the student was being curious, not confrontational.

Often challenges are nonverbal. Students who question your competence may sigh or moan when you give assignments, roll their eyes, glance knowingly at their peers, shake their heads, fall asleep at their desks, skip class, or engage in other types of disruptive behavior in class. I have seen many TAs react to such disrespectful behavior by "getting tough," adopting the position that students will respect their authority more if they start to quiz them every day, grade their papers more harshly, or adopt a sterner classroom persona. Sometimes these responses can help, but not usually. Instead, students tend to respect teachers who (1) use class time wisely, (2) offer valuable instruction, and (3) are organized and fair. If you feel that your students misbehave in class because they do not respect your authority, examine your teaching methods first and the way you interact with your students. Making adjustments along these lines may get you better results than becoming a "bad cop" teacher.

If a student questions your expertise, and you feel that you need to respond, be honest about your qualifications to teach. Let the student know about your educational background, your experience as a writer and teacher, the selection process the department used to choose TAs, the training procedures you went through, the relevant course work you have taken, or the degree work you have completed. As always, have these conversations with students *outside* of class, never in class.

You may find challenges to your qualifications distressing because of your own insecurities. Many new TAs question their own readiness to teach—they do not yet feel like "real" teachers themselves. However, these feelings usually dissipate during the TA's first semester of teaching: grading that first set of student papers usually assures new TAs that there is a lot they can teach their students about writing. If you continue to feel uncertain about your ability to teach, talk to your supervisor. Most of the faculty members who supervise TAs are strong teachers themselves, interested in helping you become a more effective instructor. Also, talk to your peers. Many of them likely feel or have felt the same way themselves and can offer their support.

Other times students may challenge your fairness as an instructor. For example, some may accuse you of treating them unfairly in class. These complaints often rest on precedent: "You didn't act this way with student X, so why are you acting this way with me?" or "My high school teacher did or did not do X, so why are you?" In most cases, you can answer these challenges by pointing out how the situations are not the same: this student's case is, in important ways, different than the case of student X, or the actions of high school teachers will necessarily differ from the actions of college teachers. But if a student makes a persuasive case, be willing to reconsider your position. Tell the student you will look at the work again and give him or her a final decision later. Take as much time as you need to think through the issue. If you doubt the course of action you took, ask your faculty supervisor or peers for advice. Give them the facts of the matter and see if they agree with what you did or if they can offer an alternative. Once you reach your final decision, inform the student and explain your reasons.

If a student becomes belligerent or overly aggressive when challenging your authority or fairness, tell your teaching supervisor. If you ever feel threatened or intimidated by a student, get help immediately. Do not ignore the situation, hoping it will just resolve itself. It will not. You should never feel like you have to address these problems alone. There is always help and support available. Go see your teaching supervisor.

STUDENTS WHO DISPUTE GRADES

Do not be surprised when students dispute grades. This happens to almost every instructor. However, grade disputes pose particular problems if you are a new, inexperienced TA evaluating student work for the first time. Experienced teachers have developed standards for evaluating student work; most new TAs have not. As a result, many TAs lack confidence in their ability to evaluate student work and feel uncomfortable addressing student complaints (see Chapter 6 for advice on how to grade student papers fairly and on developing standards of evaluation). Dealing with disputes over grades can be emotionally taxing. New TAs especially tend to feel that their judgment is being questioned—which might well be true—and react defensively. TAs who are unsure about their grading standards or insecure about assuming authority as an evaluator of student writing may opt to give complaining students the grades they want. Others give all of their students high grades, believing that will prevent complaints. There are better courses of action to take.

If a student questions a grade in class, make an appointment with the student to discuss the matter further. When the student arrives at your office, assume control of the meeting. If a student is irate, abusive, or unwilling to listen, end the conference. Tell the student to leave and schedule a new meeting when he or she has calmed down. If a student is ready to discuss the grade calmly, ask the student if there is anything you marked or wrote on the paper that he or she does not understand or any error he or she does not know how to correct. Answer any specific questions the student has about your comments on the paper. Then go through the paper with the student, pointing out what you marked and why, offering suggestions on how to fix any problems you see and build on any strengths. As you talk through the paper together, most students come to see why the paper received its grade. If they still have questions, summarize the grading standards you use in the course and your particular expectations for this assignment, and then point out specific places in the paper where the student did or did not meet those standards and expectations. If the student is still not satisfied at that point, there is little else you can do except to offer your help on the next assignment.

Because you are a TA, some students may ask you to let someone else (probably a professor) review a disputed paper to see what grade that person would give it. Behind this request is the unstated assumption that as a TA, you are not a "real" teacher—a "real" teacher would have given the paper a different (i.e., higher) grade. Whether you ask someone else to look at the paper is up to you. Most TA supervisors are willing to review a disputed paper and tell you what grade they would have given it. Just be sure to conduct this consultation outside the student's presence.

If the student remains unsatisfied, you have a few options left: tell the student the matter is over and advise the student to move on to the next assignment, allow the student to rewrite the paper, or refer the student to your supervisor. Rewriting the paper allows the student to take advantage of your comments and conversations. The final grade for the assignment is either the rewrite grade or an average of the first grade and the second—the choice is yours. There are times when rewriting a graded paper helps the student mature as a writer, but these rewrites greatly increase your workload, so consider carefully whether you want to make this a common practice. Finally, if a student is just not going to be satisfied with any course of action you take, refer him or her to your teaching supervisor.

Sometimes when reviewing a paper, you may decide you assigned the wrong grade. If you feel you graded too harshly, you can give the student a higher grade; just be sure to explain the basis of the change. Do not, however, lower a grade on review. That type of action seems vindictive. If you realize the grade is too high, just leave it, tell the student the grade is more than justified, and revise your standards as needed for the next set of papers.

STUDENTS WHO MAKE INAPPROPRIATE COMMENTS IN CLASS

Occasionally you will have students say something inappropriate in class, comments that are rude, ignorant, or prejudiced. Addressing students who make inappropriate comments in class can be challenging: you do not want to stifle discussion, yet these comments actually squelch debate, creating an uncomfortable atmosphere that works against the free flow of ideas.

When students make inappropriate comments, you can either ignore them or address them. If you choose to address them, you have several options: say something to the offending student in class, talk to the student outside of class, or invite other students to voice their opinions. If you choose to address the comments in class, decide how confrontational to be. Some teachers like to speak directly to the student, telling him or her that such comments are not acceptable. However, a public confrontation like this can be risky. While it may embarrass the student into silence, it may also cause the student to argue with you in class. As a teacher, you must consider how well you could handle such an argument and how it would affect the other students.

Other teachers prefer to address the situation in class more subtly. A common technique is to paraphrase the student's comments, giving the student an opportunity to clarify his or her position. Students speaking off the cuff often misstate their opinions in class, choosing language that misrepresents their true positions. Paraphrasing the comments helps students hear what they have actually said or implied, giving them a chance to restate their views. Once the student clarifies or explains his or her position, you or the student's peers can respond. The goal of this strategy is to use the student's comments as a teaching opportunity, to get the student to rethink his or her position, and to model for all the students how to confront and debate controversial or biased comments.

Finally, some teachers rely on peer pressure to address the problem of inappropriate comments. They encourage students to speak up if they disagree with or object to a peer's statements or, after paraphrasing such a comment, directly ask other students whether they agree with their peer's position. Students often reconsider their comments if several peers voice dissenting views.

If a student habitually makes disruptive comments in class, you need to address the problem differently. Ask the student to meet you in your office. During this conference, describe the behavior you find objectionable, explain why it is not acceptable, and ask the student to stop. Give the student a chance to respond, but let him or her know that these comments will not be tolerated in your class. If they do not stop, contact your teaching supervisor—the student might need to be removed from class. If you think the student is likely to be confrontational during the conference, have another TA in the office with you when the student comes. If you fear at all for your safety, have your teaching supervisor present for the meeting.

Never tolerate harassment of any kind in your class. If a student makes racist, sexist, or other offensive comments to you or to any student, see your teaching supervisor immediately. Also, keep a record of what was said in case the student ever faces disciplinary action. Never let a student make you feel uncomfortable as a teacher, and never let a student intimidate other students. As the classroom instructor, you need to stand firm and resolve the situation.

STUDENTS WHO PLAGIARIZE WORK

Plagiarism can be a difficult problem to address because it can assume many forms, some more serious than others. Plagiarism can range from a student's failure to supply proper citations for paraphrased material to deliberate fraud, such as turning in an essay purchased from an on-line paper mill. How to address an incidence of plagiarism in your class depends largely on the particulars: who the student is, what he or she did or failed to do, and when in the course it occurs.

Forms of Plagiarism

For most academics, plagiarism involves passing off another person's work as your own. This definition sounds simple enough until you begin to look at particular instances. Consider, for example, differences between intentional and unintentional plagiarism. In introductory-level college classes, students unfamiliar with the documentation conventions of academic discourse may plagiarize work unintentionally. These are all forms of plagiarism:

1. *In his paper, a student copies material from a source text word for word without placing it in quotation marks and without documenting it.*

This seems to be a fairly straightforward example of plagiarism: copying material from a source text and presenting it as your own work. But what if the student truly believes that copying material from a source text is sometimes acceptable? Several students have told me that in high school, they were taught that copying material from a reference work, such as an encyclopedia, without quoting or documenting it is acceptable because the information is "common knowledge." Most college teachers would consider the practice plagiarism, but the student thought he was acting in an acceptable manner.

2. *In her paper, a student copies a passage from a source text word for word, provides proper documentation, but does not place the material in quotation marks.*

Again, most college teachers would say this practice constitutes plagiarism. The student gives the author credit for his or her ideas through the documentation but fails to give the author proper credit for his or her language (no quotation marks). This form of plagiarism frequently results from faulty note taking. As they conduct research, students copy passages from source texts into their notes but fail to place quotation marks around the material. When they write their paper, they simply copy the passages from their notes, supply the proper documentation, and turn in the essay. They are not trying to deceive anyone—they supplied the proper documentation. They simply have poor note-taking skills.

3. *In his paper, a student paraphrases a passage but fails to provide proper documentation.*

In this case, the student uses his own language to convey information but commits plagiarism when he fails to give the author of the source text proper credit for his or her ideas through proper documentation. Again, this form of plagiarism occurs frequently because students are unfamiliar with the conventions of academic discourse. When you inform them that all paraphrased material needs to be documented, they often moan, "But that means EVERYTHING in my paper will be documented!" To avoid this problem, students need to learn how to blend their ideas and language with material from their source texts, properly documenting every passage.

While these first three forms of plagiarism usually result from inattention or unfamiliarity with the standards of academic discourse, other forms are clearly more fraudulent in nature. Consider these examples, any of which might occur in your class:

1. *A student purchases a paper from an on-line or mail-order company and turns it in as her own.*

In this case, the student has actively searched out a company that provides students with complete papers on the topic of their choice. She bought the paper, put her name on it, and turned it in for a grade. This student has deliberately perpetuated an academic fraud. (See Chapter 8 for more information on paper mills and plagiarism detection sites on the Internet.)

2. *A student has a friend or roommate write a paper for him or "borrows" his friend's paper and turns it in as his own.*

This form of plagiarism occurs frequently. Students taking different sections of the same composition course may turn in identical papers, believing that their teachers will not detect the fraud. You may even run into cases where students in different sections of the same course you teach turn in identical papers, again believing that you will not notice (these students believe that their teachers do not actually *read* all those papers!).

3. *A student takes another student's paper without that student's knowledge and turns it in as her own.*

I faced this situation recently. A TA suspected plagiarism—the paper he was reading just did not sound like the other papers this student had written and the student had switched paper topics a day before the essay was due. I looked at the essay and recognized it as a paper one of my students had turned in two weeks earlier. I asked my student about it, and he was genuinely amazed: he had not shared his paper with anyone and did not even know the other student. A little investigation by the TA determined that his student knew my student's roommate. The roommate had downloaded my student's paper and passed it along to the TA's student without my student's knowledge. Clearly, attempts to plagiarize work can result in complex intrigue!

Plagiarism covers a range of academic infractions; in fact, it may be one of the most ill-defined concepts in academics. At the same time, though, it carries some of the most serious consequences: plagiarizing work can result in a failed paper, an "F" for the course, or even dismissal from a degree program. Teachers can help their students avoid these problems if they take a few simple steps.

Helping Students Avoid Plagiarism

Discuss plagiarism frequently in your classes, not just once at the beginning of the term or once when your students begin a research project. In these discussions, define which acts constitute plagiarism and teach your students how to avoid these problems. Employing a case approach is often helpful. Provide your students with a range of plagiarism scenarios (see Figure 9.1 for samples) and discuss their responses. Which acts, in their view, constitute plagiarism? Which do not? Why? Which constitute it in your mind? Explain your answers. These discussions allow you to address any misconceptions your students harbor about plagiarism.

Editing exercises also help. Ask your students to revise several plagiarized passages, identifying and correcting the errors. You can create these samples yourself or pull them from your students' work.

Finally, you can discourage students from plagiarizing work by making it more difficult to accomplish. For example, you can require students to submit their paper topics for your approval and not allow them to change topics

---

FIGURE 9.1   Plagiarism Scenarios

Read each scenario below and decide if you think the student is guilty of plagiarism. Be ready to explain your decision when you discuss your responses in class.

1. A student copies part of his paper from an encyclopedia and documents it.
2. A student copies part of his paper from an encyclopedia, places it in quotation marks, but does not document it.
3. A student borrows a friend's paper, copies the opening paragraph, but writes the rest of the essay herself.
4. A student purchases a paper from an on-line service, puts her name on it, and turns it in for a grade.
5. A student paraphrases a passage from a magazine article but does not document the material in his paper.
6. A student copies several passages from a source text and properly quotes and documents all but one of them.
7. A student quotes and documents a passage but lists the wrong page number in the documentation.
8. A student turns in a paper she originally wrote in high school without telling her current teacher.
9. A student borrows a friend's paper and organizes his exactly the same way without copying any material and without documenting the fact that he follows his friend's outline.
10. A student turns in the same paper in two different classes without telling the teachers.

---

without your permission. Many students put off writing papers and, in desperation, purchase, borrow, or download an essay a day or two before it is due, regardless of the topic. You can also require students to turn in rough drafts of their work: if students buy or borrow someone else's work, they have to write or obtain a rough draft for it too, which might encourage them to do their own work from the beginning. I also require students to turn in photocopies of every source text they cite in their paper. If I think a passage might be plagiarized because it lacks quotation marks or is poorly paraphrased, I can check it against the photocopied source material. With this requirement in place, if students want to purchase their papers, they also have to gather and duplicate the paper's source texts. I do not accept a paper without the photocopies.

Dealing with Plagiarism

Despite a teacher's best efforts, however, students will plagiarize work. Handling instances of plagiarism requires tact and sound judgment. First, let your teaching supervisor know if you suspect a student has plagiarized a paper and get his or her advice on how to proceed. Most writing programs have specific procedures they want you to follow. Next, have evidence in hand before you directly confront a student: accusing someone of plagiarism is serious. If you suspect plagiarism, ask to see the student's rough draft or notes and ask the student to explain the process he or she followed when writing the paper. The material and answers the student supplies may help confirm or assuage your concerns.

Handling instances of unintentional plagiarism is typically left to your discretion as the classroom teacher. As you decide on a course of action, keep in mind your primary goal as a teacher: instead of simply failing the essay, consider making the student revise it and fix the errors. Revising the paper teaches the student more than just receiving an "F" does. If, however, you suspect the student is trying to perpetrate an academic fraud—that he or she has purchased, borrowed, or stolen a paper—and you have proof, talk to your supervisor. Your department or school likely has procedures for you to follow.

COLLEGE STUDENTS:
A DEVELOPMENTAL PERSPECTIVE

First-year college students can be a real joy to teach, but they can also be a real challenge. Most are undergoing substantial changes in their lives, learning to live on their own, making new friends, choosing a career. Better understanding your students' intellectual development in college can help you better understand their behavior in class and teach them more effectively.

Over the past five decades, many researchers have charted the intellectual development of college students. Such pioneering work as William Perry's *Forms of Intellectual and Ethical Development*, Mary Belenky and colleagues' *Women's*

Ways of Knowing, and Patricia King and Karen Kitchener's *Developing Reflective Judgment* offer useful insights into the way college students view themselves, their peers, their teachers, and their education. Though they couch their findings in different terms, these researchers all recognize similar broad stages of development most college students pass through on their way to graduation: dualism, multiplism, relativism, and commitment.

Dualism

Many students enter college viewing knowledge and authority from a dualistic perspective. They tend to believe that all questions have a single correct answer and that all problems—abortion, global warming, crime—have a single valid solution. They believe their task as college students is to learn these right answers and valid solutions. Little thought is necessary on their part: the faculty members are "experts" who teach the facts and tell them what is right and true. If teachers do not do this in class, these students tend to have one of two responses: they either dismiss the teacher as incompetent or believe the teacher is playing a game—the teacher knows the right answer but wants students to find it on their own.

In an introductory writing class, students who view knowledge and authority dualistically tend to believe there is one right way to compose a paper. If they follow the right "process" when writing their paper, they will get an "A." For them, writing is a rule-driven activity: everything about writing should be as definitive as the requirement to place a punctuation mark at the end of a sentence. If these students get low grades on their papers, they may confront their teacher with the common plea: "Just tell me what I have to do to get an 'A' in here." Again, they expect a simple, direct answer. The instructor's job is to teach them *the* writing process, to tell them exactly how to compose successful papers. They may severely question the authority of teachers who do not provide these guidelines, especially if these teachers are young TAs. In their minds, these teachers are either incompetent or are playing games by refusing to tell them the answer.

Students who view knowledge and authority dualistically often find college overwhelming because so few simple answers exist. College challenges their world view and the adjustment can be difficult.

Multiplism

Many students cope by moving into multiplism, the next stage of development. Students who view knowledge and authority from a multiplistic perspective have abandoned the dualistic notion that single correct answers exist for every problem. Instead, they recognize that people can maintain a range of equally valid positions on issues: "You have your ideas, I have mine, and we can both be right." They do not draw qualitative distinctions among positions; all views are equally sound or good. In a writing class, a student may have one way of organizing a paper and her roommate a different way, and they can both be right. In a debate over abortion rights, her roommate may be pro-choice and she may be pro-life, but neither has a right to call the other person wrong. In fact, from this point of view, college is a time of growth because students get exposed to so many different perspectives on issues.

Problems occur for these students in class, though, when teachers grade their work. From a multiplistic perspective, the teacher's claim to "truth" is no more valid than anyone else's claim: "I have my way of writing and the teacher has hers. Both are equally valid." These students tend to see grading as arbitrary and idiosyncratic. While they might agree that "rules" govern grammar and punctuation, everything else about writing is a matter of personal taste and choice. Teachers give low grades because (a) they do not like a student's "style" of writing, (b) they want to punish anyone who does not "write like them," or (c) they simply do not like the student personally.

Relativism

Over time, students begin to understand how their grades are related to disciplinary standards and conventions, an insight that eases their transition into the next perspective on knowledge and authority, relativism. Moving from class to class in college, they learn how to gather and critique evidence and information, evaluate positions, form arguments, and defend interpretations in discipline-specific ways. In fact, qualitative reasoning is the hallmark of this developmental perspective: students viewing knowledge and authority from a relativistic perspective understand that claims must be based on commonly accepted, disciplinary standards of evaluation. In their classes, students viewing the world from a relativistic perspective can make qualitative judgments about writing, including their own, and become fluent in the discourse and inquiry practices of their major.

Commitment

Commitment is the final position in most schemes of student intellectual development. Students viewing knowledge and authority from this perspective define their own positions on issues, commit themselves to particular ideologies, and develop their own philosophy of life. A hallmark of commitment is what educator John McPeck calls "reflective skepticism." People operating out of reflective skepticism understand the tentative nature of knowledge. They can commit themselves to a position but remain open to change: new information or experience may cause them to change their minds. They do not maintain positions with the blind passion of a dualistic thinker. Instead, they understand that the search for knowledge never ends and actively question what they understand to be true and just. They are not afraid to grow and change; in fact, they often seek out diverse points of view just to test the validity of their current beliefs. For them, teachers represent one of the best sources of intellectual challenge—they understand that teachers and students work together to investigate topics, question perspectives, debate positions, and clarify thought.

Teachers working in introductory composition and literature classes should understand how their students' perspectives on knowledge and authority can affect their work in class. How students define their role in the classroom, how they interpret the instruction you offer, how they respond to grades, and how they interact with their peers are all influenced by their level of intellectual development. As a classroom teacher, you should design curricula that promote your students' growth. For example, students viewing knowledge and authority dualistically should learn how to recognize and grant validity to alternative points of view; those operating from a multiplistic perspective should learn how to evaluate alternative points of view; students viewing knowledge and authority relativistically should learn how to make commitments in their lives yet remain open to change. All studies agree that intellectual development is slow and individualistic. Yet it also seems to be fairly predictable: if students stay in college, these changes will likely occur, though when they happen and how they manifest themselves will vary greatly. Supporting your students' intellectual development is easier if you understand the struggles they face as they learn to think about knowledge and authority in increasingly more sophisticated ways.

CONCLUSION

As a teacher, you need to help your students learn how to succeed in college—how to set goals, meet deadlines, and work with others. To accomplish this goal, set clear classroom policies and enforce them fairly. When conflicts arise in the classroom, remember to stay calm, decide nothing rashly, and look for teaching opportunities. Treating students with respect and consideration is the best course of action—how you interact with your students models the behavior you expect from them.

WORKS CITED

Belenky, Mary Field, et al. *Women's Ways of Knowing: The Development of Self, Voice, and Mind.* New York: Basic Books, 1986.

King, Patricia M., and Karen Strohm Kitchener. *Developing Reflective Judgment: Understanding and Promoting Intellectual Growth and Critical Thinking in Adolescents and Adults.* San Francisco: Jossey-Bass, 1994.

McPeck, John E. *Critical Thinking and Education.* New York: St. Martin's, 1981.

Perry, William G., Jr. *Forms of Intellectual and Ethical Development in the College Years.* New York: Holt, 1970.

ADDITIONAL READINGS

Brookes, Gerry H. "Exploring Plagiarism in the Composition Classroom." *Freshmen English News* 17 (1989): 31–5.

Dethier, Brock. *The Composition Instructor's Survival Guide*. Portsmouth, NH: Boyton/Cook, 1999.

Howard, Rebecca Moore. "Plagiarisms, Authorships, and the Academic Death Penalty." *College English* 57 (1995): 788–806.

Klausman, Jeffrey. "Teaching about Plagiarism in the Age of the Internet." *Teaching English in the Two-Year College* 27 (1999): 209–12.

Kroll, Barry M. "How College Freshmen View Plagiarism." *Written Communication* 5 (1988): 203–21.

McKeachie, Wilbert, J. *Teaching Tips*. 10th ed. Boston: Houghton, 1999.

Robinson, Jennifer Meta. "A Question of Authority: Dealing with Disruptive Students." *In Our Own Voice: Graduate Students Teach Writing*. Ed. Tina Lavonne Good and Leanne B. Warshauer. Boston: Allyn & Bacon, 2000. 119–127.

Wells, Dorothy. "An Account of the Complex Causes of Unintentional Plagiarism in College Writing." *WPA: Writing Program Administration* 16.3 (1993): 59–71.

Whitaker, Elaine E. "A Pedagogy to Address Plagiarism." *College Composition and Communication* 44 (1993): 509–14.

Wilhoit, Stephen. "Helping Students Avoid Plagiarism." *College Teaching* 42 (1994): 161–64.

CHAPTER 10

Holding Conferences
with Students

WHY CONFERENCES ARE IMPORTANT

One of the most effective ways for students to learn is to work individually with a teacher. However, in most American universities, offering such instruction is difficult: too many students, too few teachers. Yet teachers know that covering material for five minutes with an individual student is often more productive than covering that same material for an hour with the entire class. During those five minutes, the teacher has the student's total attention and can respond to that student's specific questions and concerns. Meeting one-on-one with a student changes the dynamics of instruction—physical barriers between teacher and student are reduced, the pressure of performance on both sides is diminished, interactions are less formal. Holding conferences with your students can help you establish a more comfortable classroom atmosphere, improve discipline, and meet your students' individual needs.

REASONS TO HOLD
CONFERENCES WITH STUDENTS

Teachers meet individually with students for a variety of reasons, and at different times throughout the semester.

Getting Acquainted

Some like to hold brief meetings with every student in the class early in the semester. These get-acquainted conferences offer you and your students a chance to chat informally and get to know each other and can pay large dividends later in the course. First, having visited your office once, your students are more likely to return later when they need help. Second, meeting one-on-one helps you form personal relationships with your students. Third, after conferences, students often feel more comfortable speaking up and participating in your class and you feel more comfortable working with them individually.

Discussing Papers

During the term, many teachers like to meet with students individually to discuss their work on particular papers. They talk about the student's choice of topic, review a preliminary outline, or discuss a completed draft. During these conferences, you can answer specific questions the student has about his work, assure a student that she is on the right track, or steer a student in a more productive direction. Occasionally students may ask you to edit or proofread their papers for them. Avoid the temptation to do this. When you edit or proofread student papers, you are doing work they ought to be doing. Students improve as editors and proofreaders only through practice—when you do the work for them, you deny them vital opportunities to learn and grow. But at the same time, if they need help, you do not want to turn them away. There are some compromises.

For example, you might carefully proofread or edit one paragraph in the paper with the student watching. Explain the reason for every change you make and point out any pattern of errors you see. Then have the student proofread and edit the next paragraph in the paper while you watch and ask her to explain the reason for each change. When the student finishes, you can correct any mistakes she has made, point out errors or problems she has missed, and discuss the strengths and weaknesses of the student's proofreading practices. The student must then proofread and edit the rest of the paper on her own. Other teachers like to meet with the student, read the entire paper, circle significant errors, and then watch as the student makes the needed corrections.

Discussing Personal Matters

Sometimes students will want to talk to you privately about matters totally unrelated to class. Yours may be the smallest, most intimate class students take. Consequently, many of your students will come to feel closer to you than they do to any other instructor they have. If you are young, there may be an even greater identification. It is not unusual, then, for first-year students to turn to you when they need help or advice. Often they will want to discuss academic matters—they may need a recommendation letter for a scholarship, for example, or want advice on choosing a major. Help the students as much as you can and, if necessary, steer them toward people on campus who can offer additional advice and guidance.

The same advice holds true for students who want help with personal matters. Students may want to talk with you about problems they are having adjusting to college life, difficulties they are having with a roommate, or confrontations they have had with another teacher. Mature judgment and discretion are called for in these cases. Sometimes students just need to vent and will feel better after talking to someone. Other times, though, students may need more help than you can provide. If a student is facing severe emotional problems, refer him to the appropriate campus office or administrator for help. If necessary, help the student set up the appointment. Do not assume responsibility for your students' psychological or emotional well-being. That is not your job. Every college has staff and administrators who are trained to help students work through problems like these. Be supportive and get your students the help they need.

ARRANGING CONFERENCES

Students will sometimes drop in to see you during your posted office hours. The students usually set the agenda for these meetings—they have something specific to discuss with you. Other times you may require your students to schedule conferences with you—some teachers want every student to meet with them outside of class at least once during the term; other teachers establish more specific expectations, requiring every student to see them once during the first month of class, once around midterm, and once during finals.

Occasionally, you may need to ask specific students to see you in your office. Sometimes these students need individualized tutoring to improve as writers; other times you need to discuss their behavior in class. When you want to hold an individual conference with a student, ask the student to stop by during your office hours. If the student cannot meet you then, set up an appointment at a mutually convenient time.

WHERE TO MEET WITH STUDENTS

One of the reasons conferences work well as a teaching tool is because they are so flexible: where you meet with students can change as the need demands. You can hold conferences in class or outside of class, in your office or elsewhere on campus. Each location has its own benefits and limitations.

Meeting with Students in Class

Although most conferences take place outside the classroom, some teachers like to hold "mini conferences" with students during class. Here is how it typically works. On a day when students are writing in class, each student meets individually with the teacher for a brief, highly focused conference. Sometimes the students bring their work up to the teacher's desk for the conference; other times the teacher circulates around the room, talking to each student individually.

These short conferences can be surprisingly effective teaching tools. Five minutes or less may not seem like much time to spend with a student, but when the conferences are focused on a specific task or question, you can accomplish a lot. Meeting during class helps you address the needs of students who cannot meet with you during office hours and gives you a good sense of the progress your students are making on particular assignments.

Meeting with Students in Your Office

Like most teachers, you will frequently talk with students in your office, which can be problematic for TAs. At many schools, TAs lack adequate office space—they either have no offices or must share space with several TAs in a central "bull pen." When completing my master's degree, for example, I shared a room with around twenty other TAs. Holding private conferences with students there was difficult and at times impossible. If this is the case at your school, some commonly accepted rules of etiquette apply. First, you need to talk with your officemates about which activities take precedence in the office: Should TAs holding conferences leave the room if other TAs are working quietly, or vice versa? Second, if another TA is working in the office while you are holding a conference, try to keep your voice down; if you have something private to discuss with the student, find a more private place to talk. Finally, coordinate your office hours with the other TAs. Try not to let them overlap: if you want to hold office hours early on Monday, Wednesday, and Friday, see if your officemate can come in later on those days or on Tuesday and Thursday. Making decisions like this early in the semester will help you avoid problems later.

Because this is a litigious age, you need to take some commonsense precautions when you meet with students in your office. Some of these recommendations may strike you as silly or extreme, but recent experiences of teachers around the country make them necessary. For example, except under extraordinary circumstances, keep your office door open during conferences. You can still hold private conversations with your students if you keep your voices down. Second, during a conference, if a student says anything that makes you feel uncomfortable, tell your teaching supervisor right away. If a student makes a sexist, racist, homophobic, or other offensive remark, tell the student that such speech is not acceptable and immediately let your teaching supervisor know this has occurred. Likewise, if a student flirts with you or makes sexual advances, discourage the behavior and tell your teaching supervisor. If you feel uncomfortable talking to your supervisor about this sort of student behavior, tell your officemate and write up a report of the incident that you both sign and date. If it happens a second time, see your teaching supervisor immediately. During a conference, do not become too familiar with your students—standards of professional conduct apply inside your office just as they do in your classroom. Sexual harassment charges can easily arise if you talk to or touch students inappropriately during conferences. Always remain professional in your demeanor and in your interaction with students.

Finally, arrange the furniture in your office to facilitate student conferences. Make sure you and your student can sit next to each other as you look over a paper and that you can speak to each other in a normal tone of voice. If you have a computer in your office, place it where you and your student can both see the screen. If your school puts you in a TA bull pen, decide with your officemates where students should wait for their appointments and set aside space for their coats and book bags.

Meeting with Students Outside Your Office

Sometimes you may find it better to have conferences with students outside your office. For example, you might want to hold some office hours in dorm lounges or meeting rooms so that it is easier for students to meet with you. Getting together in dorm lounges also helps you understand the life your students lead—you get a better sense of your students' experiences outside the classroom. You could occasionally meet with your students in the school's cafeteria, sharing a cup of coffee as you talk about class. The campus library is also a good place, especially if your students are working on a research project; you can help your students conduct searches, locate material, or write their papers.

Meeting outside the office has some strengths, but it also has a couple of drawbacks. First, meeting outside the office means you may not have access to some needed resources, such as dictionaries, sample texts, old handouts, or computers. Second, holding these conferences can be demanding on your time. Unless you meet with students around campus during your regular office hours, you will need to set aside extra time for these conferences. In my experience, though, students truly appreciate your willingness to move outside the office. Because these meetings usually take place during off hours—in the evening or on weekends—which the students may find more convenient than your office hours, the students know you are setting aside special time for them and make a concerted effort to see you.

A word of warning: always make sure you hold these conferences in a public place. As a TA, do not meet with students privately in your home or in their dorm rooms. Though your interactions with these students might be totally professional and innocent, meeting with students privately outside the office is not wise.

MEETING WITH GROUPS OF STUDENTS

For several reasons, you may want to hold conferences with more than one student at a time. If your students are working on group projects, for example, you may want to meet with each group of students to answer their questions and check on their progress. When you do, make sure every group member understands the meeting time and place and choose a location that can accommodate the entire group comfortably. You may need to meet in a dorm meeting room or in an empty classroom. During the conference, solicit comments from each group member—this is the group's best opportunity to get your advice and your best opportunity to gauge how well the group members work together as a team.

Even if your students are not working together on a project, you may want to schedule group conferences. During these sessions, in addition to talking with you, the students have an opportunity to talk with and help each other. The students may hesitate to play this role during a conference, but with your encouragement, they will. TAs who have used this conferencing technique in the past report more and better class participation afterward: during the conferences their students learned how to listen and respond to each other, lessons they carried into the classroom. On a more practical level, while group conferences last longer than one-on-one meetings, you have to hold fewer of them to meet with every student in class. At certain points in the term, group conferences may best fit your schedule—holding fewer conferences frees up time for your own research and course work.

HOLDING CONFERENCES WITH STUDENTS: A SURVIVAL GUIDE

Regardless of when or where you meet with your students, here are some tips that can make your conferences more productive and manageable.

1. *Keep the conferences short and focused.*

Generally, individual conferences should run ten to twenty minutes, not longer. If a student needs more help than you can offer in twenty minutes, set up another appointment when you can start fresh. Conferences function best when you and your students can work intently on a few specific tasks.

2. *Let the student talk and work.*

Guard against monopolizing the conversation during a conference or doing work the student should be doing. Encourage your students to ask questions during a conference and to talk about their writing strategies. Noted composition teacher and researcher Donald Murray has written extensively about students' ability to teach themselves during a conference—as they explain a problem they are facing, they frequently find their own solution. At that point, you only need to confirm their plans if you agree with them.

Also, avoid the temptation to write or rewrite your student's paper during a conference. For example, if you and a student are trying to find the best wording for a thesis statement, talk it out with your student, but have the student write it. The same holds true for editing a text—in most cases, have the student do the work. You may correct a sentence or two as you model the right procedures to follow, but then insist that the student edit the rest of the paper. Your students will learn more by doing the work themselves than they will by watching you do the work.

3. Schedule appointments.

During open office hours, meet with students on a first-come, first-serve basis, but when you plan to meet with a number of students on any given day, use a sign-up sheet. Schedule conferences to start at fifteen- to twenty-minute intervals and have the students sign up for a slot. Keep one copy of the schedule with you in your office and post another copy outside your office door. Keep to this schedule; if a student comes late for the appointment, do not extend the time scheduled for her conference. Ask that student to sign up for another appointment.

4. Treat appointments like class meetings—expect attendance.

As a TA, few things are more frustrating than students skipping appointments. This behavior is especially frustrating if you have made a special trip into the office to meet with them. To avoid these problems, let your students know that this sort of behavior is not acceptable in college, that they must keep the appointments they make. If they have to miss an appointment, tell them to let you know so you can change your plans. To reinforce this policy, some TAs like to treat scheduled appointments like class meetings: missing an appointment is like missing a class and counts against the student if a course attendance policy is in effect. If a student makes a habit of missing scheduled appointments, stop arranging them. Tell the student to come see you during your regular, posted office hours.

5. Schedule breaks.

When new TAs schedule conferences with a large number of students, many forget to set aside time for breaks. They quickly discover that they have no time to take notes, head to the restroom, or eat lunch. A TA will only make this mistake once, but it can be a miserable lesson to learn. You might as well avoid the problem all together by scheduling breaks when you put together your conference sign-up sheet and spreading the conferences out over two or three days.

6. Change venue every once in a while.

To avoid falling into a rut when you hold conferences, try meeting with students in a variety of locations—your office, a dorm meeting room, an empty classroom, the cafeteria, the library. Changing where you meet often changes the dynamic of the conference. Certain students may respond more positively than usual in certain venues—they may feel more comfortable talking to you in a dorm commons or school cafeteria. Plus, a change of venue helps you stay fresh.

7. Record the results of conferences.

Find some way to keep track of what you and your students discuss in these conferences. Such record keeping is standard practice for writing center tutors today; learn from their experience. After a conference has ended, briefly summarize the session in a teaching or conference log (many TAs like to keep these records on computer disks for easy storage). You might also require your students to submit a summary of every meeting they have with you. Writing these summaries will help your students remember what the two of you discussed during the conference and help you maintain a complete record of each meeting.

These conference survival tips are summarized in Figure 10. 1 below.

FIGURE 10.1   Conference Survival Tips

---

1. Keep the conferences short and focused.
2. Give the student a chance to talk and work.
3. Schedule appointments.
4. Treat appointments like class meetings.
5. Schedule breaks.
6. Change venues every once in a while.
7. Record the results of your conferences.

WORK CITED

Murray, Donald. "The Listening Eye: Reflections on the Writing Conference." *College English* 41 (1979): 13—18.

ADDITIONAL READINGS

Anderson, Carl. *How's It Going? A Practical Guide to Conferring with Student Writers.* Portsmouth, NH: Boyton/Cook, 2000.

Clark, Beverly Lyon. *Talking about Writing: A Guide for Tutor and Teacher Conferences.* Ann Arbor: University of Michigan Press, 1985.

Harris, Muriel. *Teaching One-to-One: The Writing Conference.* Urbana, IL: NCTE, 1986.

Newkirk, Thomas. "The Writing Conference as Performance." *Research in the Teaching of English* 29 (1995): 193–215.

Rule, Rebecca. "Conferences and Workshops: Conversations on Writing in Process." *Nuts and Bolts: A Practical Guide to Teaching College Composition.* Ed. Thomas Newkirk. Portsmouth, NH: Boyton/Cook, 1993. 43–66.

Walker, Carolyn P., and David Elias. "Writing Conference Talk: Factors Associated with High- and Low-Rated Writing Conferences." *Research in the Teaching of English* 21 (1987): 266–85.

CHAPTER 11

Teaching Literature

INTRODUCTION

Many TAs eagerly look forward to teaching literature. After all, this is why they entered the profession. Other TAs are less enthusiastic about the prospect; though they have taken many literature classes, these TAs question their ability to be good literature teachers themselves. Although teaching literature successfully does require instructors to employ a unique set of skills, TAs usually improve quickly with practice, drawing on their knowledge and experience as readers. This chapter should help you get started.

OPPORTUNITIES FOR
TEACHING LITERATURE

TAs usually get the opportunity to teach literary texts in one of three ways: by teaching a lower-level literature class, by assisting a professor who is teaching a literature course, or by incorporating literary texts into their introductory writing courses. These circumstances are often tied to the TA's degree program, years of service in the department, and interests.

Teaching a Literature Course of Your Own

TAs in a master's program rarely get the chance to teach a literature class of their own. Most of those opportunities go to TAs who are advanced doctoral students. These experienced TAs typically develop their own course syllabus, choose their own texts, and design and grade their own assignments.

If you obtain one of these teaching assignments, expect little additional training. Most departments do not offer advanced workshops for TAs teaching literature classes for the first time. Therefore, you will need to take advantage of whatever informal support systems you have developed, getting advice and guidance from your teaching supervisor, professors, and fellow TAs. Selecting texts the first time you teach a literature class can be especially difficult; you have to decide if the readings are too difficult, too easy, too traditional, too idiosyncratic, too canonical, or too experimental. Check with instructors who have taught the course; see if you can examine syllabi they developed for the class, and ask them to comment on the texts you are considering. In addition, gather as much information as you can about the papers and exercises teachers commonly assign in the course and the grading standards they employ.

Assisting a Professor in a Literature Course

Leading a discussion section of a large literature class is perhaps one of the few times you will truly be a teaching "assistant" in graduate school. At many universities, professors and TAs jointly teach these classes: once or twice a week the professor lectures to all the students taking the course and once or twice a week TAs meet with smaller groups of students in discussion sections. TAs may serve many roles in these classes, depending on what the professor asks them to do. In addition to leading class discussions, TAs may design and grade essay assignments and tests, grade papers and tests the professor designs, calculate the students' course grades, develop Web pages, or lecture to the entire class on occasion. Some professors meet regularly with their TAs to talk about the course, answer their questions, and coordinate the instruction being offered in the various discussion sections; others do not.

As a TA, you have an important function in these courses. If students have any problems or questions, they will turn to you for help. You will be expected to master the course material, attend every lecture, and teach the required texts. You will often find yourself explaining what the professor said in a lecture, explicating texts, and teaching students how to write their papers or prepare for their tests. In most courses, you will assign midterm and final grades. In short, you will be responsible for the day-to-day business of teaching your students.

Incorporating Literature into a Writing Course

Many TAs teach literary texts in their introductory composition classes. Whereas some writing programs structure their courses around the study of literature, most do not. More commonly, instructors in these programs teach one or two literary texts in a course that otherwise focuses on other types of assignments. In many cases, the instructors do not get to choose the literary texts they teach—all of the students in the writing program study the same texts. Some programs, though, allow instructors to choose the literary texts. When you teach literature in a writing course, the real challenge is integrating that assignment with the others on your syllabus. Also, you cannot assume that your students already know how to read literature critically, write about literary texts, or adhere to the conventions of literary analysis. You will likely have to teach these skills.

PRESENTING MATERIAL IN A LITERATURE COURSE: A RANGE OF OPTIONS

Successful instructors know how and when to vary the way they teach literary texts. Below are just some of the options available to you.

Lectures

The most traditional way to teach literature is for the professor to lecture on the texts. Lectures are the most efficient way to present course material— you can cover a lot of ground in an hour-long presentation. In fact, sometimes lecturing is the best way to present certain material, such as the historical background of a text, the author's biography, and trends in critical interpretation. But there are trade-offs for this efficiency and coverage. For your students, lecturing is a passive activity: while you talk, they sit silently and listen.

Chapter 7 offers several tips on how to lecture effectively—here is some additional advice that applies specifically to lectures on literary texts. First, if your lecture includes references to specific dates, names, locations, or titles, prepare a handout or overhead that contains this information. Having this material at hand increases the likelihood that your students will pay attention to your lecture instead of fretting that they misspelled a name or missed a date. Second, when lecturing about a literary text, make frequent references to the text itself, including page numbers. Third, explain why you are lecturing on this material. Why is this information important? How will it help your students understand the text? Do not expect your students to make these connections themselves. Starting your lecture with an overview of what you will cover—perhaps even placing an outline on the board—and explaining what your students should learn from the presentation will make the lecture more productive.

Close Readings

Close readings involve leading your students through a small section of the text—a chapter, a paragraph, or even a sentence—offering commentary as you proceed. Your goals can include teaching the students how to read literature carefully and critically, how to tease out the meanings and implications of the language, how to make connections between various parts of a text, how to understand the relationship between a text and its author or between a text and its broader culture, or how to articulate a personal response to a text.

Close readings can resemble lectures—the teacher stands in front of the class, speaking at length on passages in the text. Although close reading a text this way is efficient, it is also passive; students are only listening to and watching the teacher. To address this problem, make close reading more interactive, offering your commentary on a passage and then asking for your students' responses. If students are reluctant to speak, call on them, and through your questions, lead them to a fuller understanding of the text. When your students offer an opinion, keep them tied to the text and ask them to explain their reasoning process: how, exactly, did the words on the page lead them to this particular position or interpretation?

Class Discussions

Students usually like to discuss literature. You can capitalize on this enthusiasm in several ways. For example, you can alternate between focused and open discussions. With focused discussions, you set the agenda for your students, identifying a question or a passage to talk about. Sometimes these discussions lead to a consensus of opinion; other times they just complicate and enrich your students' understanding of the material. With open discussions, the students talk about whatever aspects of the text strike them as interesting or important. The students may focus on a particular question or passage for a while, but the next speaker may draw their attention to an entirely different aspect of the text. Open discussions allow students to determine the direction of the class, often increasing their interest and motivation. This type of discussion also gives you the chance to find out what aspects of the text most interest your students. For additional tips on leading class discussions, see Chapter 7.

Student Oral Presentations

Brief oral presentations increase student participation in class. Students can offer reports on the historical or cultural background of the literary text or on the life and career of its author. Reports can focus on specific chapters or stanzas of a work, specific characters, particular elements of literature, or particular scenes or lines. They can present the students' personal response to the material, their critical reading of the text, or their synthesis of relevant criticism.

If you require oral presentations, offer your students instruction on how to prepare and present them and decide how you will evaluate or respond to their presentations (see Chapter 7 for advice on these matters). The presentations do not have to be graded, but unless they affect the course grade, students may not take them seriously. One possibility is to incorporate some material from the oral presentations into your tests or quizzes. Specify time limits for the presentations and enforce them. With some guidance and support, oral presentations can be a valuable addition to the course, resulting in interesting, imaginative projects.

Group Projects

For variety, you might occasionally assign group projects. Groups of students can present the results of their work orally or in writing, and their projects can be graded or ungraded, completed in class or out. You can place students in groups or have them self-select—limit each group to five or fewer members, though. As your students work on their projects, meet with each group occasionally to answer their questions, help them resolve problems, and offer advice (see Chapter 7 for more tips on using group work in class). You can require your students to complete their projects outside of class, but devote some class time to the assignment as well.

For many reasons, students sometimes object to group work, especially in a literature course. Some simply do not like to debate literary interpretations: they know what they think a text means and are not interested in discussing or questioning their views. Others feel that the work load gets unevenly distributed in group projects—some students do more work than others. Still other students resent the forced sociability of group work; they prefer to work alone and do not like being forced to collaborate with others. If you are committed to employing group work in your literature class, address these objections and accommodate these students as best you can. Most students who object to group projects will complete them; they may just need more guidance and reassurance, and perhaps a chance to vent some of their frustrations.

Multimedia Presentations

When teaching literature, consider using multimedia presentations to supplement your instruction. For example, show your students film versions of the works you are studying. If class time does not allow you to show the entire film, show certain scenes. Films help students visualize the work they are reading and enable them to compare genres: what are the differences between the print and the film versions of the work? What are the differences between the director's vision of the literary work and their own? Another option is to find the work on audio tape and play parts of it for your students. Hearing the words spoken aloud helps students understand the material and often generates interesting class discussion. It is especially helpful to play a recording of the author reading his or her own work—students hearing the author's own voice often remark that it makes the work more "real" or immediate.

Along with showing films and playing audiotapes, consider other ways you can supplement your instruction in a literature class. For example, when I teach my course on the literature of the Vietnam War, I bring in maps of Vietnam, diagrams of battle sites, combat photographs, pictures of aircraft and weapons frequently mentioned in the works, pictures of the Vietnamese landscape and people, and reprints of newspaper and magazine articles from the war years. I also share with my students music from the Vietnam War years, old network news casts, and current documentaries. All of this supplemental material helps students understand the texts they are reading, making it more accessible and placing it in a historical and cultural context.

Informal Writing Exercises

Teaching literature presents many opportunities for informal, ungraded writing assignments. These assignments help focus the students' attention on particular aspects of a text or on particular literary interpretations and can prepare them to write longer, more formal papers. Described below is a range of informal writing exercises useful when studying literature.

Responses Essays

With these assignments your students explore their personal reactions to the literature they are reading. The actual assignment can be stated several ways. Below are just a few examples:

- What did you find interesting in the reading? Why?
- What did you find confusing about the text? Why?
- What part of the reading best relates to your life? How so?
- Which parts of the reading seem most or least believable to you? Why?

Even though these essays are not graded, and there is no "right" or "wrong" answer, they should exhibit certain qualities. Successful response essays should be:

Clear: students articulate their responses in language that is understandable and precise.

Specific: students tie their responses to specific passages in the text.

Explicit: students explain the link between the passages and their responses.

While responsed cannot be "right" or "wrong," they can be clear or unclear, grounded in the text or not grounded in the text, fully developed or underdeveloped.

Response essays encourage students to make personal connections to the texts they are reading, to explore what the text means to them, to pay close attention to the words on the page, and to develop ideas for future, more formal papers. The responses can be written in class or out of class and shared with the teacher, with other students, or with no one at all: you do not need to read every response essay your students write, especially those completed in class. Teachers often employ these assignments to help students develop their critical reading skills, to help them learn to question their responses to a text, or to generate class discussion—when the students finish their response essays, the teacher may open the class for comments, encouraging students to talk about the responses they have just written.

Predictions

Making predictions promotes reflective reading. With these assignments students are asked to speculate in writing on the direction a text will take before or as they read it. As a prereading strategy, ask students to predict what will happen in a book, story, or poem based only on its title or author. This exercise brings to the students' conscious attention the expectations they make as readers, expectations that influence how they read and respond to texts. You might also ask your students to make predictions as they are reading the text: at the end of a chapter, for example, ask them to guess what will happen next and to explain their predictions. These exercises encourage students to read texts closely and critically.

Questions

At the beginning of class, ask your students to write down any questions they have about the literature they are reading, collect and quickly scan them, read a few aloud, and then spend the rest of the period working out answers. Alternatively, collect the questions, read them outside of class, and choose a few to address the next time the class meets. Some teachers like to have students write down questions at the end of class, after a lecture, discussion, or presentation. Quiet students then have an opportunity to ask questions they might not ask in class, and you get the chance to gauge how well your students understand the material. Writing out questions also helps students think critically about the texts. Oftentimes students who are struggling with material do not understand why they are struggling until they are asked to articulate their questions. This exercise gives them that opportunity.

Dialogues

This creative exercise asks students to write a dialogue involving characters from the works they are studying. In these dialogues, students can imagine what characters from different works might say to each other if they happened to meet, or they can ask characters questions. These role-playing exercises promote empathetic readings of literary texts and help

FIGURE 11.1   Presenting Material in a Literature Course: A Range of Options

Lectures

Close Readings

Class Discussions

Student Oral Presentations

Group Projects

Multimedia Presentations

Informal Writing Exercises

   Response Essays

   Predictions

   Questions

   Dialogues

students develop a deeper understanding of characters and themes. To complete dialogues successfully, students have to assume a new perspective; they have to see the world through the character's eyes and assume the character's voice.

The various ways of presenting course material in a literature course are summarized above in Figure 11.1.

FORMAL PAPER ASSIGNMENTS IN A LITERATURE COURSE

Formal literature-based essays usually require students to respond to, analyze, critique, or synthesize the texts they read. When designing an assignment in a literature class, pay particular attention to your own intentions: Why are you requiring this assignment? What do you expect your students to learn by writing this essay? What skills do they need to complete the assignment? Do your students currently have those skills or will they need instruction? Below are just a few of the formal, literature-based assignments you might consider using in class, based on Tim O'Brien's *The Things They Carried*, a collection of stories about the experience of American soldiers in the Vietnam War. Chose ones that meet your students' needs and suit your course goals.

Response Essays

As with informal response essays, these assignments ask students to examine their personal reactions to literary texts. In their papers, students articulate their reactions to a reading and explain the link between the text and their responses. Possible response essay assignments might include:

- When reading the story "Love," how did you react to the way Martha treated Lt. Cross on his return from the war? Why did you respond this way?

- What was your response to Rat Kiley killing the baby water buffalo in "How to Tell a True War Story"? What aspects of the story most influenced your response?

These assignments ask students to examine their personal reactions to characters, events, and themes in the texts they read. But they also require students to consider how their knowledge, feelings, prejudices, and life experiences influence their reading. These essays are usually evaluated in terms of their clarity and development.

Analytical Essays

Analytical essays usually ask students to explore how an author achieves a particular end through the use of a certain literary device or technique, such as characterization, symbolism, foreshadowing, allusion, setting, or rhyme. To complete the assignment, students have to focus on one aspect of the text, examine it closely, form their interpretation, and relate their conclusions to the work as a whole. Here are some possible analytical paper topics:

- How does O'Brien employ setting in "Speaking of Courage" to help readers understand Norman Bowker's psychological trauma and feelings of isolation?

- Kiowa's death is described quite differently in two stories, "Speaking of Courage" and "In the Field." How does O'Brien's use of point of view in these stories further his argument that truth is often hard to pin down in a war?

- Courage is an important theme in *The Things They Carried*. Choose one story out of the collection and explain how it addresses the question of what it means to be courageous.

These assignments call on the students to focus on one or two stories, isolate for examination a particular element of fiction or a particular theme, examine it closely, then articulate and defend an interpretation. The students would, of course, be expected to support any contentions with evidence from the text and to explain how that evidence actually supports their interpretation or claim.

Critiques

Here students evaluate the quality or worth of a literary text. To complete these complex assignments, students have to understand the standards critics typically employ to critique literature. If they do not know those standards, you need to teach them in your class. If they know the standards but have little practice applying them to literary texts, you may also need to offer guided practice and response. Here are some sample critique assignments:

- According to the standards it lays out, is "How to Tell a True War Story" a true war story?

- In "Sweetheart of the Song Tra Bong," O'Brien portrays Mary Ann Bell's descent into a state of brutishness. Is he successful in this characterization?

- In *The Things They Carried*, Tim O'Brien creates a character named Tim O'Brien. Is this an effective narrative technique in "Lives of the Dead"? Why or why not?

Critiques call for an argumentative thesis: students have to articulate and defend a claim or interpretation. They typically support their thesis with explicated examples from the source text and/or references to other critics.

Synthesis Essays

These assignments ask students to work with more than one literary text in their papers. The essays can require students to respond to, analyze, or critique the readings. Here are some sample synthesis assignments:

- Which story did you like better, "Sweetheart of the Song Tra Bong" or "On a Rainy River"? Why?

- In several vignettes or "intercalary" chapters, O'Brien discusses the nature of storytelling. Which discussion was clearer, the one contained in "Spin" or the one contained in "Good Form"?

- O'Brien claims that sometimes "story truth" is truer than "happening truth." Which story better illustrates this theme, "How to Tell a True War Story" or "Ghost Story"? How so?

- Many critics have highly praised the story "The Things They Carried." Summarize the arguments of at least three critics who praise the piece. Which critic is most convincing or enlightening?

To complete these assignments, students have to examine more than one story, synthesizing material from the literary texts and perhaps from critics to support their thesis.

COMMON PROBLEMS STUDENTS ENCOUNTER WHEN WRITING ABOUT LITERATURE

Learning how to write literature-based essays takes time and practice; like any other academic genre, it has its own conventions that students need to master. Knowing the kinds of errors students typically make when they compose literature-based essays can help you teach this type of writing more effectively—you can let your students know the pitfalls to avoid as they write and revise their papers.

Summarizing the Plot

Instead of explaining an assertion or developing an argument in their papers, students often summarize the text's plot. Plot summary typically comes in two forms. Sometimes the entire paper is nothing but plot summary—the student simply retells the story. Other times plot summary is used as evidence to support a claim. The students know they need textual support for their assertions, so after they make a claim, they summarize a relevant passage from the text. However, instead of articulating the relationship between the passage and their claim—explaining how the passage does, in fact, support or illustrate their assertion—they let the summarized text "speak for itself," relying on their readers to draw the connection between the assertion and its support.

Learning how to use plot summary effectively takes instruction and practice. Explain what plot summary is, acknowledge why it appears so often in student papers, and provide examples of plot summaries used effectively and ineffectively in essays. Teach students how to properly support assertions in literature-based essays without resorting to this technique.

Employing the Proper Tense

For students new to literary criticism, tense poses special problems. The students' natural inclination is to use past tense in their papers—after all, the author wrote the work some time ago. Explaining why literary critics use the present tense can be difficult. Of course, you can require students to use it because it is a convention, but it is best to explain how this choice of tense relates to the way one reads and understands literary texts: because the action of the work unfolds as one is reading it, one discusses those events in the present tense. Past tense is saved for discussing past events in the work itself. Employing this convention as you discuss literary texts in class can help your students learn to use it in their writing. Through repeated exposure and correction, using present tense in their literature-based essays will become habitual for your students.

Quoting Material

Teaching your students how to quote and document material from literary texts correctly takes time. First, cover the conventions of quoting that apply to the literary genre your students are reading. If you are studying poems, for example, teach your students how to indicate line breaks when quoting material and how to employ block quotations; if you are reading plays, explain how to block-quote passages involving more than one speaker; if you are teaching a novel or short story, show how to quote dialogue. The same holds true for documentation conventions: depending on which texts you are studying, teach your students how to document lines of poems, scenes and acts of plays, and page numbers of novels and short stories.

Second, explain how to use quoted material effectively in literature-based papers. Teach your students when to quote and paraphrase material, how to quote and paraphrase it, how to integrate quoted and paraphrased material into their essay, and how to avoid misquoting texts.

Supporting Assertions

Only a few students in most introductory-level classes fully understand how to support assertions in literature-based essays. The most common techniques they employ include quoting and paraphrasing material from the text, citing specific examples, and summarizing the plot. Any of these techniques can, of course, help support a claim, and every critic uses them to some degree. However, you need to teach your students how to support their claims using a wider variety of evidence (including secondary sources and even personal experience, depending on the assignment), how to choose the best kinds of support for their claims, how to locate and evaluate literary criticism, and how to draw clear, strong connections between a claim and its evidence.

Misreading Texts

Never assume that your students understand what they read, even if you think the text is accessible and your students assure you they have no questions. The best approach when discussing literature: move from the literal to the interpretive. When discussing a literary text for the first time, do not immediately leap into interpretation. Instead, first make sure your students can identify the work's characters, summarize its plot, and identify its point of view. Students cannot successfully analyze, critique, or interpret a text they misread.

PROBLEMS TO AVOID WHEN
TEACHING LITERATURE

When teaching literature for the first time, most TAs make up for their lack of experience with their enthusiasm—when you are excited about the material you are teaching, most of your students will be excited too. However, even the most enthusiastic instructor can fall into some common traps when teaching literary texts. Avoiding these problems will improve the quality of your teaching.

Monopolizing Discussions

Even TAs who describe their teaching style as discussion-based rather than lecture-based can monopolize class time when they teach literary texts by answering their own questions or elaborating at length on their students' remarks. Because many teachers hate silence in the classroom, when one of their questions goes unanswered, they jump in with the response they hoped to receive from their students. Silence, of course, is not necessarily bad in a literature class. If you ask a particularly thought-provoking question, students will need a few moments to formulate their response. If you too quickly supply the answer, you deny your students an opportunity to add their voice to the discussion. Other teachers monopolize classroom discussion by elaborating at length on their students' comments. Instead of asking the students to elaborate on their statement, the teacher uses the students' response as a starting point for a lengthy commentary of his or her own.

To avoid these problems, first, learn to be patient when you ask a question in class—wait for your students' answers. If your students look puzzled, rephrase the question or call on a student for a response. Second, listen to your students. Too often when paraphrasing what a student has said, teachers misrepresent the student's point. Whenever you paraphrase a response, ask the student if your restatement is fair and accurate. If it is not, ask the student to repeat his or her comment and try to paraphrase it again. Repeat the process until the student accepts your articulation. At that point, the discussion can continue. Third, ask follow-up questions. Rather than elaborating yourself on a student's comment, ask the student to do it. You can guide the student through the process by asking good questions. Fourth, broaden discussions by pulling in other students. If a student makes a comment, ask another student to paraphrase it and see if the first student agrees that the paraphrase is fair and accurate. Encourage the free exchange of ideas. If one student contradicts what another has said, point out the contradiction and see if the two students can more fully express their differences. In good class discussions students are talking with each other; your job is to referee and record—to keep the conversation flowing and civil and to take notes on the board to record what the students have said.

Mishandling Discussions

Sometimes discussions of literature fail because the students have not read or understood the assigned texts; other times they fail because the teacher has not asked the right kinds of questions. For example, do not try to spur class discussion by asking a question that has only one correct answer. Instead, ask questions that have more than one valid response. *"Who marries Hamlet's mother after Hamlet's father dies?"* will generate less discussion than *"Why is Hamlet so hesitant to kill Claudius?"* In the best discussions, you and your students will work out answers together.

Class discussions can also falter if they lack focus. Most of the students in introductory writing or literature classes are not experienced critics; they probably do not know how to analyze and evaluate literary texts the way you would like them to. Consequently, open-ended questions such as *"What did you find most interesting about these poems?"* typically result in only one or two insightful responses before the class falls silent. To get beyond these initial comments, teach your students how to analyze literary texts or lead them through a systematic close reading of the text yourself.

Designing Poor Writing Assignments

Many literature-based writing assignments fail because they are too specific—they constrict the students' ability to develop and write about a topic that interests them. Of course, some teachers have good reasons for using these assignments: experience has taught them that their students usually have a hard time finding appropriate topics for papers on their own or that their students will avoid difficult interpretative questions when left to their own devices. Yet if the assigned paper topic is too constrictive, students may never learn how to generate good paper topics on their own.

To avoid this problem, offer your students a range of topics for each writing assignment, letting them choose the one that most interests them. You still maintain some control over the topics, but the students have some choice. If you leave the topic of the assignment open, review and approve your students' choices early in the writing process. If you think a topic is not appropriate, talk to the student and help him or her develop a new assignment. This procedure can help ensure that your students are addressing good topics that interest them.

Getting in a Pedagogical Rut

A final problem literature teachers often face is falling into a pedagogical rut—before they know it, they are always lecturing, always explicating texts, or always employing group work. Although there is something to be said for predictability—the students quickly learn how to prepare for class—routines can also breed boredom: with nothing new ever happening in class, students tend to become less interested, less motivated learners. Also, though some students will love the routine you establish because your preferred pedagogy matches their preferred way of learning, students who learn differently may not fully benefit from your instruction. Additionally, your preferred way of teaching may slight some course content. Sometimes lecturing is the best way to present material in class, but other times the best choice is group work or discussion. Good instructors are comfortable with a range of pedagogies and each day employ techniques they think will be most effective. Such variety helps you provide appropriate instruction for every student.

QUALITIES OF EFFECTIVE LITERATURE TEACHERS

You know from your experience as a student that some literature teachers are better than others. If you were to identify the qualities that distinguish effective literature teachers, the list would likely include the traits described below.

Preparedness

Good literature instructors go into every class having *thoroughly* reviewed the material they are teaching that day. Studying literature as a teacher is different than studying it as a student. As a teacher, when you read and reread a text, you must consider how you will teach it to your students: which aspects of the text will you address in class, which aspects will you skip, what might your students struggle to understand, what instruction do they need, how can you help them draw connections between the text they are studying and other course material? Being prepared means studying texts like a teacher, not like a student.

Organization

Being prepared also means being organized. Few good literature teachers just "wing it" in class. Though their teaching style may be informal, most good literature teachers have a defined agenda for each class meeting, a clear set of goals and objectives. They also have a game plan, a sense of how they will structure their time in class. Some teachers prepare formal teaching plans; other rely on informal lists; still other just mentally rehearse their plans. Good literature teachers always spend time before class organizing their thoughts and plans to make the most effective use of the brief time they have with their students.

Flexiblity

Good literature teachers also know when to set their plans aside. If a class takes an unexpected yet productive turn, they are able to change their plans quickly. If a class discussion, lecture, or presentation is not going well, they can try something new. If their planned activities do not match the teaching conditions that day—if, for example, the students have not read the material or if the VCR breaks—they can quickly develop new activities for class. To be flexible, you must be able to read the moods and responses of your students, assess the effectiveness of your instruction as you are teaching, and choose the best teaching tools for each situation you face. The more pedagogical tools you have at your disposal, obviously, the greater your flexibility as a teacher.

Openness

The best literature teachers do not believe they have all the answers—they remain open to learning something new. Sometimes being open means engaging in research, discovering what other critics have said about the literary texts you are teaching. Sometimes it means being willing to question and change your own interpretation of a text. Still other times it means listening carefully to your students. Good literature teachers listen to their students and take seriously their interpretations of and responses to the texts. Every opinion in the class—the teacher's, the students', the critics'—receives the same respect and the same critical scrutiny.

Curiosity

Not only are good teachers open to learning more about the texts they teach, but they *want* to learn more. The best literature teachers are deeply curious about the texts they study and teach. They are fascinated by how writers write and how readers read. Something happens to a person while reading great literature, something great teachers want to understand. They want to understand how literature "works," how it affects readers, and what it teaches about human nature, the world, and the readers themselves. Most importantly, though, they want to find the best way of teaching the text and the best way of helping others learn to love literature too. Cultivating this sort of curiosity will help you become a successful literature teacher.

WORK CITED

O'Brien, Tim. *The Things They Carried*. New York: Penguin, 1990.

ADDITIONAL READINGS

Birenbaum, Harvey. *The Happy Critic: A Serious but Not Solemn Guide to Thinking and Writing about Literature*. Mountain View, CA: Mayfield, 1997.

Clifford, John, and John Schilb. "Composition Theory and Literary Theory." *Perspectives on Research and Scholarship in Composition*. Ed. Ben W. McClelland and Timothy R. Donovan. New York: MLA, 1985. 45–67.

Comprone, Joseph J. "Literary Theory and Composition." *Teaching Composition: 12 Bibliographic Essays*. Ed. Gary Tate. Forth Worth: Texas Christian University Press, 1987. 291–330.

Horner, Winifred Bryan, ed. *Composition and Literature: Bridging the Gap*. Chicago: University of Chicago Press, 1983.

Jacobus, Lee A. *Teaching Literature*. Upper Saddle River, NJ: Prentice Hall, 1996.

Lindemann, Erika, and Gary Tate. "Two Views on the Use of Literature in Composition." *College English* 55 (1993): 311–21.

Roberts, Edgar V. *Writing about Literature*. 9th ed. Englewood Cliffs, NJ: Prentice Hall, 1998.

Steinberg, Erwin R., Michael Gamer, Erika Lindemann, Gary Tate, and Jane Peterson. "Symposium: Literature in the Composition Classroom." *College English* 57 (1995): 265–318.

CHAPTER 12

Growing and Learning as a Teacher

INTRODUCTION

The first time you teach a class, professional development is likely the last thing on your mind—you're probably more concerned with simple survival. Like any teacher, though, you want to do a good job in the classroom and offer your students the best instruction possible. As a TA, you may feel that goal is a long way off, that you lack the skills and knowledge necessary to make a difference in your students' lives. Developing those skills and gaining that knowledge is the essence of professional development. This chapter discusses several ways you can become a more effective teacher throughout your academic career, starting from the first class you teach.

STAGES OF TA DEVELOPMENT

In their article "Thinking Developmentally about TAs," researchers Jody D. Nyquist and Jo Sprague claim that TAs typically pass through three stages of development: senior learner, colleague-in-training, and junior colleague. As senior learners, TAs still identify themselves more strongly as graduate students than as teachers. Their primary concern in the classroom is survival—they want to perform well and be accepted by their students. In the next stage of development—colleague-in-training—these concerns shift. TAs become more interested in mastering the basic skills of classroom teaching, such as designing and evaluating assignments, leading class discussions, and delivering effective lectures. Finally, as junior colleagues, TAs try to understand the effect their instruction is having on their students. They actively investigate whether they are providing their students the best possible education, and they learn to adjust their pedagogy to meet their students' needs.

TAs at different stages of development also define their authority as teachers in different ways. Senior learners tend to draw their authority from their teaching supervisors and program requirements—they follow their supervisor's lesson plan or teach the department's syllabus. As they gain more experience, TAs tend to become more independent. Colleagues-in-training begin to form their own views about what and how to teach and may even defy their supervisor's authority. Junior colleagues understand the collegial nature of college teaching—they begin to relate to faculty on a more equal footing, sharing and borrowing ideas as peers.

Nyquist and Sprague found that TAs at different stages of development interact differently with their students. Senior learner TAs take their jobs very personally—they want to be liked or even admired by their students and are often hurt or angered when that does not occur. As colleagues-in-training, TAs become more detached from their students. They learn how to analyze student behavior and the relationships they form with their students. Being respected becomes more important than being liked. As junior colleagues, TAs find ways of combining these first two stages: they care about their students' education without feeling personally hurt if students reject them or their instruction. They learn to form strong relationships with students as *teachers*, not as friends or peers, establishing professional relationships with them.

Nyquist and Sprague point out that their model of TA development does not imply value judgments: one stage is not "better" than another. Instead their model is descriptive: this is how most TAs grow into their positions, each stage being a necessary step in their development as instructors. TAs tend to pass through these stages rather quickly, even in M.A. programs. With experience, TAs tend to become less egocentric in the classroom and more concerned with student learning, less dependent and more interdependent, less concerned with being liked and more concerned with being respected, less of a graduate student and more of a professional educator.

Most of these changes are inevitable—TAs will pass through these stages regardless of the training or supervision they receive. Simply working in the classroom helps them develop as teachers. Nyquist and Sprague point out, though, that these changes can be personally challenging and even painful at times as TAs redefine who they are as graduate students and teachers. Taking a few steps can ease the transitions and help you develop into a more confident, professional instructor.

WHAT YOU CAN DO IMMEDIATELY TO IMPROVE YOUR TEACHING

As a TA, many aspects of your professional life may be out of your control. Depending on your program, you may not choose your teaching supervisor, your officemates, or even your textbook and course syllabus. In most programs, though, you will have some say in many important aspects of teaching. Recognizing what you have the power to change is the first step in your professional development as a TA. Three such areas are described below.

Changing How You Prepare for Class

One aspect of teaching entirely under your control is the way you prepare for class. Some TAs like to wing it in class and give little thought to preparation. They believe that being spontaneous heightens their energy and solicits more genuine responses from their students. Others, however, script almost every second they spend with their students in class. They bring in mountains of notes and follow their detailed lesson plan faithfully. They believe that such preparation makes their teaching more organized and comprehensive.

Both approaches to preparation have their advantages, but both are also seriously flawed. You need to find the middle ground most successful teachers occupy. Few good teachers wing it in class. Experience has taught them that some preparation is always necessary. Good teachers also know the dangers of overplanning. Effective instruction is flexible, addressing the students' current needs. If you are too highly scripted, you become inflexible, pressing on with your agenda even if your students are confused or have questions. Effective teachers assess the mood of the room every time they teach, adjusting their pedagogy to their students' temperament and response.

How much should you prepare for each class you teach? It depends—usually more if you are teaching something new and less if you are covering material you have taught before. As a teacher, you can improve the instruction you offer your students by improving the way you prepare for class in the following ways.

Engage in Research

This is especially important if you are teaching something for the first time. Educate yourself on the topics so you have something to offer your students beyond what they can find in their textbooks. For example, if you plan to discuss invention techniques in your introductory writing class, consult textbooks, journal articles, and your peers. The more you know, the better your position in the classroom: your expertise will benefit your students and earn you the respect and authority you want and need.

Prepare Effective Lesson Plans

Lesson plans can be simple or elaborate, informal or formal. Formal lesson plans, like those education majors are taught to prepare, often list educational objectives for every class, teaching methods for achieving those objectives, and assessment procedures to determine how well the students learn the material. Lesson plans do not have to be so elaborate to be effective, however. For example, before every class I teach, I simply list what I plan to cover. Preparing this list helps me organize my thoughts; referring to it in class reminds me what I need to teach next. Do not let a lesson plan straightjacket you, though. If your class is doing productive work in ways you did not anticipate—ways that do not fit your lesson plan for the day—abandon the lesson plan and follow your students' lead. Good teaching is organized, but it is also flexible. Lesson plans should serve as a guide to your teaching, not as a strict mandate.

Rehearse

Another important aspect of course preparation is the degree to which you rehearse your teaching. Sometimes rehearsing can be collaborative. For example, before you deliver a lecture to your students, rehearse it in front of your peers. Other TAs like to rehearse in private. They talk through their presentation alone to familiarize themselves with the material. Still others prefer mental rehearsal. As they prepare their lesson plan, they run through the class session in their minds, practicing what they will say and how they will use the time they have with their students. Rehearsal of any kind will likely result in better classroom teaching.

Anticipate Questions or Problems

Think about questions your students might ask and develop answers. As you plan each class, ask yourself: if I were a student learning this material for the first time, what questions or problems would I have? Being able to adopt your students' point of view when preparing for class will make you a more effective teacher.

Changing How You Present Material in Class

A second important aspect of teaching you have the power to change is the way you present material in class. While many programs will dictate *what* you teach in class, few dictate *how* you teach it. Chapter 7 outlines a wide range of pedagogical options for teachers. One key to developing and growing as an instructor is to utilize a variety of instructional activities to determine which work best for you and for your students.

You will not expand your repertoire of skills without experimenting, yet experimentation implies risk and possible failure. Assignments and activities sometimes fail to achieve their ends even for the most successful teachers. You have a decision to make: avoid failure by always playing it safe or take risks and learn from both your successes and your failures. If an activity or assignment does not go well, take time to reflect on what happened and develop a way to avoid similar problems in the future. Remember, though, that failure is much less likely with adequate preparation. As noted above, new pedagogies or assignments are more likely to succeed with adequate research, planning, and rehearsal.

Changing How You Interact with Students

A final aspect of teaching you have the power to change is the way you interact with students on a daily basis. Do you see yourself as the authority in the classroom, lecturing while your students sit quietly, study hard, and learn? Or do you envision establishing a more informal relationship with your students, perhaps turning your classroom into a writing–reading workshop? Will you assume sole responsibility for designing the course or will you collaborate with your students to develop assignments and classroom activities? What tone will you adopt in class? How will you encourage your students' growth—will you nurture and support them or confront and challenge them? Below are some of the crucial questions you should ask yourself as you define your role in the classroom and your relationship with your students:

1. *What degree of control will you maintain in the classroom?*

    Will you share with your students any responsibility for designing the course?

    Will you share with your students any responsibility for choosing course readings or assignments?

    Will you share with your students any responsibility for evaluating student work?

    Will you allow your students' voices to be heard in class?

    Will you allow students to be in charge of the class at times?

    Will you allow students to work together on projects?

2. *What tone will you assume when dealing with students?*

    How formal or informal will your dealings with students be?

3. *How much of your life will you share with your students?*

4. *How much will you want to know about your students' lives outside the classroom?*

5. *How will you expect your students to treat you?*

6. *How will you define "appropriate" conduct in the classroom?*

7. *How will you expect the students to treat each other?*

8. *How will you define your expertise?*

Will you see yourself as the "expert" in the classroom?

Will you see yourself as the sole authority in the classroom?

What will you assume your students already know about writing and learning?

Will you be responsible for student learning in the classroom or will the students themselves have some responsibility too?

What do you think you will have to offer your students?

How will you share your expertise with your students: through lectures, through comments on their work, in conferences?

9. *How will you define your job?*

Will you be in the classroom to "teach" your students?

Will you be in the classroom to help your students learn?

Will you be trying to teach students what it means to be a college student?

Will you be trying to get your students to accept a set of values?

Will you be trying to get students to question the values they currently hold or accept as true?

Will you be trying to get students to think in certain ways?

Will you be trying to get students to use language in certain ways?

Will your job be overtly political, nonpolitical, or somewhere in between?

How will the work you do with students effect the work they do in their other classes?

Will you be preparing students for college, for life, or for both?

Your answers to these questions will be influenced by your personality, your experience, and your students' needs. Just be aware that when it comes to interacting with your students, you have more options than you might at first think.

PROFESSIONAL DEVELOPMENT RESOURCES

Teachers interested in professional development have at their disposal a wide range of resources. From books and journal articles to Internet Web sites, they can consult publications that address almost every aspect of the profession—theory, pedagogy, administration, student development, employment, campus politics. On every campus, they can also turn to a variety of people for advice and instruction—peers, colleagues, staff, administrators. Finally, they can learn from their own experience through reflection and introspection.

Books and Journal Articles

There are books and journal articles on every topic pertaining to professional development. For example, you can consult writing textbooks to help you master the material you are teaching and develop more effective assignments and exercises. Most departments maintain a library of composition texts they receive for examination or have used in the past. If your department does not maintain such a collection, your teaching supervisor can likely lend you copies of texts. These books offer a range of perspectives on the material you teach and provide you alternative ways of presenting information to your students.

Another important aspect of professional development is becoming more conversant in the theories underlying your pedagogy and discipline. No one teaches theory-free—every instructor is guided by some theory of language, learning, and instruction that dictates how they define their job, interact with students, evaluate student work, and design their class. The best teachers consciously examine the theories that guide the instruction they offer. Reading widely in composition theory can give you a much greater awareness of your options as a classroom teacher, make your teaching more logical and consistent, and help you assess your successes and failures in the classroom. (See "Additional Readings" at the end of Chapter 2 for a list of several books and articles that offer an overview of current theories of rhetoric and composition.)

Several books also offer practical tips on teaching. Much like this book, many of these instructional guides suggest various ways you can prepare for class, design and evaluate assignments, present material in class, and address student problems. You may turn to these books for advice at certain points in your class, for example when you grade that first set of essays or when you suspect a student paper has been plagiarized. (See "Additional Readings" at the end of this chapter for a list of some helpful teaching guides.)

While the last few decades have seen an explosion of journal articles that address the theory and practice of reading and writing instruction, actually locating the material can sometimes be difficult. As a relatively new specialty in English studies, much of the early work in rhetoric and composition theory was not included in standard disciplinary indexes such as the *MLA Bibliography*, which focuses on literary theory and interpretation. The best way to find articles on reading and writing theory and pedagogy is to conduct an on-line search of three databases: Educational Resources Information Center (http://www.accesseric.org), CompPile (http://compile.tamucc.edu), and the CCCC Bibliography of Composition and Rhetoric (http://www.ibiblio.org/ccc). You can conduct key word searches of any of these databases ("grading" or "plagiarism" for example) and find citations for a large number of helpful journal articles and conference papers. See Chapter 8 for more information on locating on-line resources such as these.

The Internet

The number of helpful Internet sites in rhetoric and composition is growing every year. The Internet, in fact, offers a wide range of resources you should explore. For example, many professional organizations maintain sites that give you access to current standards and practice in the field: the Modern Language Association (http://www.mla.org) provides links to the newest versions of its citation and publication guidelines; the National Council of Teachers of English (http://www.ncte.org) offers official standards for teaching, TA employment, and professional ethics; and the Council of Writing Program Administrators (http://wpacouncil.org) includes its highly influential outcomes statement for introductory writing classes.

Also useful are the many on-line writing centers available. Several schools, such as Purdue University and the University of Missouri, support extensive on-line writing labs (OWLs) that offer information on composition instruction, answers to frequently asked questions, and even tutorial services. Other writing programs have developed Web sites that include course policy sheets, grading guidelines, plagiarism statements, and other helpful documents you may want to consult as you plan your own course. Some of the helpful sites include those maintained by Indiana University (http://www.indiana.edu/~wts/wts/home.html), Texas A & M University (http://www.english.tamu.edu/wcenter/), Washington State University (http://owl.wsu.edu/), and Colorado State University (http://writing.colostate.edu/). Colorado State University also maintains Academic.Writing, one of the best on-line collections of material related to writing across the curriculum (http://aw.colostate.edu/index.html).

See Chapter 8 for a more complete list of on-line resources in rhetoric and composition, literary studies, and professional development.

Colleagues

Your fellow teachers can be invaluable instructional resources as well. Never hesitate to ask a more experienced faculty member or peer for advice on teaching. Most teachers like to talk shop, to share their experiences and offer advice. Ask for old course syllabi, writing assignments, and exercises. Get their response to your course plans. Talk to them about any problems you face—chances are they found ways to address similar situations in the past.

Just remember to consider their advice in light of what you know about your students. Good teaching is context specific: what worked for one teacher in the classroom may not work for you. As you learn your craft, gather course material and advice from others, but shape it to your own needs and the needs of your students.

Your Own Experience and Knowledge

When you get ready to teach something new, first examine your own knowledge about the topic. Novice instructors often know more about the material they are teaching than they realize. As you prepare your lesson plans, consider the following questions: What do I already know about the topic? When did I learn it? What helped me learn it? If I were a student learning this material for the first time, what would I need to know? What instruction would I find helpful? What questions would I have? Answering these questions will help you teach this material more effectively and improve as an instructor.

TAKING RISKS AS A TEACHER

Growth implies risk taking—teachers who play it safe in the classroom, who never take risks, rarely develop their full potential. But taking risks is, well, risky. Experiments sometimes fail. Every experienced teacher knows the frustration of lessons plans that *should* have worked, assignments that *should* have succeeded, classroom activities that *should* have been a hit. However, instead of giving up when something fails, successful teachers analyze the situation, identify how to teach the material more effectively, and try again. More often than not, though, classroom experiments succeed, partially or wholly, which can bring real joy to your teaching. As you begin your teaching career, consider experimenting with the way you present course material, interact with students, and evaluate their work.

Experimenting with Classroom Pedagogy

This the best way to combat the dulling effects of routine. Change keeps your students alert and you fresh. Chapter 7 offers advice on different ways of presenting course material (see "Additional Readings" at the end of this chapter for other teaching guides you can consult for ideas). Your goal is to develop the pedagogy that best meets your students' needs. This sounds simple enough, but good teaching is rarely a simple enterprise. The real art of teaching is determining the best instructional technique to use each class, assessing its effectiveness, and making necessary adjustments. As a TA, the best way of developing these skills is to experiment with different ways of presenting course material and to determine how well they help your students learn.

Experimenting with the Way You Interact with Your Students

For example, try meeting with them outside of class, either individually or in groups, in less formal settings, such as the library or cafeteria. Get to know your students and let them get to know you. Developing an interest in your students' lives and a concern for their education will make you a better teacher. The risk here, though, is in becoming too involved in your students' lives (you should not, for example, go to parties with your students, date your students, or try to solve your students' personal problems). You must always maintain a professional relationship with your students—but "professional" does not have to mean "distant."

Experimenting with the Way You Evaluate Your Students' Work

From assignment to assignment or course to course, experiment with the way you grade student work (see Chapter 6 for a discussion of various ways you can respond to and evaluate your students' writing). For example, use scoring sheets on one assignment and taped responses on another. One semester, grade individual papers as students complete them, and the next semester employ a system of portfolio evaluation. As you experiment, get your students involved. Let them know which techniques you are using and ask for their response: what techniques do they find most helpful? Why? How can it be improved? What do they suggest doing differently? Collaborating with your students in this enterprise will increase their interest in your course, increase their interest in their work, and help you make more informed decisions in the future.

TEACHING AND ADMINISTRATIVE OPPORTUNITIES OUTSIDE THE CLASSROOM

In many programs, TAs are limited to teaching introductory composition classes; in other programs, experienced TAs can teach more advanced writing classes. Some may assist faculty who are teaching a lower-level literature course, and others may teach such a course themselves (see Chapter 1 for a detailed discussion of the tasks TAs typically perform in these classes). While a TA, take advantage of whatever teaching opportunities are available in your program; the experience will make you a better instructor. Also look for opportunities to develop your skills outside the classroom that involve tutoring, service learning, and administration.

Tutoring

Many TAs work as tutors in their university's writing center. In fact, some schools require new TAs to do this before they teach a class on their own because they believe that the experience TAs gain working closely with students as writing center tutors helps them become more effective classroom instructors. At other schools, only experienced TAs serve as writing center tutors. Either way, as a tutor in a writing center, you work with a wide range of students in a wide range of majors, offering advice, guidance, and support.

However, the writing center may not be the only place on campus that hires tutors. Others may include the Office of Student Services (hiring tutors to work in the dorms), the Office of Minority Affairs, the Office of Learning Assistance, the basic skills program, and the athletic department. Investigate these teaching opportunities, but before you accept a tutoring position outside your department, check with your teaching supervisor—some writing programs will allow you to take on these appointments, others will not. Also, look into all of these programs for summer employment. Few writing programs offer TAs summer employment; you may be able to find a summer job as a tutor, though, somewhere at your school.

Service Learning

Check out community service opportunities. Even as a first-year TA, you have valuable skills to offer others. Many community literacy programs would be glad to have you join their efforts. You may need to go through some additional training, but literacy programs give you the chance to work with an entirely different sort of student than you might encounter at your school. Volunteering your time and talents to serve others offers tremendous rewards and personal satisfaction. Many schools even offer course credit for your work with these agencies, recognizing that service learning can be an important part of your professional development. Just be careful with your time—you may find your work in the community so interesting you neglect your studies.

Administration

Look into any opportunities you have to work as an administrative assistant in your department. TA administrators perform a wide range of tasks as they help faculty run programs or provide student services. For example, as the assistant to the director of composition, you might help place students into appropriate courses, assess the writing program, or administer exit examinations. You could also help select texts for the program, train TAs, develop departmental syllabi, or handle student complaints or questions. These positions typically make great demands on your time and are usually open only to experienced TAs who have completed all or most of their degree requirements. The positions are also commonly competitive, involving a detailed application and screening process. However, if you are planning a career in academia, administrative experience can be invaluable; it prepares you for the kinds of tasks you will likely perform as a professor and makes you a more marketable job candidate.

REFLECTIVE TEACHING

Perhaps the most powerful aid to life-long improvement as an instructor is developing the capacity for reflective teaching. Reflective teachers actively and systematically critique their curriculum and pedagogy, identify strengths and weaknesses, explore alternative practices, and make needed changes. Developing your reflective teaching skills is one of the most important steps you can take to ensure you grow as a teacher throughout your career.

In his important work *The Reflective Practitioner*, Donald Schön draws a distinction between "reflection-in-action," which takes place while teaching, and "reflection-on-action," which takes place afterward. Good teachers constantly reflect-in-action. As they present information in class, they gauge their students' responses; if they feel their students are confused or unengaged, they quickly choose a new way to present the material and try again. They know when to pause, when to offer illustrative examples, when to reiterate information students may not have understood, and when to move on to a new topic or activity. Reflecting-in-action occurs quickly and often unconsciously as teachers match pedagogy to student response. Reflecting-on-action, however, occurs after the fact—it involves critically assessing your lesson plans, actions, thoughts, and feelings after a class is over. Reflecting-on-action can help you determine the quality of your course design and instruction and make the changes necessary to improve both.

Reflecting-in-action is an individual act performed spontaneously in the classroom and leads to immediate decisions and actions. You usually see the results of those decisions and actions at once—your students' responses help you gauge the success of your decisions. Reflecting-on-action, however, takes place away from students, often long after a class is over. It can be performed at leisure and can involve several instructors collaboratively assessing their curriculum or classroom performance. You usually see the results of this reflection later, when you return to class and teach your students again.

Schön maintains that as teachers learn their trade, they can improve their ability to reflect-in-action if they routinely reflect-on-action. In other words, teachers who carefully analyze and reflect on their teaching outside the classroom become more adept at teaching reflectively in the classroom.

Aspects of Teaching Open to Reflection

To make reflective teaching activities a regular part of your professional development, consider all the aspects of instruction open to reflection—your course, your teaching, your students, your own career goals. Below is just a partial list of the topics open to serious, thoughtful reflection and the kinds of questions you might ask:

1. *Your Course Content*
     Are my course goals clear?
     Does the material I cover in my class help me achieve those goals?
     Is the course content appropriate for my students?
     Is the material relevant to my students' lives?
     What changes in the course content would make the class better?
     What needs to be cut from the course and what needs to be added?
     Is there an adequate balance among the various skills I need to cover in
        the course?

Are some skills being emphasized more than others inappropriately?

How are my students responding to the material we are covering in class?

How can I better educate myself about the topics I cover in class?

What do I expect my students to gain by taking my course?

2. *Your Pedagogy*

Am I presenting the course material as effectively as possible?

Am I presenting material in a way that engages my students and involves them in their own education?

Am I presenting material in a variety of ways to appeal to different learning styles?

Have I fallen into predictable patterns of teaching that makes instruction stale and uninteresting?

Am I responding to my students' work effectively?

Am I using the best evaluation methods?

What alternative procedures might work better?

How can I find out how my students are responding to the class?

3. *Your Students*

How well do I understand my students?

What are my students' needs?

What are my students' educational backgrounds and interests?

Why are my students in this class? Why are they in college?

What are my students' strengths and weaknesses as readers and writers?

How do my students prefer to learn?

How can I find out this information?

What do my students expect to gain by taking my course?

How can I create educational experiences that better address their needs and challenge their understanding and abilities?

How would answers to these questions help me shape my course, in terms of both content and pedagogy?

How will answers to any of these questions influence my future as an instructor?

4. *Your Experience as a Teacher, Graduate Student, and Scholar*

What roles do I play in my department or program?

How do I define myself: as a teacher? as a student? as a scholar?

Do these roles conflict for me? If so, how can I resolve the conflict?

How can I combine roles to be mutually beneficial?

Which role takes most of my time? Is it taking too much time?

What aspects of my professional life do I find most and least rewarding?

Which roles do I want to investigate further or spend more time on?

Who are my role models? What do I find in them worth emulating?

What help do I need performing certain roles? What help do I need balancing the roles?

5. *Your Future in the Profession*

What are my career goals?

What job do I want to hold in the future?

Do I want to stay in academics or obtain employment outside the academy?

What specialization do I want to pursue in my degree work?

What resources are available on campus to help me decide on a career or area of specialization?

Who can I talk to if I want to learn more about a career in and out of academia?

How am I preparing myself for my future career?

What steps can I take in graduate school to prepare myself for the job market?

How can I best document the work I am doing in graduate school?

Is my vita up to date? Is my teaching portfolio current? What needs to be added?

Activities that Promote Reflection

Several activities can help you reflect on these central aspects of teaching and professional development that can improve the instruction you offer your students and prepare you for your career. Below are just a few. Experiment with them to see which you find most helpful and productive.

Assembling and Maintaining a Teaching Portfolio

Assembling a teaching portfolio (a collection of course material, letters, and essays) is one of the best aids to reflection. Many new TAs are required to maintain a teaching portfolio as part of their training and education. They often find the experience so helpful that they continue to add material to the collection every year. Although the content of teaching portfolios can vary, Chris Anson, a long-time TA educator and writing program director, suggests that they include:

- Course syllabi—a copy of every syllabus you develop for every class you teach

- Writing assignments—copies of every assignment you ask students to complete in every course you teach

- Course rationales—brief descriptions of every course you teach and explanations detailing why you designed the course this way and required these assignments
- Course examinations—copies of every test you ask students to complete
- Graded student essays—a copy of one or two graded student essays from every course you teach with your written comments
- Evaluation reports—a copy of any letter or report produced by a supervisor or peer who watched you teach and evaluated your performance
- Student evaluations—the results of any required or voluntary student course evaluations, including the written comments
- Teaching philosophy statement—a brief but detailed statement of your teaching philosophy, including your beliefs about the course design, evaluation, student learning, and the aims of education
- Self evaluations—statements you write at the end of every term assessing what worked well in your classes, what did not work well, and any changes you plan on making in course design or instruction

Maintaining a teaching portfolio aids reflection in several ways. First, simply selecting material for the portfolio promotes reflection: you have to decide what goes into your portfolio and what does not because you only want to include material that is central to your teaching. Second, as you get ready to teach a class, reviewing the material in your portfolio will help you set course goals, decide on a particular pedagogy, select a particular text, revise syllabi, develop new assignments, choose new readings, or change evaluation procedures. With the help of the documents in your portfolio, you can design more effective classes and improve your teaching.

Keeping a Teaching Log

In addition to compiling a portfolio, you might also keep a teaching log, a daily record of your experiences as an instructor. A teaching log resembles an instructional diary because it gives you a place to record your thoughts, examine problems, work out solutions, speculate on future directions, or just vent on a daily basis. You can begin writing entries in your log even before your classes start. For example, during orientation you might write about your expectations for the classes you are about to teach—your hopes as well as your reservations. Stating your expectations will help you design the course; articulating your apprehensions will help you know what questions to ask your teaching supervisor and more experienced peers.

During the semester, you may write about specific class meetings, activities, assignments, or students. Writing down your thoughts when a class goes well or when one falls short of your expectations is especially helpful. In these entries, describe what happened in class and consider how you will build on your successes and avoid future problems. Entries can also be linked to class observations (see below). As you watch others teach—peers or faculty—write down your reactions. What worked well for them and what did not? What can you learn from watching these other teachers work? What can you learn from watching the students' reactions in class? If someone comes to watch you teach, write about that experience as well.

At the end of the term, log entries enable you to reflect on the course as a whole. This is an especially helpful exercise for first-time teachers. Review all of your log entries. What concerns did you have? Which ones were warranted and which were not? What proved most successful in class? Why did some assignments or activities succeed more than others? What did you learn about teaching that you did not expect to learn? You might also want to respond in writing to any course evaluations you receive. Identify the criticism and praise you think is deserved and speculate on how the evaluations might change the way you teach. This analysis might be part of a larger project, a self-evaluation you write at the end of the term as a part of your teaching portfolio.

Other entries can address your graduate courses, your professional goals, your interactions with peers and faculty, or your seminar papers and research projects. Any aspect of your life as a TA is open to occasional reflective log entries.

Observing Others Teach and Being Observed

Observation can be a powerful spur to reflection. When possible, watch your peers or supervisor teach, then respond in writing to what you observed—describe what took place in class, evaluate the effectiveness of the instructor's teaching, speculate on why the instructor taught class that way, and suggest how the instructor or you might teach similar material differently. If possible, visit instructors who are teaching the class you are currently teaching and instructors who are teaching a class you will teach in the future. For example, if you are currently teaching English 101 and know you will be teaching English 102 the following semester, find an instructor who is currently teaching English 102 and see if you can visit her class. Watching this instructor and talking to her about the course will prepare you to teach the class yourself.

Also ask peers or faculty to come watch you teach. Meet with that person before class to review your plans for the day and your general course goals. In addition to offering a critique of your lesson plan and classroom performance, the observer can tell you how your students are responding to your instruction. After class, meet with the observer, listen carefully to what he has to say, and ask any questions you want answered. Consider responding in writing to the observation, recording your thoughts and reactions in your teaching log for later reflection.

An alternative is to have someone videotape you as you teach a class. As you watch this tape—either alone or with your supervisor—evaluate your performance, identifying what you can do to improve your teaching. However, such evaluations can be difficult. First, these critiques can be intensely personal. If you are not used to seeing yourself on film, you may have to watch a tape several times to get past the awkwardness of seeing yourself at work. Second, producing the video tape can drastically disrupt a class. Many students are camera shy and the presence of the video equipment may so distract the class that the TA learns little about his or her teaching. However, critiquing your class on tape can be productive as well. Watching yourself on tape can help you objectify your experience and critique your performance from a detached perspective. You will see aspects of your teaching—both positive and negative—you could not identify any other way. Plus, you can watch the tape repeatedly, if necessary, and at different points in the semester. Every viewing offers you the opportunity for further reflection.

Meditating

All of these reflective teaching activities have the same goal—to help you think critically about what you do in the classroom. The worst teachers approach their jobs thoughtlessly. They do not prepare well for their classes, do not consider the needs and responses of their students, do not examine their own performance in class, and do not restructure their course in light of the evaluations they receive. The best teachers continually assess the quality of the instruction they offer their students. They set aside quiet moments in their office, in the car, or at home to reflect candidly on the classes they are teaching. For most teachers, the central questions are always the same: How well is the class going? Are my students learning what they need to learn? What can I do to teach the course more effectively? Setting aside just a few minutes a day to reflect quietly on your teaching can result in insights that may drastically improve the quality of the instruction you offer your students and your own job satisfaction.

CONCLUSION

Once your TA orientation programs are over and you have completed all of your required courses in writing theory and pedagogy, how will you continue to learn your trade? As educator Robert Tremmel notes in his article "Beyond Self-Criticism: Reflecting on Teacher Research and TA Education," no teacher education program can prepare you for all the classroom challenges you will face; instead, the best programs give you the skills and knowledge you need to learn and grow on your own:

> even the world's greatest teacher education program cannot prepare a beginner for all the situations and problems that will arise in practice. Therefore, beginning teachers should learn how to "reflect" on their teaching experiences so they can figure out for themselves how to act in developing their teaching practices. (47–8)

Professional development is a career-long enterprise. Genuine growth depends on your ability to adopt a self-critical, reflective attitude toward your teaching, the willingness to seek out the best that is known and thought in the discipline, and the courage to experiment with your classroom instruction. Most of all, to grow you have to care about your students. Good teachers continue to evolve as instructors throughout their careers because they know failing to do so only cheats the students in their classes, a violation of trust they are never willing to commit.

WORKS CITED

Anson, Chris M. "Portfolios for Teachers: Writing Our Way to Reflective Practice." *NewDirections in Portfolio Assessment: Reflective Practice, Critical Theory, and Large-Scale Scoring*. Eds. Laurel Black, Donald A. Daiker, Jeffrey Sommers, and Gail Stygall. Portsmouth: Boyton, 1994. 185–200.

Nyquist, Jody D., and Jo Sprague. "Thinking Developmentally about TAs." *The Professional Development of Graduate Teaching Assistants*. Eds. Michele Marincovich, Jack Prostko, and Frederic Stout. Bolton, MA: Ankor, 1998. 61–88.

Schön, Donald. *The Reflective Practitioner*. New York: Basic Books, 1983.

Tremmel, Robert. "Beyond Self-Criticism: Reflecting on Teacher Research and TA Education." *Composition Studies* 22.1(1994): 44–64.

ADDITIONAL READINGS

Brinkley, Alan, et al. *The Chicago Handbook for Teachers: A Practical Guide to the College Classroom*. Chicago: Chicago University Press, 1999.

Clark, Beverly Lyon. *Talking about Writing: A Guide for Tutor and Teacher Conferences*. Ann Arbor: University of Michigan Press, 1985.

Fry, Heather, Steve Ketteridge, and Stephanie Marshall. *A Handbook for Teaching & Learning in Higher Education: Enhancing Academic Practice*. London: Kogan Page, 1999.

Prégent, Richard. *Charting Your Course: How to Prepare to Teach More Effectively*. Madison, WI: Magna Publications, 1994.

Vesilind, P. Aarne. *So You Want to Be a Professor? A Handbook for Graduate Students*. Thousand Oaks, CA: Sage, 2000.

APPENDIX 12.1 Some Useful Rhetoric and Composition Journals

CEA Forum

College Composition and Communication

College English

College ESL

College Teaching

Composition Chronicle

Composition Forum

Composition Studies: Freshmen English News

Computers and Composition

English Education

English for Specific Purposes

English Journal

English Language Teaching Journal

Exercise Exchange

Focuses

JAC: A Journal of Composition Theory

Journal for College Writing

Journal of Basic Writing

Journal of Educational Research

Journal of Reading

Journal of Teacher Education

Journal of Teaching Writing

Language and Education

Language and Style

Language Arts

Philosophy and Rhetoric

Reading and Writing

Research in the Teaching of English

Review of Educational Research

Rhetoric Review

Rhetoric Society Quarterly

Teaching English in the Two-Year College

Technical Communication

Technical Communication Quarterly

Visible Language

WPA: The Journal of the Council of Writing Program Administrators

Writing Center Journal

Writing Instructor

Writing on the Edge

Written Communication

CHAPTER 13

Preparing for the Academic Job Market

INTRODUCTION

"What do you plan to do with that degree, teach?" That is a question most graduate students in English hear repeatedly from family and friends. In truth, many do not pursue academic careers. For example, graduate students leaving the master's program at the school where I teach have found jobs in government and industry as technical writers, editors, personnel managers, case workers, sales persons, and journalists. Others have gone on to get degrees in law, library science, marketing, and business administration. Graduate students who want to become teachers typically look for employment at high schools, community colleges, and technical schools if they enter the market with their M.A. and at community colleges, comprehensive universities, and research institutions if they enter the market with their Ph.D.

This chapter addresses the questions graduate students typically ask as they prepare to enter the academic job market. Finding the right job usually requires planning, goal setting, research, diligence, and timing. Although no one can guarantee that you will land the teaching position you want, taking the right steps can make your job search easier and more successful.

HOW PROFESSORS GET JOBS: AN OVERVIEW

There is no single route people follow to find employment as a professor, but most graduate students in English will be hired into tenure track positions through interviews at the annual Modern Language Association (MLA) Convention. The first thing to do is to consult the *MLA Job Information List*, published four times a year— October, December, February, and April. Applicants typically begin their job search by looking in the October job list. (Departments that belong to the MLA receive a print copy of the job list in the mail. You can also access the job list on-line at [http://www.mla.org].) The job list is a collection of academic want ads organized by state. Schools that are hiring faculty place ads in the lob list indicating their area of need (a Shakespeare scholar, a specialist in nineteenth-century American literature, or a writing center director, for example), the type of position (tenure-track, non-tenure-track), the qualifications applicants should have, how applicants should apply, and whom to contact for more information.

When examining the job list, pay particular attention to the type of position mentioned in each advertisement. Some schools will be looking to fill tenure-track positions with assistant, associate, or full professors. If you are hired as an assistant professor in a tenure-track position, you will be eligible for tenure in seven years. (If you have previous experience as an assistant professor, you may be credited for those years of service and come up for a tenure vote more quickly). Schools that want to hire associate or full professors want highly experienced applicants who can be granted tenure when they are hired.

Other schools will be looking to fill non-tenure-track positions. These schools might want someone to serve as a visiting professor to replace a faculty member on leave for a year or two. They might also advertise for an "ABD" position ("ABD" stands for "all but dissertation" and refers to graduate students who have completed all of the requirements for their doctoral degree except for the dissertation). ABD graduate students who land non-tenure track positions can expect to gain valuable teaching experience as they complete their dissertation and may reenter the job market when their degree work is complete. Be warned, however, that the teaching load for ABD positions is usually high and finding time to complete your dissertation may be difficult. Still other schools might advertise positions for lecturers or instructors. Full-time lecturers or instructors teach a heavy course load but typically receive higher pay than part-time instructors and usually receive full benefits. They are not expected to publish and may or may not serve on department and university committees. Those hired into non-tenure-track positions will not receive tenure.

Study the job list carefully and decide which positions interest you. Next, contact those schools by sending them the material they request in their ads. Some schools will only ask for a letter of application (discussed below). Others will want a letter and a vita (an academic resume, also discussed below). Still others may want a complete dossier, which includes the letter of application, your vita, letters of reference, transcripts of your graduate course work, and sample publications. Send the school exactly what it requests, nothing more and nothing less.

Once the application deadline specified in the ad has passed, faculty in the department placing the ad will review all the submitted material and set up interviews with a few applicants. Most of these interviews take place at the MLA Convention held annually the week after Christmas (the city hosting the convention changes year to year). At the MLA Convention, the chair and/or a group of faculty from the department interview applicants and decide who they want to invite for a second round of interviews on campus (discussed below). After the campus interviews, usually conducted in January and February, the department makes a formal job offer to the candidate they want to hire. (A sample time line for the process is provided in Appendix 13.1.) Although the process may be abbreviated for some applicants—a few strong candidates may get job offers at MLA or during the campus visit—most graduate students can expect to go through this lengthy series of steps. Below you will find more detailed information on particularly important aspects of this complicated process: writing your letters of application, preparing your vita and dossier, and sitting for interviews during the MLA Convention and your campus visits.

WRITING A JOB APPLICATION LETTER

Once you compile a list of job openings that interest you, you need to write your letters of application, a task that takes a lot of time, care, and research. In this letter you announce your interest in the position the school is advertising, indicate where you saw the ad, introduce yourself, summarize your qualifications for the position, and highlight important aspects of your vita.

Because this letter introduces you to the faculty on the hiring committee, a bad application letter means you may not make it through the first cut of candidates. Therefore, you should learn more about each school on your list and customize every letter you send. You can find the information you need in several ways, but the most convenient is to consult the university's Web site. Here is some of the basic information you want to gather.

- Is the school private or public?
- What degree programs does the department offer?
- What is the size of the department? How many majors do they have and how many faculty members?

- Where did the current faculty get their degrees?
- What courses do they offer, both graduate and undergraduate?
- What is the university's mission statement?
- What is the department's mission statement?

I have reviewed hundreds of application letters written by graduate students seeking employment in the department in which I teach, and no one makes it through the first round of cuts if they indicate they are interested in working with doctoral students (my institution grants only the M.A.) or look forward to working in a public institution (it is a private university). These letters show that the applicants took no time to learn about the university before asking us to learn about them. Demonstrate that you know something about the department and its course offerings and indicate what you can offer to enhance their programs.

The Letter

Though the content of your letters will be tailored to specific schools, most will employ a similar structure. In the first paragraph, indicate why you are writing this letter (to apply for an advertised job opening), the position for which you are applying (be specific—many departments conduct multiple job searches each year), how you learned about the position (e.g., read the advertisement in the *MLA Job Information List*, found it on-line), and why you think you are qualified for the job. In the next paragraph, if you have your doctoral degree, discuss your dissertation—describe the nature of your study and your conclusions. If you are applying for a college position with an M.A., briefly discuss your thesis (if you wrote one) and describe your graduate work (its scope, depth, and focus, for example). Next, discuss your publications—highlighting what members of the hiring committee should notice in your vita—and your research interests, articulating your agenda for the next few years. In the following paragraph, describe your teaching experience and your plans for the upcoming years, focusing on what you would like to teach in that institution's program. Those applying to comprehensive or community colleges often flip-flop the sections on teaching and research, discussing their teaching first and in greater detail.

Close your letter with a final statement of your interest in the position. If the ad states that the school will be interviewing applicants at the MLA Convention, indicate whether you will be attending. If you cannot go to MLA, let the hiring committee know that you can be interviewed by telephone. Letters should run no more than two pages, single spaced. If at all possible, write them on department letterhead.

Tone is also an important consideration in these letters. You want to show your interest in the position, but you do not want to be obsequious; you want to make the case that you are well qualified for the job, but you do not want to brag; you want to show that you are serious and academic, but you do not want to sound stiff and stilted. The best course of action: write a letter that accomplishes all that is necessary but still sounds like you. Letters with some individualized voice stand out from the crowd. One warning though: comical, confessional, or pleading letters usually prove ineffective.

Faculty reading application letters have several questions in mind, among them:

- Is this person qualified for the position?
- Is this person so well qualified that we ought to ask for his or her dossier?
- Will this person bring to the department attributes, skills, and knowledge we need and currently lack?
- Does this person seem focused enough to make satisfactory progress toward tenure?
- Will this person make a good colleague—is he or she someone I would like to work with and have in the department?

Write your letter knowing that these are the questions your readers will be asking. If after reading your letter their answers are yes, you will make it through the first cut. The hiring committee will contact you and ask for a vita and dossier if they have not already requested them in their advertisement.

PREPARING A VITA

A vita is an academic resume that offers potential employers an overview of your qualifications for the position they are filling. Some schools draw a distinction between a short vita and a long vita. Both offer the same types of information, but a long, or extended vita goes into more detail. For example, a short vita lists the courses you have taught; a long vita also includes a brief synopsis of each course. Unless a school specifically asks for an extended vita, a short vita will suffice. There is not a standard format for a vita, but Figure 13.1 offers a general template you can use or modify as needed. For example, you may change the order of some headings to highlight your strengths, leave out some sections entirely if they do not apply, or change the format.

The Vita

At the top of the vita, center your name. Somewhere near the top, give your campus and home addresses, your home and office telephone number, and your e-mail address. Under the heading "Education," list the schools you attended, the degrees you earned, and the dates you graduated or expect to graduate. Also indicate your area of specialization at each institution and the subject or area of any qualifying examinations you passed. If you are applying for a job with a master's degree, under "Thesis," provide the title and a brief summary (one or two sentences) of your thesis. If you are applying for a job with a Ph.D., provide the title and a brief summary of your dissertation under

FIGURE 13.1   Sample Vita

VITA
Your Name
University Affiliation
E-mail Address

Campus Address/Telephone   Home Address/Telephone

Education

Thesis / Dissertation

Employment

Administrative Duties

Publications

Conference Presentations

Honors

Professional Activities

Teaching Experience

Desired Teaching Duties

References

---

the heading "Dissertation." Under "Employment," list the academic jobs you have held: the job title, the place of employment, and the years of employment. In a long vita, also briefly describe the job duties for each position. Include your work as a teaching assistant, research assistant, or tutor. List under "Administrative Duties" any committees on which you served, departmental positions you held (for example, assistant to the director of composition), and any academic or governance activities you completed (for example, evaluating student portfolios or proctoring placement examinations). Always include the dates you held these positions or completed these tasks.

If you have no publications or conference papers and currently do not have any work under consideration or accepted for publication, leave the "Publications" section out of your vita. Otherwise, provide the works-cited entry for any article, chapter, or book you have published or edited, any work accepted for publication but not yet in print (give the title of the piece and the place of publication, followed by the phrase "accepted for publication"), and any work that is currently under review (give title of the piece and the place of possible publication, followed by the phrase "under review"). List the citations in chronological order, the most recent first. Under "Conference Presentations," give the works cited entry for any conference papers you have presented, listing them in chronological order, the most recent first.

Under "Honors," indicate any awards you received (e.g., Dean's List, grants, fellowships) and under "Professional Activities," include any conferences you attended, any professional organizations you have joined (e.g., National Council of Teachers of English, Modern Language Association), and any other activities that indicate your engagement with the profession (e.g., reviewing manuscripts for a publisher, helping a professor edit a book or journal).

List the courses you have taught under "Teaching Experience." Be sure to include the course title, not just the course number, and indicate your role in the classroom (e.g., teacher, assistant to a professor, discussion leader). In a long vita, also provide a brief description of the course (a sentence or two long). Finally, indicate under "Desired Teaching Duties" which courses you would like to teach as a professor. Place these in rank order—those you are most interested in teaching first. Be prepared to discuss your plans for these courses in detail should you be asked for an interview.

"References" can be handled in one of two ways. Some people prefer to write "References available upon request" on their vita, whereas others list the name, position, address, telephone number, and e-mail address of each person who has agreed to write letters of recommendation for them. Be sure to contact faculty about writing letters of recommendation before you start your job search and choose people who know you well, faculty or administrators who can describe and attest to the quality of your teaching and research.

PREPARING A DOSSIER

A few years ago, job ads rarely asked candidates to send dossiers with their letters of application; they only asked for the vita. Increasingly, though, hiring committees are asking for dossiers in their ads instead of requesting them only from applicants who make it through the first cut. Therefore, you should begin to compile material for your dossier early in your academic career, updating it as you progress toward your degree.

The Dossier

Think of your dossier as an academic portfolio or scrapbook, a collection of material that testifies to your accomplishments as a teacher, researcher, and administrator. As a record of your teaching accomplishments, include a syllabus for every class you have taught along with a copy of any writing assignments you designed. Add summaries of your student course evaluations and copies of any letters from faculty or peers who observed you teach. Also enclose a copy of your "teaching philosophy," a statement of the goals you set for your teaching and your students and the strategies you employ to achieve them. To document your accomplishments as a researcher, include copies of your publications and conference papers and manuscripts of any work currently under review. Finally, to document your accomplishments as an administrator, include a description of any administrative positions you have held, copies of any documents you produced (handbooks, Web material, letters, brochures, and so on), and letters from faculty or peers who can comment on the quality of your work.

Your dossier will also include your letters of recommendation. These letters, written by faculty and others who know your work well, are extremely important. Hiring committee members usually give great weight to these letters. They look to the letters for frank appraisals of your strengths and weaknesses as a teacher, researcher, administrator, and colleague. Choose your letter writers carefully. A letter from a "big name" in the field who does not know you well and cannot offer specific examples to support his or her assessments will be less impressive than a letter from a less famous professor in your department who does know you and can provide particular details about your scholarship and teaching abilities. Also, because no single letter writer may be able to comment on every aspect of your academic achievement and potential, think about the letters *collectively*: what *group* of faculty can write the most effective set of letters for you?

All of the material in your dossier should be well organized, labeled, and sent to prospective employers in a manila folder or binder. Many graduate programs will send dossiers for you—a central office holds your dossier until you request a copy be sent to a particular school. This service is frequently free, though some schools may impose a small fee, especially if the dossier contains an official university transcript.

THE JOB INTERVIEW

Most graduate students on the job market face two types of interviews: initial interviews at the MLA Convention and final interviews on campus. These interviews play a crucial role in the hiring process of most schools. Although you may look good on paper with your letter of application, vita, and dossier, you also need to make a strong impression in person during these interviews. Interviewing well or badly can make the difference between getting the job you want or not getting it.

The MLA Interviews

After you send out your letters of application indicating that you will be attending the MLA Convention, be ready to set up your interview schedule. On a chart, list the days you will attend the convention and the times you will be available for interviews. Interested schools will either call or e-mail you to ask for an appointment. Schedule only one interview an hour; that gives you time to talk with the representatives of one school and make your next appointment without being late. Establish the date and time of the interview, the location, and the identity of the interviewers. Expect to talk to two or more people at each interview; as mentioned above, many schools send a team of faculty to interview candidates, including the chair of the department and members of the hiring committee.

MLA sets aside space in the convention hall to hold interviews, but most schools interview candidates in hotel rooms or suites. Therefore, when you get to MLA, locate the sites of all your interviews so you know how long it will take you to reach each location. Arrive on time for every appointment and dress professionally. A few minutes before each interview, review your notes on that school. Be sure you know the department's degree programs, the courses they offer, and the size of their faculty.

Some interviewers will start asking you questions as soon as you sit down; others will start by asking you to talk about yourself and your research or teaching; and other interviewers will chat informally with you before beginning the formal interview. The best advice: relax, listen carefully, and respond honestly. A smile and an easy manner can go a long way in an interview. Remember that you applied for this job because it interests you and you believe you are well suited for the position. Demonstrate this awareness in your attitude and in your answers. Respond to the interviewer's questions as thoroughly and as honestly as you can. If you do not have an answer to a question, do not fake it; just admit that you do not have an answer. With some preparation, though, this will rarely occur.

Having thought through your answers to some commonly asked questions can help lower your anxiety. Here are some questions you can expect to be asked. Have responses ready.

- What are your research goals for the next few years? How do these goals compliment the mission of our department and university?

- What types of courses would you like to teach? How do they fit into the courses our department currently offers?

- Where do you situate yourself in terms of current debates over theory in your field?

- What theorists or writers in your field do you most admire? With whom do you most strongly disagree? Why?

- What is your teaching philosophy?

- What courses have you taught? What was successful? What was not? What texts did you use? Why?

- What was the focus of your dissertation? What publications will come from your work on this project?

- What are your strengths as a researcher and a teacher? What are your weaknesses?

- What is your approach to teaching writing?

- What graduate courses would you like to offer?

- How do you see yourself fitting into the department?

As you can see, developing answers to many of these questions requires you to do some homework first.

At the end of the interview, it is your turn to ask questions. You might ask your interviewers which courses they would like you to teach at their school, what role they see you playing in their department, how well their graduates do on the job market, or what changes they see in store for the department or university. These questions demonstrate your interest in the school; the interviewers' answers give you a better sense of the department, its programs, and its students. Remember, the job search is a two-way street: the interviewers want to determine whether to offer you a job and you want to determine whether you would accept an offer should it come. Finally, thank the interviewers for their time before you leave. After MLA, you will return home and wait for the telephone call requesting a campus visit.

Campus Interviews

If you make their final list of candidates, most schools will invite you to visit their campus for a final round of interviews. Campus visits usually last a day or two and are packed with activities. You will likely be interviewed by a dean and a provost; meet informally with the department's faculty, graduate students, and undergraduate students; discuss your research interests and teaching philosophy with a group of faculty members; and tour the campus. You might also be asked to teach a class with faculty observing.

Preparing for the campus visit begins with the telephone call you get extending the invitation. If you are no longer interested in the position—if you would not accept the job even if it were offered you—let the school know. Campus visits represent a tremendous investment in time, money, and energy for the school hiring new faculty. Courtesy requires you to help them avoid unnecessary expenditures. If you are still interested in the position though, establish the date of the visit, find out who will arrange and pay for travel and housing, and ask for a copy of the agenda.

Before the trip, review the research you compiled on the school, paying particular attention to the department's degree programs, mission statement, and course offerings. This information will help you talk knowledgeably about the department and school when you are on campus. During your visit, expect a lot of questions about the courses you would like to teach, the texts you like to use, and the teaching strategies you find most effective. Also expect a lot of questions about your research agenda and your willingness to serve on campus and department committees. Many of the people you talk to on this visit—faculty, administrators, and even students—will meet later to assess your qualifications for the position, your ability to complete the tenure requirements, and your potential to excel as a teacher, researcher, colleague, administrator, and mentor.

During your visit, you have a lot of questions to ask too. If you have more than one job offer, the information you gather on this visit will help you choose which position to accept. Below is a list of the questions you should ask on your campus visit.

1. *What will my teaching load be my first year? What will it be after that?*

Many schools give new faculty a reduced teaching load. If the regular load is three courses a semester, new faculty may teach only two their first term. Be sure you understand how many courses you will teach your first semester and how many you can expect to teach after that.

2. *What courses will I teach the first year?*

Make sure you find out what courses the department would like you to teach that first semester. You may need time to work up material for the class. Also, the courses the department assigns you to teach that first term can give you a good indication of what you are likely to be teaching the first few years you work in the department.

3. *What, exactly, are the tenure requirements and by what process is tenure granted?*

Answers to these questions can be complicated, but they are also very important. Who oversees tenure review—a department committee, a college committee, or a university committee? Who sits on these committees? What are the tenure requirements? Where are they explained in writing? What are the teaching, research, and service expectations for new faculty? What is the time line for tenure: how often will your work be reviewed and when will decisions be made? Every school and department establishes unique tenure review standards and procedures. During your campus visits, gather as much information as you can about the process in place at each institution.

4. *How will my teaching, research, and service be reviewed? How often will it be reviewed?*

Most departments have in place fairly clear procedures for reviewing the teaching, research, and service of non-tenured faculty. You can expect to have tenured faculty watch you teach and to have the department chair review your student course evaluations. Many departments also require non-tenured faculty to submit a yearly summary of their teaching, research, and service activities. A department tenure review committee may examine these documents and submit yearly evaluations of tenure-track faculty. On your campus visit, clarify the review procedures in place at each school.

5. *What is the salary? How are pay raises determined?*

Do not be shy when it comes to asking about money. In conversations with the chair, find out what salary comes with the position and how pay raises are figured. If you have more than one job offer, the salary available at each school may be a determining factor in your choice. It does not have to be, however. The better-paying position may not be the best choice of jobs for you. If you face this dilemma, contact the chair to see if the school that truly interests you can negotiate the salary. If they want to hire you, they may be able to match the other school's offer. There is no harm in asking. If the answer is no, they cannot match the offer, you still have the option of accepting the position at the original salary.

6. *What benefits are available? What insurance plans are available?*

Salary is only one financial consideration when choosing a job. Ask about other benefits too. For example, what health insurance plans are available? What are their costs? What retirement plans are available? How much does the university contribute to each plan? Can faculty spouses and children attend the school tuition-free? Are employment benefits extended to married spouses only or are they also available for unmarried partners and life companions? How often do faculty get sabbatical leave? How often do they get to teach abroad? Are their expenses covered when they move to campus? Try to get a full sense of all the benefits that come with the position.

7. *How is research supported? What release time is available? What funds are available to support research?*

If the department expects faculty to publish as a requirement for tenure, how does the department support the faculty's research efforts? Find out whether the department offers faculty release time from teaching to complete research projects, whether summer research funding is available, and whether offices outside the department offer research funding (for example, whether funds are available from the dean, the provost, or the campus development office).

8. *What level of committee work is required of new faculty? When will that change?*

Again, most departments like to relieve new faculty of most committee work. They prefer that new faculty devote their time to developing their teaching and research agendas first. However, this is not always the case. During your campus visit, ask the department chair what your service obligations will be during your first year at the school. How much time do department faculty tend to devote to committee work and other forms of service?

9. *What role will I play in advising majors?*

Finally, ask about your advising duties. Most faculty members advise majors, so find out how many advisees you will be assigned and when that work will start. Also, ask about the training the department offers to teach you how to advise students effectively.

You will have a chance to ask several people on campus these questions, so do not rely on faculty and administrators alone for information. If possible, find out what the students think of the program. Ask them about the strengths and weaknesses of the department, whether they are happy at the school, and whether the faculty generally work well with them.

In short, while you are on campus, ask enough questions of enough people to get a clear idea of what job duties the position will entail, how you will be compensated for your work, and how you will fit into the department. Armed with this information, you will be in a much stronger position to make a final decision about accepting the job, should an offer be made.

At the end of your visit, ask the chair about the department's timetable, how soon they will reach a decision, and how they will inform you of its outcome. When you get home, send the department chair and each faculty member you met with a thank-you note, then wait. If you visit more than one campus and get other offers, as a courtesy let each school know right away. This gives them the opportunity to match it if they like. If you accept a position, let the other schools know you are no longer on the market.

FINDING HELP

Some schools do an excellent job of preparing their graduates for the job market. The university at which I did my graduate work, for example, set up a series of workshops for those of us going to MLA, teaching us how to apply for positions, build dossiers, and prepare for interviews. A few of the professors even ran mock interviews for us so we would know what to expect. If your university does not offer these services, do not hesitate to ask your professors for help and advice when applying for a position. For example, as you put together a list of jobs that interest you, ask your teachers what they know about the programs, about the faculty at those institutions, and about the reputations of the schools. Most faculty will give you frank and helpful answers. You might want to ask faculty for sample vitae or sample letters of application—these models can be invaluable starting points for you as you put together your own material. Also, never send out a letter of application, vita, or dossier without having someone else review it for you. Your teachers are usually the best people to ask for this kind of help; they have been through the process themselves, know the profession, and may have served on hiring committees. Listen carefully to any advice they offer.

You can gather information about a school any number of ways. As previously stated, you might start by logging onto the university's Web site and reading about the department. You can also consult books such as the *Princeton Review's Best Graduate Programs: Humanities and Social Sciences* or *Peterson's Graduate Programs in the Humanities, Arts, and Social Sciences*. When writing your vita and letter of application, consult the guidelines furnished by the Modern Language Association in its publication *The MLA Guide to the Job Search* and on its Web site at [www.mla.org/infocan.htm]. The MLA Web site also offers general advice for job candidates and a list of acceptable and unacceptable questions faculty can ask you during job interviews. Think long and hard about accepting a position at any institution whose representatives violate these basic standards of professionalism and courtesy.

CONCLUSION

The typical job search process is lengthy and complicated; however, with adequate planning, organization, and care, it should not be overwhelming. As you go on the job market, you want to find a position that best matches your interests, talents, and life goals; colleges and universities want to hire faculty who can make significant contributions to their program and serve their students' needs. The length and detail of the job search process helps ensure that everyone involved can make sound, informed decisions.

APPENDIX 13.1   Typical Job Search Time Line

October-early November	Read the MLA Job Information List
	Compile a list of job openings that interest you
	Conduct research on these schools
	Update your vita
	Write your letters of application
Early November-mid December	Mail out your applications
	Schedule interviews at MLA
	If not attending MLA, schedule telephone or personal interviews
Late December	Attend MLA Convention
	Sit for interviews
January-February	Campus visits
March-April	Job offers

WORKS CITED

Peterson's Graduate Programs in the Humanities, Arts, and Social Sciences. Princeton, NJ: Peterson's, 1997.

Showalter, English, et al. *The MLA Guide to the Job Search.* New York: MLA, 1996.

Spaihts, Jonathan, ed. *Princeton Review's Best Graduate Programs: Humanities and Social Sciences.* 2nd ed. New York: Random House, 1998.

ADDITIONAL READINGS

Barron's Profiles of American Colleges. 20th ed. New York: Barron's, 1994.

Bay, Libby. "Teaching in the Community College: Rerouting a Career." *ADE Bulletin* 114 (1996): 27–9.

Cass, James, and Max Birnbaum. *Comparative Guide to American Colleges.* 15th ed. New York: Harper's, 1991.

Feirsen, Robert, and Seth Weitzman. *How to Get the Teaching Job You Want.* Herndon, VA: Stylus, 2000.

Formo, Dawn, and Cheryl Reed. *Job Search in Academe.* Herndon, VA: Stylus, 1998.

Thomas, Trudelle. "Demystifying the Job Search: A Guide for Candidates." *College Composition and Communication* 40 (1989): 312–27.

Index